Sociolinguistics and contemporary French

SOCIOLINGUISTICS AND CONTEMPORARY FRENCH

D. E. AGER

PROFESSOR OF MODERN LANGUAGES
ASTON UNIVERSITY

The right of the
University of Cambridge
to print and sell
all manner of books
was granted by
Henry VIII in 1534.
The University has printed
and published continuously
since 1584.

CAMBRIDGE UNIVERSITY PRESS
CAMBRIDGE
NEW YORK   PORT CHESTER
MELBOURNE   SYDNEY

Published by the Press Syndicate of the University of Cambridge
The Pitt Building, Trumpington Street, Cambridge CB2 1RP
40 West 20th Street, New York, NY 10011, USA
10 Stamford Road, Oakleigh, Melbourne 3166, Australia

First published 1990

Printed in Great Britain by the University Press, Cambridge

British Library cataloguing in publication data

Ager, D. E. (Dennis Ernest), *1934–*
    Sociolinguistics and contemporary French.
    1. French language. Sociolinguistic aspects
    I. Title
    448

Library of Congress cataloguing in publication data

Ager, D. E.
    Sociolinguistics and contemporary French/D. E. Ager.
        p.   ca.
    Includes bibliographical references.
    ISBN 0 521 39335 3 – ISBN 0 521 39730 8 (pbk.)
    1. French language – Social aspects. 2. French language – Social
    aspects – Foreign countries. 3. Sociolinguistics. I. Title.
    PC2074.75.A37   1990
    306.4′4′0944 – dc20   90-33162   CIP

ISBN 0 521 39335 3 hardback
ISBN 0 521 39730 8 paperback

Transferred to
Digital Reprinting 1999

Printed in the
United States of America

Contents

Glossary of terms   x

1 Overview
1.1 Sociolinguistics   1
   1.1.1 Langue and parole: system and data   1
   1.1.2 Individual and group variation   2
   1.1.3 Variation and correlation   3
   1.1.4 Language as cooperation   5
   1.1.5 Languages in contact   7
   1.1.6 Languages in competition   8
   1.1.7 Language planning and control   9
1.2 France and the French   10
   1.2.1 French to 1600   10
   1.2.2 Modern French   13
   1.2.3 France and the French   14

2 Regionalism
2.1 Overview   18
2.2 Dialects of the North   19
   2.2.1 Zone 3   20
   2.2.2 Zone 2   21
   2.2.3 Zone 1   22
2.3 Regional French   22
2.4 Dialectology and sociolinguistics   26
2.5 Sociolinguistics and regional variation   28

3 Occitan
3.1 Occitan: history   37
3.2 Occitan: politics   42
3.3 Occitan: language and the sociolinguistic situation 43

4 Regional languages

4.1 Alsatian	50
4.1.1 History	50
4.1.2 Politics	52
4.1.3 Language	53
4.2 Basque	60
4.2.1 History	60
4.2.2 Politics	61
4.2.3 Language	62
4.3 Breton	64
4.3.1 History	64
4.3.2 Politics	66
4.3.3 Language and culture	69
4.4 Catalan	73
4.4.1 History	73
4.4.2 Politics	74
4.4.3 Language	74
4.5 Corsican	75
4.5.1 History	75
4.5.2 Politics	76
4.5.3 Language	77
4.6 Flemish	79
4.6.1 History	79
4.6.2 Politics	79
4.6.3 Language	80

5 French abroad

5.1 Historical situation	82
5.2 Countries, regions and territories	86
5.2.1 Europe	86
5.2.2 Near East	89
5.2.3 North Africa	89
5.2.4 Sub-Saharan Africa	91
5.2.5 West Indies	92
5.2.6 Pacific and Indian Oceans	94
5.2.7 Indochina	96
5.2.8 North America	96

5.3 Canada 97
   5.3.1 Historical situation 97
   5.3.2 Quebec: corpus and status planning 99
   5.3.3 Quebec: French regional and social varieties 102
   5.3.4 Quebec: attitudes of speech communities 103
5.4 Attitudes and policies in France 104
5.5 Attitudes and policies abroad 109
5.6 French in international organisations 110

6 Social variation: age and sex
6.1 Age 113
   6.1.1 Children's language 114
   6.1.2 Adults and the old 118
6.2 Sex 118

7 Social categories
7.1 Models of society 126
7.2 Social class in France 127
7.3 Upper- and lower-class usage 135
   7.3.1 Pronunciation 136
   7.3.2 Lexis 137
   7.3.3 Syntax 138
   7.3.4 Style 139
7.4 Interpretations of social-category differences 140

8 The outsider
8.1 Jews 144
   8.1.1 Historical situation 144
   8.1.2 Present situation 146
   8.1.3 Linguistic situation 147
8.2 Gypsies 148
   8.2.1 History and present situation 148
   8.2.2 Language 151
8.3 Armenians 152
   8.3.1 History and present situation 152
   8.3.2 Language 153
8.4 Other immigrants 154
   8.4.1 History and present situation 154
   8.4.2 Language(s) 157

8.5 Social outcasts   159
   8.5.1 Present situation   159
   8.5.2 Language   160

9 Social variation: occupations
9.1 Professional discourse   163
   9.1.1 Tasks and groups   163
   9.1.2 Analysis of professional discourse 165
   9.1.3 The study of language at work   166
9.2 Legal language   168
   9.2.1 Sources   168
   9.2.2 Characteristics   169
   9.2.3 Attitudes   173
9.3 Science and technology   175
   9.3.1 Sources   175
   9.3.2 Characteristics   176
   9.3.3 Text types   179
   9.3.4 French and English in scientific language 180
   9.3.5 Control of scientific language   182
9.4 Commerce and management   182
   9.4.1 Sources   182
   9.4.2 Characteristics   186

10 Interaction
10.1 Approaches and methods   194
10.2 The communication situation   195
10.3 Monologue and group interaction   198
   10.3.1 Monologue   198
   10.3.2 Group interaction   200
10.4 The structure of dyadic interaction   201
   10.4.1 Purposeful interaction   201
   10.4.2 Conversation   203
10.5 Formality levels   208
   10.5.1 Stereotypes   208
   10.5.2 T/V oppositions and forms of address 209
10.6 Written and spoken differences   210
   10.6.1 Differences of code   211
   10.6.2 Other differences   212
10.7 Registers   213

11 Language policy

11.1 Historical overview   218

11.2 French opinions and attitudes   222

    11.2.1 Awareness of language questions   222

    11.2.2 The general public   223

    11.2.3 Politicians   226

    11.2.4 Intellectuals   227

    11.2.5 Linguists   231

    11.2.6 Pressure groups   235

    11.2.7 A language crisis?   236

11.3 The norm   238

11.4 Contemporary language legislation   241

    11.4.1 General language laws   241

    11.4.2 Terminology arrêtés   242

    11.4.3 Ministerial control in education   243

11.5 Contemporary official language policy   244

    11.5.1 1981-1986   244

    11.5.2 The Chirac government   245

    11.5.3 The Rocard government   246

11.6 Language control and support mechanisms   246

Index   250

Bibliography   254

List of maps

France: regional languages and dialects   23

Alsace: dialects of German   59

Brittany: dialects of Breton   70

Francophonie   90

Glossary

This glossary provides French or English translations for technical terms, most of which are printed in bold in the text. It excludes French expressions not normally translated, such as *Langue d'oc*.

accent *accent (m)*
alemannic (dialect) *(dialecte (m)) alémanique (m)*; *bas/haut alémanique*: low/high alemannic
allophone *variante (f) combinatoire (d'un phorème)*
argot (m) slang

bilingualism *bilinguisme (m) See* societal, individual
biological gender *genre (m) biologique, humain*
borrowing *emprunt (m)*
boundaries (between social groups) *frontières (f)*

channel *canal (m)*
coalescence *coalescence (f)*
codification *codification (f)*
coherence *cohérence (f)*
cohesion *cohésion (f)*
communication *communication (f)*
communication situation *situation (f) de l'acte (m) de parole, de la communication*
communicative competence *compétence (f) communicative*
communicative practices *pratiques (f) langagières*
communicative style *façon (f) de parler; pratique (f) langagière, style (m), registre (m)*
community *communauté (f) See* language, political, speech, symbolic
competence *compétence (f)*
conceptual system *système (m) conceptuel*
contact *contact (m) de langues*
context *contexte (m)*
conversation analysis *analyse (f) de conversations*
core *centre (m)*
corpus planning *aménagement (m) linguistique*
creole *créole (m)*
cultural assumptions *préjugés (m) culturels*
cultural identity *identité (f) culturelle*
culture *culture (f)*

deficit theory *thèse (f) du déficit (m) linguistique*
dialect *dialecte (m)*
dialectology *dialectologie (f) See* geographical, historical
difference theory *thèse (f) des différences (f) linguistiques*

diglossia *diglossie (f)*
discourse *discours (m), pratiques (f) langagières*
discourse analysis *analyse (f) de discours*
distinctiveness *distinction (f)*
dominated language *langue (f) dominée*
dynamic *dynamique*

elaborated code *code (m) élaboré*
ethnography of communication *ethnographie (f) de la communication*
ethnography of speaking *ethnographie (f) du discours*
ethnomethodology *ethnométhodologie (f)*
ethnic group *groupe (m) ethnique, ethnie (f)*

franconian (dialect) *(dialecte (m)) francique; francique rhénan palatin/mosellan*: Rhine
   Palatinate/Moselle franconian
Francophonie (f) French-speaking countries
Francophonie of the borderlands *des frontières (f)*, of emigration *de l'émigration (f)*, of
   expansion (ie of colonialism) *de l'expansion (f)*
French *français (m), langue (f) française See* old, middle, modern, standard
functional linguistics *linguistique (f) fonctionnelle*
functions *fonctions (f)*

geographical dialectology *dialectologie (f) géographique*
gender *genre (m) See* biological, grammatical, social
grammatical gender *genre (m) grammatical*
group *groupe (m) See* ethnic, human, primary, reference, secondary, task
group identity *identité (f) du groupe*

Habitus (m) Behaviour patterns
historical dialectology *dialectologie (f) historique*
human group *groupe (m) humain*

idiolect *idéolecte (m)*
immediate situation *situation (f) immédiate (de l'acte de parole)*
individual bilingualism *bilinguisme (m) individuel*
individual mobility *mobilité (f) de l'individu*
information *information (f)*
insecurity *See* linguistic insecurity
interaction *interaction (f)*
intergenerational mobility *mouvement (m) entre les générations (f)*
interlanguage *interlangue (f)*
isogloss *isoglosse (m)*

javanais (m) (type of) slang

langage (m) language usage, choice of words
language *langue (f)* (as a system); *parole (f)* (as use of language); *langage (m)* (as usage);
   as object *objet (m)*; as symbol *symbole (m)*; as tool *outil (m)*
language community *communauté (f) linguistique*
language contact *contact (m) de langues*
language (dialect) continuum *continuum (m) linguistique (dialectal)*

language for specific purposes *langue (f) de spécialité (f)*
language levels (ie phonetics, syntax etc) *branche (f) de la linguistique*
language loss *perte (f), disparition (f) d'une langue*
language maintenance *maintien (m) linguistique/ d'une langue/ de langues*
language mixing *mélange (m) de langues*
language planning *planification (f) linguistique, d'une langue;* or *politique (f)* (status
    planning) or *aménagement (m)* (corpus planning) *linguistique, d'une langue*
language repertoire *répertoire (m) verbal, linguistique*
language shift *déplacement (m) de langue*
language/code switching *alternance (f) de langues, de codes (m)*
langue (f) language (as a system)
largonji (m) (type of) slang
legitimacy *légitimité (f)*
legitimate language *langue (f) légitime*
levels of language (ie colloquial, formal etc) *niveaux (m) de langue, style (m), registre (m)*
linguistics *linguistique (f)*
linguistic capital *capital (m) linguistique*
linguistic insecurity *insécurité linguistique*
linguistic market-place *marché (m) linguistique*
loucherbem (m) (type of) slang

message *message (m)*
middle French *moyen français*
minorisée (la langue minorisée), minorisation (f) marginalised, denigrated, marginalisation,
    denigration
mobility *See* individual, intergenerational, social, structural mobility
modern French *français (m) contemporain*
monolingualism *unilinguisme (m)*

nation *nation (f)*
nation-state *état-nation (m)*
neologism *néologisme (m)*
normative pressure *pression (f) de la norme (f)*

official language *langue (f) officielle*
old French *ancien français, vieux français*
onomatopoeic form *onomatopée (f)*

parole (f) speech, (use of) language
performance *performance (f)*
periphery *périphérie (f), régions (f)*
phoneme *phonème (m)*
physical proximity *voisinage (m) physique*
pidgin *pidgin (m)*
political centralisation *centralisation (f)*
political community *communauté (f), corps (m) politique*
power relationship *rapport (m) de pouvoir (m), de force(s) (f)*
primary group *groupe (m) primaire*
professional culture *culture (f) de la profession (f)/du métier (m)*

receiver *interlocuteur (m)*
redoubling *dédoublement (m)*
reference group *groupe (m) de référence*
regional French *français (m) régional*
regional language *langue (f) régionale*
restricted code *code (m) restreint*

secondary group *groupe (m) secondaire*
secret language *langue (f) secrète, cachée, privée*
sender *émetteur (m)*
sexism *sexisme (m)*
slang *argot (m), javanais (m), largonji (m), loucherbem (m), verlan (m)*
social categories *catégories (f) sociales*
social class practices *pratiques (f) de la/des catégories sociales*
social equilibrium *équilibre (m) social*
social gender *genre (m) social*
social mobility *mobilité (f) sociale*
social network *réseau (m) social*
social process *processus (m) social*
social role *rôle (m) social*
social strata *couches (f) sociales*
social system *système (m) social*
societal bilingualism *bilinguisme (m) social*
sociolect *sociolecte (m), dialecte (m)* or *varété (f) social(e)*
socio-occupational categories *catégories (f) socio-professionnelles*
speech community *communauté (f) de discours*
standard French *français standard, parisien, correct, courant; la norme du français*
state *état (m)*
status planning *planification (f), politique (f) linguistique*
structural mobility *transformation (f) de la structure des classes*
symbolic community *communauté (f) symbolique*

task group *groupe (m) de travail*
terminology *terminologie (f)*
territorial monolingualism *unilinguisme (m) territorial*
text *texte (m)*
text typology *typologie (f) de textes*
transactional analysis *analyse (f) transactionnelle*

unifying symbols *symboles (m) unificateurs*
utterance *énoncé (m)*

variable *variable (m)*
variant *variante (f)*
vehicular language *langue (f) véhiculaire*
verlan (m) (type of) slang
vernacular language *langue (f) vernaculaire*

wider situation *situation (f) générale, culture (f)*

1 Overview

1.1 Sociolinguistics

1.1.1 Langue and parole: system and data

Two complementary approaches are needed when we study language: we need to be aware of the raw data - what people actually say; and also aware of the underlying systems - the grammar, the sound system, how to classify words and expressions. The system can be described as a more or less abstract structure, whereas the things people say are best analysed as ways of behaving, subject to all the pressures of the moment and varying according to the situations in which people find themselves and the sort of people they are.

Language in use, the data, was labelled *parole* by Saussure and contrasted with the system, *langue*. *Parole* is the sum of all the variations used in a language, whether caused by chance or by (conscious or unconscious) choice, so some of the individual preferences, differences of pronunciation and selection of terms will correlate with a speaker's individuality and personality, his memory and physical capacities, his knowledge and experience, expertise in language use; others with aspects of the situations he finds himself in and the people he converses with.

Chomsky's term for this raw data was **performance**; his term for *langue* was **competence**. The competence of an idealised speaker/hearer is a systematised abstraction from the data, reducing them to order in grammatical, lexical, phonetic or phonemic terms and imposing both constraints and explanatory structures on real usage, rejecting some items as being 'ungrammatical' or 'irrelevant' to the analysis. *Langue* can therefore be predictive and permit discussion of abstract structures or things people might conceivably say, *parole* can only treat what has actually been produced and must concern itself with the closed object, usually called a **text** or an **utterance** (whether written or spoken), as its object of study.

Sociolinguistics and other disciplines such as psycholinguistics are concerned with questions of variation in performance and hence with *parole,* but whereas psycholinguistics is concerned with variation based on personality variables such as the skill of the user, sociolinguistics looks for systematic choice of language items correlating to identifiable social factors. These are usually classified as those relating to the speaker and the recipient: regional or social origin, age, sex, personality; those concerned with the context or situation of the utterance: participants, setting, purpose and nature of the interaction; and those concerned with the medium (spoken or written channel) or the message (genre and register). Sociolinguistics is hence concerned both with the study of language and also with the study of society: with the range of language items used, and the reasons why they are used, but also with the social characteristics of speakers, their attitudes and their use of language to convey meaning and to effect social functions.

1.1.2 Individual and group variation

Every individual human being speaks and writes in a different way from others: he chooses words, expressions and textual structures which are different from those even close relatives, colleagues or friends choose. His **idiolect** (lect, or isolect) is a reflection of his personality, which itself reflects his upbringing, knowledge, experience and the situations he finds himself in. But human beings must nonetheless communicate, so personal choices are limited by the necessity to ensure the successful reception of messages.

People live in groups, and these groups themselves make choices from the range of expressive possibilities. Sometimes these choices are systematically the same throughout a geographical region, which is thus differentiated from other regions by an **accent** or by a **dialect**.

Choices are also made collectively by groups united by their work (soldier talk, schoolboy slang) or activity (the language of football or *pelote basque*), by families and generally in any face-to-face or **primary group.** **Secondary groups,** of people not necessarily in face-to-face contact, such as lawyers or scientists, also have their own 'dialects'. Some linguistic choices seem also to correlate to membership of social categories, such as age, sex or profession: children and adults, women and men, aristocrats and labourers, thus have identifiable **sociolects.**

These choices are systematic and characteristic: a human being who uses *alors* or *n'est-ce pas* frequently in conversation, or who uses *vous* to his wife, finds it difficult to give up these linguistic habits and is recognised by friends and colleagues through such mannerisms. Likewise it can be statistically shown that children's speech is different from that of adults, and that scientists collectively make the same linguistic choices, whereas an occasional mispronunciation, the choice of one word rather than another is impossible to measure.

· Sociolinguistics is mainly concerned with systematic measurable linguistic variation and its relationship to social groups. The basic data are obtained from observation, or with more accuracy from surveys, interviews and questionnaires applied to a representative sample of the population whose behaviour is being studied. These methods, which do not exclude qualitative approaches to the same phenomena, are essentially those of any social-science discipline. Sociolinguistics is not concerned solely with description, however, but also with the evaluation of the nature and practices of social groups using language and their language attitudes, with more general questions of the social use and value of cultural symbols such as language, and with the social **processes** involved in language use.

1.1.3 Variation and correlation: variation in language, variation in society and variation in language use

The sounds of a language can be pronounced in a number of different ways, some conditioned by the (linguistic) context and others less so. Thus the [k] sounds in *car* and *qui* are phonetically distinct, and are regarded as **allophones** of the **phoneme** /k/. Likewise the consonant /r/ can be pronounced in any one of four different ways in French without losing its linguistic meaning. But these phonetically distinct forms of /r/ are recognised and associated by a French hearer with certain expectations and hence have different social meanings:

> the zero form [kat] with the familiar or popular level of speech;
> the trilled form [katr] with a provincial or old-fashioned form of speech;
> the fricative [katʁ] as the normal standard;
> and the uvular trill [katR] with emphatic or (over)careful speech.

The four forms are **variants** of a speech **variable**, the consonant /r/. Similar variables are the presence or absence of the consonant /l/ at the end of words like *il*, the *liaisons*, the presence or absence of the negative particle *ne*, the pronunciation or non-pronunciation of the '*e muet*', the use of *je peux* as against *je puis* and innumerable others. The choice of variant in each case, correlated to a variant within a social variable like age or sex, provides the basic data of sociolinguistics. Linguistic variables are not of course limited to pronunciation, but occur in the choice of words, syntactic constructions, style and throughout language use, so variation in language is identified in all the **language levels**: phonetics, lexis, syntax and discourse structure.

Social variation can be analysed in two ways: by examining the traditional **social categories**, such as age, sex, class, geographical origin, occupation, which affect the identity of the participants in language use; and by investigating situational variables. These latter are the factors which affect a specific **communication situation**, typically a dialogue: the factors (variables) which are relevant to the linguistic choices made are for example the political, economic and social setting, the time when the interaction occurs, the relationship between the participants, the nature and purpose of their interaction, and the channel (medium: spoken or written) of the exchange.

The archetypal sociolinguistic study therefore identifies an independent social variable, such as social class, and measures the correlation between it and a dependent linguistic variable such as the pronunciation of /r/. The results are presented in a statistical table, which often shows the percentages of the total cases in which a particular variant is used. Thus:

Pronunciation of children of parents in manual and non-manual occupations.

Opposition	Manual occupations	Non-manual occupations
tache/tâche	52.27	30.51
brin/brun	11.36	28.81

The figures are percentages of cases in which the opposition is retained, and the study demonstrates that the 'lower' social class retains one opposition and dispenses with the other.

Such simple correlative methods suffer from a number of drawbacks such as problems in defining social variables such as 'class' and in the use of insufficiently sophisticated statistical techniques. More refined statistical methods and approaches have been developed, **social networks** rather than dubious social variables have been used; and researchers have studied the **language repertoire** of individuals, or **linguistic continuums** rather than discrete linguistic variants.

Sociolinguistics has also moved away from studying correlation towards interpretation of the basic correlational data, for example by measuring attitudes and opinions towards language use, by examining the nature of sociolinguistic situations, particularly interaction, by considering the functions of language choices in interaction ('**ethnography of communication**') or by studying social processes as exemplified by language use. Although the aims and methods of study are many and varied, all follow, or should follow, basic 'scientific' methodology in establishing hypotheses which can be tested against data, in attempting to identify and measure observable data in repeatable experiments/observations, and in drawing conclusions from all the available data, and which account for all the data.

1.1.4 Language as cooperation: the concept of language community

All those who speak the same language form a **language community**, so all those who speak French are part of the French language community, including members of the French-using States in **Francophonie** and those many people who are learning the language. But many of those included in this definition feel they belong to a community which differs radically from that of the Parisian native speaker: the African or Algerian, the inhabitant of New Caledonia, of Switzerland or Belgium, the second-generation Tunisian or Portuguese immigrant in Marseille differ in their political, cultural and economic traditions, their history and interests. Is language alone therefore a sufficient link to form a community?

Many communities are bi- or multilingual, and indeed many French speakers only use the language for defined and limited purposes such as trade or administration. In this way bilingual areas such as Alsace, Algeria or Senegal contrast with mainly monolingual France. Similarly the use of certain varieties, particularly socially defined varieties such as the language of the bourgeoisie or the slang of a prestigious Higher Education institution, create 'bi-dialectal' subcommunities which may regard themselves as distinct from the mainstream one. In addition, the form of the French language used in Canada, and more particularly in Africa, has characteristics which often render it nearly incomprehensible to a standard French speaker: how far can there be a sense of community between such groups?

A more subtle and complete definition of a language community would therefore include not only a common language, but (a) common meanings: common political, cultural, economic or social histories and situations;

common attitudes towards language use, by the rejection of certain words as vulgar or socially inferior, and the attribution of prestige to a type of pronunciation; (b) frequent interaction, whether face-to-face or via the media, with other members of the community, as with the recent meetings of Francophone or Commonwealth Heads of State; and (c) the use of a common verbal repertoire, or range of preferred linguistic and stylistic choices.

One can define **speech communities**, usually smaller than language communities, by criteria including interaction and verbal repertoire. Since every human being forms part of many different groups, both primary and secondary, it is inevitable that he will form part of different and interacting speech communities, so one and the same person for example could be a member of the French, Breton, Quimper, Catholic and maritime communities, and at an even more detailed level of his *quartier*, clubs or family groups, each of which would be identifiable in ever more circumscribed language use. The individual concerned would have available a range of distinct sublanguages which together form his verbal repertoire.

Language use relates also to **political communities** such as region, country, nation and State, and to **symbolic communities** such as an ethnic group. In such groups the use of symbols in addition to and other than language is of considerable force in fostering and maintaining loyalty and cooperation, although language is usually the main link. Thus the **State** is an objective political and territorial entity with legal and administrative structures and a set of institutions. The **nation** is both objective and subjective: its inhabitants have affective ties in addition to political links and social institutions and hence a wish to organise their affairs in common. Most French people would regard France as both a State and a nation, while Breton separatists, for example, would regard Brittany as a nation but accept that it is not a State. The **ethnic group** has the affective links but not necessarily the wish to organise the totality of its political, social or economic affairs in common and separately from others; it nonetheless expresses cultural solidarity, as for example do contemporary Bretons living in Marseille or Paris.

Some symbolic links, such as language, which unite members of ethnic groups may change or even disappear, as has happened for example with exiled Bretons in the USA; but the sense of belonging may remain. Hence definitions of communities and groups are based on both the **unifying symbols** - the content of group beliefs (the nature of the community's history, practices and traditions, its attitudes and beliefs, myths and rites;

symbolic links such as language or a flag) and also on the identifiable **boundaries** between one group and the next (skin colour or 'racial' characteristics, territory, language difference).

1.1.5 Languages in contact: problems of language interference; language borrowing

Every human being belongs to many different speech, and perhaps language communities. Although the different languages he knows are used in communication with different interlocutors or for different purposes, a speaker may nonetheless borrow terms from one language to use in another. At the frontiers of a language community - whether a region, nation or ethnic group - each language or dialect may be affected by another language or dialect used by different - or even the same - people living close together. A useful distinction here is that between **societal bilingualism** (or multilingualism), in which essentially monolingual communities may live in close contact with each other, and **individual bilingualism**, where everybody has more than one language.

In some areas of France however dialects and languages have withstood close **contact** and retained their identity: strong affective ties have been important in this process, usually associated with tightly knit communities, united by economic and administrative practices. Examples would be the wine-growers of the Var or Hérault or the fish-sellers of Brittany. Some language communities speak languages which are also used outside the French State, and thus call on affective ties to a nearby nation or region: German, in Alsace, to Germany; Catalan and Basque to the larger communities in Spain. Other communities - the Jews, for example, and more recent immigrant groups such as the Armenians or Arabic speakers from the Maghreb countries - retain their languages for reasons of religion, tradition or ethnic loyalty. Stable bilingualism in language contact situations is therefore associated with a high level of **language maintenance**.

The most widespread linguistic evidence of language contact is the presence of words **borrowed** from one language to another and which have now become part of the language: *le weekend, le smoking*; or rendezvous, toilet and cuisine in English. Evidence of closer everyday contact comes from **language mixing**, where words, whole sentences or phrases are borrowed from one language to another, even to the extent of starting a sentence in one language and finishing it in another. Internal linguistic evidence can reconstruct the detail of language contact: the devoicing of French plosives in Alsace under Germanic influence, or the denasalisation of French vowels in the South because of influence from Occitan, are two examples, as is an Arabic speaker's use of juxtaposition rather than subordination in a phrase like *je l'ai mangé je me suis pas aperçu.*

The separate identity of dialects or regional languages can suffer from the presence of a standard or prestigious form, such as standard French. This situation is hence dynamic, leading to **language shift** or **language-(code-) switching**, and perhaps eventually to **language loss.** As schooling in standard French develops, the regional language is less used by children; in the home, television and radio bring standard French and the regional language is less used by the family in talking of matters of public importance; rural dwellers move from their villages and of necessity have to use standard French for all their communicative needs; populations move, for holidays, for commerce or for war, and the community loses its distinctiveness and its language. In contemporary France, as well as elsewhere in the world, English is becoming available, particularly through television and popular songs, and one of the dangers of this dominance is the (admittedly remote) possibility of it eventually replacing French altogether. The phenomenon of **coalescence** may have similar effects: the distinctions between dialects around Paris have not been great enough to withstand 'infiltration' and gradual replacement by standard French.

1.1.6 Languages in competition: diglossia and conflict

The coexistence in a society of a 'high' and a 'low' language or dialect, with the superior one having higher prestige than the inferior, is called **diglossia.** It is now normally accepted in sociolinguistics that this distinction of prestige may be caused by or associated with a differentiation of the **functions** each language carries within the relevant society, the higher language being used for public official purposes and the lower for private domestic uses. In stable diglossia, each language is able to coexist with the other because of this distinction of functions. In some circumstances however the situation is dynamic, with one language or dialect gradually supplanting the other: increased use of French in Quebec, for example, after linguistic legislation intended to produce this effect, or French replacing Breton in formerly bilingual Brittany. All the situations in which two indigenous languages or dialects are in contact in France, and many of those involving immigrants' languages, are diglossic situations.

While bilingualism or multilingualism is the normal state for most of the world's inhabitants, France is unusual in having a mainly monolingual population. **Standard,** codified French is used for official functions and thus occupies the role of superior (public, written) language. In the regions where a local language or dialect survives, it occupies the inferior role and is marginalised (*minorisé*) into domestic, non-official, private situations; spoken and informal uses. This situation sometimes provokes social or political conflict, particularly in Corsica and Brittany but also elsewhere, where people reject the negative label of inferiority and wish to promote a positive image of the local language by seeing it used for more official, superior functions, such as on road signs or cheques. The dimension of conflict is that of prestige, acceptability and value.

Outside France French is rarely in the inferior position, with notable exceptions such as Canada, although recent language-planning decisions in Quebec have affected the situation of French there. In Belgium the situation is dynamic, with continuing tension between Flemish and French, which has led to virtual partition of the country and the creation of **territorial monolingualism**, albeit within societal, and with much individual, bilingualism. In many African countries French occupies the élitist role of official language while a range of other languages is used and defined according to their role in commerce, international trade, administration and politics, family or tribal loyalties, and diplomacy.

With occasional exceptions situations in which one language dominates lead to the eventual disappearance of the dominated languages for all except private and domestic purposes, and this seems to be as true for economic as it is for political domination. **Dominated languages** decline: the young no longer use them and mothers do not teach them to their children. Since in France French is the only accepted language for official purposes, the other languages or dialects spoken in certain regions could be expected to disappear, and have in fact massively declined, although this has not been a rapid process, and it may be a process which can be reversed or halted by deliberate planning.

1.1.7 Language planning and control

France has known language planning since 1539, when the Edict of Villers-Cotterets required French to be used in the courts and in the administration of the State. This type of official instruction, defining the status of a language, is known as **status planning**, contrasting with the **corpus planning** carried out to define the nature of the language involved and ensure its quality. The creation of the *Académie Royale* in 1635 (later to become the *Académie Française*), with its specific **codification** tasks of writing a grammar and a dictionary in order to systematise the language and render it an instrument for the arts and also for government, has led to a long and respectable tradition of state involvement in the modification of French and in specifying the conditions of its use. The methods of control lie most obviously in education, but also in other aspects of state administration, where the competitive open written examination system for entry to any state employment has required state control of linguistic correctness for over two centuries. In contemporary France governmental language policy, remarkably coherent since de Gaulle's time, is aimed at reinforcing international links through the development of the concept of *francophonie*; with ensuring efficiency and modernisation through terminology banks and lexical control; and with 'defending' French from excessive reliance on Americanisation. Language-planning instruments are however a mixture of control and persuasion, and the inbuilt conflicts of these differing aims, despite a generally supportive attitude among the French, mean that success is not guaranteed.

Further reading
Edwards, J. 1985. *Language, Society and Identity*
Fasold, R. W. 1984. *The Sociolinguistics of Society*
Garmadi, J. 1981. *La Sociolinguistique*
Wardhaugh, R. 1986. *An Introduction to Sociolinguistics*
Wardhaugh, R. 1987. *Languages in Competition*

1.2 France and the French

1.2.1 French to 1600
Julius Caesar's defeat of the Gaulish chieftain Vercingetorix in 52 BC marked the end of the Celtic occupation of Gaul, and the disappearance of Druidism. By AD 400 it is thought that no native speakers of Celtic languages remained, although modern French has retained about sixty words of Celtic origin, for example *arpent, bruyère, chemin, mouton*. The romanisation of Gaul was achieved by military force, but also by administration, trade, religion, schools, transport and effective policing, so the variety of the Latin language generally spoken there about AD 400, the sermo cotidianus or vulgaris, contrasted with the sermo urbanus of the Italian towns and the sermo classicus of the Roman aristocracy of lawyers

and poets. Our knowledge of this popular tongue of Roman Gaul is limited to the evidence provided by inscriptions or schoolbooks, together with internal linguistic evidence of developments since.

Successive waves of invaders from the East attacked Gaul, starting about AD 230. At first these were raids, but eventually deliberate settlement took place, with or without the agreement of the Romans themselves. The first were the Visigoths *(Wisigots)* from the Lower Danube, who settled over the whole of the Mediterranean coast, particularly in the South-West and in Spain. In 430 the Alemani *(Alemans)* attacked Alsace-Lorraine, followed in 440 by the Burgundians *(Burgondes)*, who settled around Lyon and Grenoble. Between 300 and 600 Celts expelled from Wales and Cornwall established themselves in Brittany, bringing their Celtic language with them: these were the only invaders who did not adopt the Latin-based local language. From before 500 and up to 700 the Franks *(Franques)* arrived in the North: the start of the Middle Ages is often dated to the crowning of Clovis as King of the Franks in Reims in AD 496. The Goths spoke Germanic languages, and many words, particularly military terms, are left in modern French, such as: *bleu, blanc, banc, auberge, guerre, guetter, garder, garant, maréchal, marcher, fourreau, fauteuil, franc, France.* Invaders came from the South, too, with the Arabs (Moors) reaching Tours in 732 and not being expelled from Narbonne until AD 759, and from the North, with the Vikings settling all round the coasts but particularly in Normandy. Both groups left borrowings in modern French: *algèbre, chiffre, chimie, coton, jupe, sucre* from Arabic, and *équipe, cingler, crique, vague* from Scandinavian languages.

Although these invaders accepted the language they found, their habits of pronunciation, the words and expressions of their original tongues all had their effect on the language, which, towards AD 800, had developed far enough away from Latin to be called Gallo-Roman. A sample of the language is conveniently provided by the oath sworn by one of Charlemagne's sons in 842:

> *Pro Deo amur, et pro cristian poblo et nostro comun salvament, d ist di in avant, in quant Deus savir et podir me dunat, si salvarai eo cist meon fradre Karlo, et in aiudha et in cadhuna cosa, si cum om per dreit son fradra salvar dift, in o quid il m i altresi fazet, et ab Ludher nul plaid nunquam prindrai ki, meon vol, cist meon fradre Karle in damno sit.*

With the break-up of control from Rome and worsening transport, the language spoken in different parts of Gaul was developing differently, to the extent of creating in effect three mutually incomprehensible languages: in the South moving to what would become known as the *langue d'oc*, from Latin *hoc*, used for 'yes', in the North to the *langue d'oïl*, from the Latin *hoc ille* used for 'yes', and in the area around Lyon and Grenoble settled by the Burgundians to *franco-provençal.*

In the **Old French** period, from AD 800 to 1300, two of the different dialects were particularly important: *francien*, spoken in the area round Paris, which was to develop into modern French due mainly to the military prowess of the Frankish kings of the North who imposed it on the rest of France, and *provençal* (other terms were also used) applied to a variety of southern dialects which were used by the wandering minstrels, artists and poets who created a literature of the first order between AD 900 and 1230. In 1230, the northern kings launched a crusade against the Cathares, the Albigensian heresy, speedily imposing their rule on the Count of Toulouse and the southern population with ferocity and cruelty, and eliminating any possibility of political opposition. *Provençal* leaves about 400 words in modern French: *aubade, amour, velours* from the earlier period, and many words since: *abeille, banquette, cable, cadastre, cigale, escalier, troubadour.*

After the thirteenth century the administration started to record its deeds in French rather than Latin; literature in French started to develop, the University of Paris was founded, and although the Gallo-Roman languages and dialects other than French were still strong in both spoken and written usage, the prestigious variety became *francien*. In Old French there was probably a word stress, falling on the last syllable but often with a following final 'e'; a trilled /r/ sound, and diphthongs for nearly all /o/ and /e/ sounds. Two nasal vowels were used /ã/ and /ɛ̃/), and /l/ and /n/ could be pronounced palatalised. An interdental sound similar to English 'th' existed and final consonants were normally pronounced. Two grammatical cases still existed from the days of Latin; personal pronouns were often not used before verbs; the simple past tense was widespread, and the order of words was much freer than in modern French.

Middle French is defined as falling between AD 1300 and 1600. The work of the French kings in extending their influence continued, with increasing sophistication in administrative and cultural matters accompanying the increasing power of the court. Constantinople fell to the Turks in 1453 and scholars fled to Western Europe, bringing learning and knowledge to centres such as the University of Paris. In the sixteenth century there were internal religious wars, again, but the war which led French armies to Italy was as important politically and much more so linguistically, bringing civilisation, grace and culture to Paris. In 1539 the Edict of Villers-Cotterets imposed French as the sole language of the law courts: Latin disappeared as an official language, and the date marks the beginning of the end for official uses of regional languages. The Edict of Nantes in 1598 put an end to religious conflicts, and the ensuing peace and tolerance aided economic growth, the rise of a middle class and the start of the main period of French influence and power in Europe.

Although Latin disappeared as an official language, it was rediscovered as a vehicle for learning: many Latin words were borrowed for learned purposes at this time, in some cases doubling a previous borrowing or a word which had been in French from the beginning: *frêle/fragile, entier/intègre, naïf/natif, nager/naviguer.* Italian is the source of many borrowed words. In the military domain: *cavalerie, colonel, caporal, infanterie;* the maritime: *remorquer, boussole;* the commercial: *banque, banqueroute, tarif;* the architectural: *balcon, façade;* and the cultural: *sonnet, fugue, parfum.*

1.2.2 Modern French

France in the seventeenth century was the principal European power, with a population of twenty million inhabitants contrasting with the twelve million of Great Britain, agricultural wealth, and a centralised and effective absolutist monarchy. The power of the Court led to the creation of a prestige pronunciation, with final consonants being dropped (to be restored later in some cases such as *il* and *courir*); the popular pronunciation [wa] of -*ais* or -*ois* in adjectival endings and elsewhere was replaced by [wɛ] or [ɛ]: *français, raide, anglais*, although this did not prevail in *suédois, boire, croire*; and the uvular [R] replaced the trilled form [r], a pronunciation which was imitated across Europe.

After the eighteenth century, a time of authority and control ended by the Revolution, three influences marked modern French as it developed. The first was the need to develop a national policy of using French, a policy clearly supported by the political Left at the Revolution, when a survey found that two thirds of the country did not speak French, the language of enlightenment, reason and progress. The political Right, including the Church, supported regionalism, thus paradoxically opposing the centralising policy of the *Ancien Régime*.

The second influence was that of increased educational provision, possible after Napoleon's administrative reforms, but not implemented until after 1882. Universal primary and then secondary education, conducted in French by state functionaries who received a normalised education and training eliminating their specifically regional characteristics, including local languages and dialects, led to a high degree of uniformity, particularly as the education offered was language- (and even rhetoric-) oriented, with success in the *baccalauréat* requiring linguistic abilities of a high order in both speech and writing.

The third influence comes from outside France. The rising power of English-speaking states, Britain and then America, has led to a continuous and continuing pressure on French to retain and strengthen the purity of the language and resist outside pressure, and yet at the same time to adapt and modernise, to borrow from and to cooperate with other French-speaking countries, and even with other Romance languages, in order to stem the increasing pressure of Anglo-American domination.   Borrowings from English are noticeable since the   seventeenth century (*ballast, brick, piquenique, paquebot*), through the eighteenth (*milord, redingote, club*) and the nineteenth (*biftek, rail, rosbif, wagon, chèque, stock, ticket, football, sport*) to the twentieth, with *shampooing, dancing, parking, leader, speaker, jeans, rock, hot, pull,* and many more.

1.2.3 France and the French

This rapid survey of the development of the language towards modern French shows how mixed are its origins: it retains similarities with the other Romance languages, likewise descendants of Latin, but has been strongly marked by its Gothic/Germanic pronunciation characteristics, its numerous borrowings from a range of other European and Mediterranean languages, its history of constant battles to establish unity and uniqueness, but perhaps most of all by its insistent history of centralisation and political control.

These historical facts not unsurprisingly affect language attitudes within France, which have clear historical origins. The Edict of Villers-Cotterets was simply a piece of good administration: it was necessary to modernise and to ensure that both administrators and administered could communicate effectively. But since most of the areas administered did not have French as a native language, one of the consequences was the growth of a class of French speakers, able to interpret between the language of power and the local vernacular, and gaining prestige from so doing. This growth of a prestigious group, an élite dominating by and through its control of language in the provinces, is paralleled by the increasing power and prestige of the Court in Paris. In the following century language attitudes became even more devoted to identifying and prizing the prestigious: the Court formed the notion of 'good French' (*le bon usage*), based on the concept of society supporting its leader and rejecting individualism. Language authorities were established and respected: Malherbe attempted to remove from the language all specialised, pedantic, provincial words in order to establish the least varied, but clearest, modes of expression. The *Académie Royale* (*Académie Française* after the Revolution of 1789), founded in 1635, at first as a private club, was assigned the task of producing a grammar and dictionary to codify the language as an instrument for the arts and sciences, but also for government. Vaugelas published his *Remarques sur la Langue française* in 1647, recommending, not the language of the people which Malherbe had accepted but tried to refine, but the language *de bonne tenue* of the Court itself, banning popular expressions. Jansenists such as Arnauld and Lancelot sought to find a rational basis for their comments, and their *Grammaire générale et raisonnée* (normally called the *Grammaire de Port-Royal*) justifies a reasoned and rational approach to codification. Boileau produced in 1674 his *Art poétique,* aimed at producing language which would neither shock nor offend.

These seventeenth-century grammarians shared the belief that French, in its clarity, reached perfection. Rivarol, in his *Discours sur l'universalité de la langue française* of 1784, repeated the message in limpid phrases known to every Frenchman:

> *Ce qui n'est pas clair n'est pas français*
> *La syntaxe française est incorruptible*
> *Sûre, sociale et raisonnable, ce n'est plus la langue française, c'est la langue humaine.*

For Rivarol, the universality of French derived from its clarity, itself derived from the direct order of its syntax - verb-subject-object; from its simplicity; and from the abstract nature of its expression. He made the point also that the prestige and hence universality of French depended on the evident superiority of French arms and culture, an approach which required him to denigrate other languages as crude, barbarous or otherwise inferior.

At the Revolution it became clear, after a report by the Abbé Grégoire, that only three million of the twenty-six million French population fully understood French. Regional languages were condemned in the report, and the proposal was clearly made that a standard French should be created, and imposed. The sentiment was reflected in a speech by Barère:

> *Le fédéralisme et la superstition parlent bas-breton; l'émigration et la haine de la République parlent allemand; la contre-révolution parle l'italien, et le fanatisme parle le basque. Cassons ces instruments de dommage et d'erreur...au moins on peut uniformer le langage d'une grande nation, de manière que tous les citoyens qui la composent, puissent sans obstacle se communiquer leurs pensées...le peuple français doit être jaloux de consacrer au plutôt, dans une République une et indivisible, l'usage unique et invariable de la langue de la liberté.*

Against this historical background it is almost inevitable that Bourhis should summarise thus the normal attitude of the French today toward regional languages, accents and dialects:

> a majority...favour one standard norm of French which happens to be the Ile de France dialect. Non-standard dialects and accents are not much tolerated as these are viewed as a threat to both the linguistic unity of France and to the purity and universality of the French language...on a prestige (high-low status) and evaluative (good-bad) continuum of speech styles in France, the Ile de France standard would be rated very favourably by both standard and non-standard speakers.   Conversely, one could expect regional accents and dialects to be rated below the Ile de France style, while urban non-standard and ethnic speech styles would be rated even lower.

It is commonly accepted that such purist and élitist attitudes are still prevalent today, among politicians, specialist linguists, the educated and non-educated alike.   Moves for the defence of French and for the maintenance of standards are widespread, the newspapers, of the Right and the Left, still have columnists providing advice on acceptable usage, and many educationalists feel that proposals for simplification of the acceptable rules, of spelling, syntax or pronunciation, in some way betray the character of French, despite the 1989 proposals for spelling reform by, of all people, the primary-school teachers. Although Zeldin (1983, 352) feels that this kind of élitism is no longer acceptable, and indeed recent editions of standard French dictionaries such as the *Petit Larousse* accept African or Canadian terms, and Larousse has revised the formality of the model letters it provides in *Le Parfait Secrétaire*, linguistic corpus planning is still a fact of life for the Linguistic Policy section of the Foreign Affairs Ministry and for the various Governmental agencies involved in terminology and in education, and language is still a topic which raises passions.

Further reading

Comrie, B. (ed). 1987. *The World's Major Languages.*
Grillo, R. D. 1989. *Dominant Languages: Language and Hierarchy in Britain and France.*
Muller, B. 1985. *Le Français d'aujourd'hui.*
Price, G. 1971. *The French Language: Present and Past.*
Rickard, P. 1989. *A History of the French Language.*
Ryan, E. B. and Giles, H. (eds) 1982. *Attitudes towards Language Variation.*
Von Wartburg, W. 1971. *Evolution et structure de la langue française.*
Walter, F. 1988. *Le Français dans tous les sens.*
Zeldin, T. 1983. *The French.*

2 Regionalism

2.1 Overview

STANDARD modern French derives from *francien*, the name now given to
the *langue d'oïl* dialects spoken around Paris after the disappearance of
Latin. France is usually divided into three main linguistic regions: the
North, where these *langue d'oïl* dialects are grouped; the South, where
langue d'oc or Occitan dialects are spoken; and the *franco-provençal* area.
In addition to Occitan, six other 'indigenous' languages, only two of them
deriving from Latin, are spoken around the geographical periphery of
France, while a number of 'immigrant' languages such as Arabic or
Portuguese are now spoken over the whole country.

The northern *langue d'oïl* dialects of French can be thought of as lying in
three zones: zone 1, closest to Paris, including the dialects of *francien*, zone
2 in a circle from *angevin, normand, picard, champenois, bourguignon,
berrichon* to *poitevin*, and zone 3, farthest from Paris including *gallo,
lorrain,* and *wallon*. Such a labelling represents the Paris-dominated world
of linguistic research, but is convenient in examining linguistic
characteristics by contrast with standard French.

In the South, dialects of north Occitan include *limousin*, north and south
auvergnat, and alpine *provençal*. South Occitan dialects are *languedocien*
and *provençal*, and the dialects of *gascon* are situated in the south-west of
France.

Franco-provençal covers the major part of French-speaking Switzerland
(Suisse romande), and the northern Alps to St-Etienne. Linguistically it
presents a mid-point between *langue d'oïl* and *langue d'oc,* with rather
more similarity to the former.

The indigenous languages of France, apart from French itself, are:

> German, in the form of three dialects: franconian (*francique*) in Lorraine and northern Alsace, and alemannic - *haut alémanique* in southern Alsace and *bas alémanique* in central Alsace;
> Basque, in the south-west part of France near Biarritz;
> Breton, in the Armorican peninsula of north-west France - with two main dialect groups: KLT (Bro-Gerne, Bro-Leon, Bro-Dreger (Cornouaille, Léon, Trégor)) and the Vannetais;
> Catalan, in the South-West from Carcassonne to Perpignan;
> Corsican;
> Flemish, in the North-East around Dunkirk;
> Occitan, with the three main dialect groups we have already described.

These seven are known as **regional languages**: each has territorial boundaries. Three are spoken only within the French State (Breton, although as a Celtic language this is very similar to Welsh and Irish; Corsican, although this is basically a dialect of Italian; and Occitan), while the others are also spoken beyond French frontiers: German in Germany, Austria, Switzerland and elsewhere; Basque in Spain; Catalan in Andorra and Spain; and Flemish in Belgium and Holland.

2.2 Dialects of the North: linguistic characteristics

THE following outline review covers the area of the *langue d'oïl* (ie it does not include Alsace, Brittany or the Flemish-speaking area around Dunkirk) and uses the names of the medieval dialects, but it should be remembered that what is being described are some major contemporary differences from standard French. Some of these should properly be classified as **regional French,** others as dialect forms; some are merely a matter of accent or pronunciation differences; some indeed represent borrowings from nearby languages, as in the case of Lorrain. All together represent pronunciations, morphology, syntax and usage which generally characterise the region today. The survey suffices only to give some hint of the contrasts with standard spoken French which are still widespread. More detailed yet still fairly general information is available in Walter 1982, Carton et al 1983, Muller 1985, Vermes 1988, and Walter 1988, and these volumes also indicate appropriate references for the detailed studies. Sample recordings appear with Carton et al 1983.

The principal differences in pronunciation from standard French include the presence of diphthongs - [iao] for [o] (*eau*), and different contexts of use of the standard French vowels - [u] for [œ] (*plusieurs*), or [ɛ] for [a] (*moi*). Some consonants which standard French does not know are used in the regions: an aspirate [h], a [w] where French uses [g] (*wetier* for *guetter*), or a palatalised [l]; and some consonants such as [ʃ] in words like *échapper* may be pronounced as their unpalatalised equivalents - [k], while French [s] may often sound closer to [ʃ] in words like *racine*. In many regions the morphology of the verb may not be the same as in French, and the past historic of the verb may be used for example instead of or as widely as the past perfect, or the *passé surcomposé* (*j'ai eu fait*) may be frequent. French vocabulary may be replaced by local terms, such as *cinse* for French *ferme*; the number system may include terms like *septante* or *nonante* where French uses *soixante-dix* or *quatre-vingts*.

2.2.1 Zone 3 (outer zone)
2.2.1.1 Wallon
Pronunciation
- The /r/ is pronounced gutturally ('*r grasseyé*').
- Some vowels are nasalised in addition to the standard French set: words such as *reine*, *jeune* and *royaume* thus have a nasal vowel.

Lexis
- The numerals *septante*, *nonante* correspond to French *soixante-dix*, *quatre-vingts*.
- Particularly in Belgium, and because of different social conditions from France, the vocabulary for many aspects of life is quite different: *athénée* for *lycée*, *aubette* for *kiosque à journaux*.
  Many other terms of everyday life are also different: *amitieux* for *affectueux*, *dracher* for *pleuvoir*.

Syntax
- *Avoir* followed by an adjective: *avoir bon de faire quelquechose* (or *facile*, *difficile*, *dur* etc), in the sense of *trouver bon de faire quelquechose*.

See particularly Baetens Beardsmore 1971 for a description of the French of Brussels.

2.2.1.2 *Lorrain*
Pronunciation
- In words such as *gage* the initial [g] of French corresponds to Lorrain [w]. Many of these words are of Germanic origin.
- Some vowels of French correspond to diphthongs in Lorrain: *après* [aprie], *vérité* [veritie], *mère* [meir].
- [ʃ] corresponds to French [s] in words like *tisserand* or *laisser*.
- A final consonant is often sounded in words which may have lost it even in spelling in French: *vertu* is thus pronounced [vɛrtyt].
- [b], in words such as *table* or *fable*, is often pronounced as [u].
- [u] is used instead of [œ] in words like *plusieurs* or *pleurs*, and instead of [o] in *chose*.

2.2.2 *Zone 2*
2.2.2.1 *Normandy*
Pronunciation
- An /ɛ/ sound like that in French *père* is used in many contexts where French uses [a] or [wa]: *moi* [mwɛ], *boire* [bwɛr], *boîte* [bwɛt].
- [k] is used instead of [ʃ] in words like *chapeau* or *chêne*.
- [ʃ] is used where French uses [s] in words like *racine* and *cent*.
- A palatalised l ('*l mouillé*') is used in words like *caillou* or *fille*.
- Diphthongs appear in words like *faut* ([fao]), *eau* ([iao]), *beau* ([biao]), *seau* and *tonneau*.
- The nasal [ɛ̃] without the preceding [j], is used in words like *bien*, to produce the well-known [bɛ̃].
- h is pronounced as an aspirate [h] in words like *hublot* or *houille*.

2.2.2.2 *Picard*
Pronunciation
- As in Normandy, [k] appears where French uses [ʃ]: *échapper* is pronounced [ekape].
- [ʃ] replaces the French [s] in examples similar to those quoted above for Normandy.
Vocabulary
- Some examples of different terms: *apothicaire (pharmacien), cinse (ferme), arbéyer (regarder), ennoyer (scruter), raviser (contempler), wetier (guetter).*

2.2.3 Zone 1 (inner zone): Ile de France and Centre

Pronunciation
- Diphthongs are used: in the pronunciation [eɥ] for *eu* (eg *j'ai eu*).
- The intercalated 'd' is not present in the future and conditional of verbs like *voudra, viendra, faudra*.

Syntax
- *Pas mais* is used where standard French uses just *pas*: *la vie, elle est pas mais belle quand on est vieux*.
- *Aucun* is used with a positive sense: *d'aucuns le disent*.
- *Devant* is used for *avant*: *devant la guerre*.
- *Autant comme* is used for *autant que*.

Vocabulary
- Regional words exist for a range of items and concepts: *heurible* for 'early' (crops); *un repas* is 'a festival', rather than 'a meal'; *guetter* is used in the sense of 'to watch over' (*garder*); *un voyage* is 'a pilgrimage'.
- Words change sense according to local usage: *la fourche* is 'a wooden hay-fork' north-west of Paris and a *broc* is of metal there, while south of Paris the only word is *fourche*; 'a scab' is *un galon* north-west and *une croûte* north-east of Paris; *macabre* is 'heavy' in the Eure-et-Loir.

2.3 Regional French: linguistic characteristics

THE medieval dialects spoken from Gallo-Roman times had practically disappeared from normal usage in the towns and in educated groups early in the present century, leaving only the accents and the type of minor differences noted above. In the areas where regional languages were spoken, and although these languages as such may have disappeared in normal use, there remain differences between the French spoken and the Parisian educated norm, particularly as far as older speakers and intimate family occasions or situations in which 'psychological or physiological control of speech is relaxed' (Muller 1985, 158) are concerned. Speakers in the regions believe however that they are speaking French, rather than any local patois; they have no sense of inferiority or **insecurity** about their regional French and diglossia is not involved. They have nonetheless finished by creating a supplementary level, 'intermediary between the regional language they spoke and the standard French they wanted to speak' (Muller 1985 159).

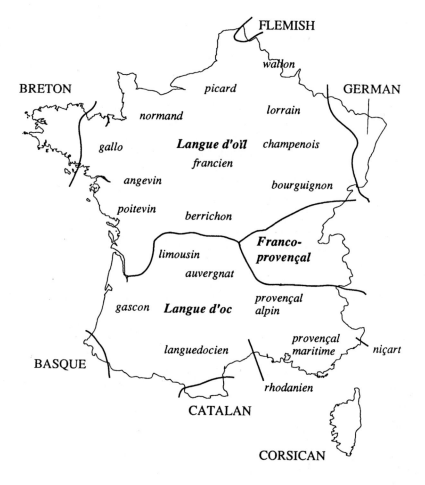

FLEMISH

wallon

BRETON

picard

GERMAN

normand

lorrain

gallo

Langue d'oïl

champenois

francien

angevin

bourguignon

poitevin

berrichon

Franco-provençal

limousin

auvergnat

provençal alpin

gascon

Langue d'oc

provençal maritime

languedocien

niçart

BASQUE

rhodanien

CATALAN

CORSICAN

French Regional Languages and Dialects

Tuaillon, however, in Vermes 1988 (299), summarises the situation thus:

> French exists in a pure form which is perceived as the model
> towards which everybody 'must' strive, correcting his accent, his
> regional grammatical errors, purifying his vocabulary. The world
> of patois and dialects is founded on tolerance and the freedom to be
> part of one's village; the world of French is that of severe linguistic
> discipline. Regional French is made up of the failure to achieve that
> discipline: it marks the points where linguistic unification has not yet
> achieved perfection.

Many individual lexical items have survived from the ancient dialects and
languages, and in some cases, morphological and syntactic differences from
standard French, and certainly pronunciation differences, can be traced
back to these earlier forms. Muller quotes the following examples
applicable to a number of regional forms of French:

- an aspirate [h], particularly noticeable in Wallonie, Lorraine,
  Alsace, but also in Normandy;
- a trilled [r], widespread in the North but also throughout the
  southern Occitan areas;
- retention of the nasal vowel [œ̃] in the South-East and South-West,
  in the North and the East;
- retention of the final *e muet* in the South-West and the West.

In vocabulary, one particularly widespread archaism is noted: the use of
the forms *dîner* and *souper* for standard French *déjeuner* and *dîner*. In
morphology and syntax fewer examples are relevant, mainly because, since
their regional French is thought by speakers to be standard French, wide
divergences from the written norm, with which all are familiar from their
education, would be more obvious. Nonetheless, such syntactic divergence
as does occur on a generalised basis is likely to be similar to the syntactic
forms of spoken, popular or vulgar French. One example is the use of *être*
as the perfect tense auxiliary for être itself - *je suis été malade*; another is
the widespread use of *que* as a linking element: *faire ce qu'on a envie, dans
la position qu'elle est, c'est une vieille dame que les dents lui bougent.*
The following outline review of some characteristics of different forms
of regional French covers the areas where regional languages are or have
been spoken: that is, Alsace, Brittany, the Flemish-speaking areas of the
North, and the South where Basque, Catalan and Occitan are used. The
differences noted here are limited mainly to questions of pronunciation, and

in each case it is clear that they arise from the speech habits of the relevant regional language: in Alsace, for example, the resulting accent is practically indistinguishable from that of a native German speaker speaking French.

Alsace
- A distinction of length in vowels: vowels followed by a 'voiced' consonant are lengthened.
- Final consonants are devoiced: *sud, gaz, village, fève* are pronounced as though they ended with [-t, -s, -ʃ,] or [-f].
- The opposition between voiced and unvoiced consonants is neutralised generally: *jeune* is pronounced *cheune* with initial [ʃ], and *pièce* sounds as though it begins with [b].
- p, t and k are aspirated as in English.
- The initial syllable is stressed, and often preceded by a glottal stop as in German.
- The intonation often rises on stressed syllables.

More detailed information is available in Wolf, 1983b.

Brittany
- e, o and /œ/ sounds followed by a consonant are pronounced 'closed': *treize* with the vowel of *les*; *notre* with that of *eau*; *coeur* with that of *jeu*.
- /r/ sounds are often very guttural, like the -ch of Scottish loch.
- Stressed vowels are lengthened.
- Stress falls on the penultimate syllable of word or group.
- Unstressed syllables are swallowed.
- Intonation often rises at the end of a phrase.

Flemish-speaking areas
- /e/, /o/ and /œ/ sounds are closed in open syllables and open in closed ones: *c'était, aurait* have the vowel of *les*, while *côte* is pronounced [kɔt].
- There is no palatalised [j] sound derived from [l], so [traval] is used for French *travail* and [viel] for *vieille*.

The South
- Pronunciation of nasal consonants, with some denasalisation of the preceding nasal vowel: *tombe* is pronounced [tɔmb] rather than [tɔ̃b].
- Final *e muet* is pronounced.
- /r/ is usually an apical trill.

- /o/ before a consonant is usually pronounced as an open [ɔ]: *saute* is pronounced like *sotte*, and *gauche* as similar to English 'gosh'.

These general characteristics are those of the pronunciation of the different Occitan dialects, and apply across southern France. In different areas of the South, however, the dialect history of the region causes additional pronunciation differences: in the Auvergne, for example, the *auvergnat* dialect of Occitan palatalised consonants freely, so *ça* might be pronounced [ʃa], and the [t] in *le matin* closer to [ʃ].

Muller (see also Nouvel 1978) also gives a list of morphosyntactic differences found in Marseille, such as:

- retention of the simple past, even in spoken forms;
- in imperatives, the direct object pronoun does not immediately follow the verb: *dites-moi-le!*;
- use of *un* as equivalent to *quelqu'un: un qui est boulanger*;
- use of the possessive adjective: *il est mien* for *il est à moi*.

2.4 Dialectology and sociolinguistics

DIALECTS and regional languages have long been studied in France, and the linguistic facts have been clearly established through the two main methods of historical and geographical study.

The apparently clear distinctions however between **accent**, a pronunciation difference from the standard, **dialect**, a subset of a language which is comprehensible to speakers of another dialect of the same language but which presents difficulties in pronunciation, grammar and lexis, **language**, distinguished from other languages because of mutual incomprehensibility, and **patois**, often used pejoratively to indicate rural or backward usage, in fact require refinement. Between each dialect or regional language the frontier or boundary of intelligibility is rarely absolute, each dialect area shading into the next, so the Romance languages distributed across Europe from Portugal to Romania and from Sardinia to Belgium show different degrees of comprehensibility between contiguous varieties, and the passage from one language to another takes place across gradually adapting dialects and dialect groups, forming a language/dialect continuum: generally there is no sharp dividing line. Only in recent years, with the development of States as political entities and nationalism as an affective tie, have language boundaries become more marked, so a second criterion for distinguishing between the terms languages, dialects and accents is a social one: whether people generally consider that they are speaking French or Normand, Breton or Vannetais, Catalan or Occitan, and whether speakers feel these are languages, dialects or accents.

The historical facts are however clear: there is general agreement that in the Gallo-Roman period, after the collapse of the Roman Empire, considerable dialectal fragmentation of the popular Latin then spoken across France occurred, and the three major dialect divisions developed, further divided into subdialectal areas. There is some dispute concerning the relationship of *langue d'oc*, variously called *provençal* or *occitan*, with Catalan, and with *langue d'oïl*, but it is the historically attested distribution of dialects, and the history of their development from Latin, which forms the basis for the identification of modern dialect areas in most contemporary reference works. The term dialect, in this historical tradition, is reserved for the forms which derived direct from Latin in parallel with French, which itself, as the *francien* dialect, is linguistically of no more importance than any other. Regional French however is a variation from standard French, a variation whose characteristics may well recall the linguistic history of the region, and one which may now have replaced the dialect itself. Some confusion is hence possible when describing local usage in the *langue d'oïl* areas of the North: the historically attested dialect may not now be represented 'on the ground'.

To identify the contemporary situation, the researcher will need to carry out direct enquiry of the inhabitants of a particular region, in a survey by questionnaire or interview, in a similar way to market research or sociological survey work. Such geographical dialectology was a reaction both to historical methods of internal re-creation and also to the 'folklore' approach to dialectology, in which much *ad-hoc* information was produced in dictionaries, glossaries and samples collected by amateurs. Dialectologists establish current patterns of language use, transfer these to maps and plot the distribution of features of pronunciation, grammar and lexical selection.   Traditionally the informants providing data for such dialect surveys are selected from older inhabitants in rural occupations, have a level of education not above the primary and have lived all their lives in the region. They provide secondary descriptions of their own or the neighbourhood's use, together with, more recently, recordings of their own speech and other primary evidence. The maps resulting from the surveys enable the plotting of dialect boundaries for individual features (the boundary line is called an **isogloss**, on the analogy with isobar for a line joining points of the same atmospheric pressure), and the line where a number of such isoglosses converge indicates the location of a major dialect or language boundary, such as for example that between the north and south of France, which forms a line joining Lyon and Bordeaux, with a curve or crescent running north of Clermont-Ferrand.

The results of **geographical dialectology** form a series of atlases, correlating pronunciation and location, the linguistic forms used for a particular concept or object ('cat', 'ploughing') and their location, and other aspects of language such as morphology or syntax with location. The oldest of the atlases is the *Atlas linguistique de la France* by Gilliéron (1902-10), and newer ones in more detail and with a more local focus continue to appear, with new technology aiding the complex task.

One of the main conclusions to draw from the study of such atlases is that dialect areas are themselves subdivided, and that although it may be possible to give a general description of a dialect, individual villages and towns within the area will show subtly different traits: the isoglosses indicating the boundaries between dialect areas by no means all coincide. Another, related, conclusion is the observation that in contemporary France there is normally no written form for the dialect; both accents and dialects are spoken forms.

Although both historical study and dialectology establish the linguistic map of France, they do not necessarily assist in identifying variation within a dialect, or provide information about the usage of social groups other than those directly investigated, or about language attitudes. A whole range of dialect forms of 'superior' levels is often excluded by the necessity to confine enquiry to rural uneducated peasants who have never left the region - a group which is becoming rarer in any case; and the necessarily atomistic data, together with the frequent use of historical data to 'explain' and sometimes to restrict understanding of the contemporary dialect or language situation, means that information on actual contemporary usage is often inadequate.

2.5 Sociolinguistics and regional variation

VERY few if any true monolinguals are left in any of the French regional languages. The young generally speak and use regional languages less than their parents did, and in no region is the regional language used by more than 70 per cent of the population. There are no accurate and dependable figures from which to identify the population of speakers of each language, but estimations, based on Tozzi 1984 and Vermes 1988 are as follows:

German: 1,100,000.
Basque: 90,000 (the Basque-speaking population in Spain is approximately 600,000).
Breton: 350,000, while 600,000 are capable of speaking it and 1,000,000 understand.
Catalan: 180,000, together with 20,000 in Andorra and a further 5,500,000 in Spain.
Corsican: 70,000 to 180,000.
Flemish: 40,000 to 100,000.
Occitan: 3,000,000, although up to 12,000,000 are said to have some understanding.

Hence between 4,830,000 and 14,650,000 of the 50 million or so of the French population, or between 10 and 30 per cent of the total, are thought to have some knowledge of the regional languages. Estimations of the number of remaining *langue d'oïl* dialect speakers are similarly vague.

We shall review each of the seven regional languages in following chapters, identifying their sociolinguistic situation, problems and concerns by examining the history of the region, its political situation and finally its language situation. Since every region is different the treatments will differ, but overall there are common factors affecting each of them:

- all language regions are geographically peripheral;
- generally speaking, the history of the regions is one of absorption into the French State: slowly, by marriage or conquest before the Revolution; more speedily, by economic domination or administrative efficiency since;
- all regional languages are in effect spoken by bilinguals;
- all regional languages are in a diglossic situation within France;
- in many areas the sociolinguistic situation is closely associated with economic and social problems, and French has been seen as the symbol of domination if not of oppression;
- the preferred areas for action by those who wish to protect or encourage regional languages are in education and the media;
- regional action is often also political action: in the past (up to 1945) this was often political action with right-wing tendencies, although since that time it has been mainly left-wing, associated

with national liberation movements, local economic freedom from
Paris domination, and worker movements;
regional action is often, but not always, associated with a wish for
federation, autonomy, separatism or independence, and hence with
views on the organisation and institutions of the State; in some
situations this has led to violent action.

How strongly rooted is language-based regionalism in France? How, and
why, do people in the regions find themselves in conflict with Paris? The
concept of dominance, which was introduced in Section 1.1.6 above,
provides the clearest approaches to understanding, although they are
necessarily based on conflict models and often on essentially Marxist views
of social processes.

There are at least six possible interpretations of the meaning of
dominance, and the resulting conflict, in sociolinguistics (cf Wardhaugh
1987, Grillo 1989), each dependent on an underlying academic discipline
and on the interests and aims of the analyst. Two analyses, one 'political'
and the second 'economic', see language as an **object** of policy and
planning: the relevant region or ethnic group must be dominated through
the political or the economic marginalisation of its language. Two more
approaches rely on psychology or sociology: analysing on the one hand the
power roles of individuals as mediated through their language and on the
other the interplay of their conceptual systems. Language is seen here as a
symbol of identity, of the person or of the group. Two rather more
linguistic or discoursal approaches complete the range: one observing and
analysing the use of language as a **tool** and method of domination by the
superior group, and the other analysing the marginalisation of the
communicative practices of the inferior group. Language is seen here as a
weapon used within social processes.

Political centralisation was a major policy of the kings of France in
their attempts to annex territory and to create a powerful European
nation-state. Their policy was followed by the French Revolution, by the
emperors and kings who ruled in the nineteenth century and by the
Republics which have followed: even today President Pompidou could say,
in 1972, '*Il n'y a pas de place pour les langues minoritaires dans une France
destinée à marquer l'Europe de son sceau*'. This linguistic centralisation,
and the conscious or unconscious language planning it involved, had the
same aim as political, military and diplomatic moves: to ensure that political
boundaries also became affective boundaries. To do this it was necessary

for the political power first to destroy local allegiances and regional symbols, among them the regional languages.

A similar process took place in economic terms, with planning being undertaken by economic and market forces rather than the political power. The insertion of French into regional economic life, as a necessary means of communication (Brun 1923), reflected the moves towards capitalist economic systems requiring investment from outside the province, with profits flowing away from the periphery to the same centres. Transport systems, allowing the movement of goods; economic structures locating manufacturing in the provinces but the head office in Paris; and the relocation of populations in Paris, added to their constant moves - even today, some 44 per cent of the population of Paris was not born there - exacerbate this domination of the **periphery** by the **core**. In the economy, the peripheral regions have suffered from the exodus of the peasantry from the countryside to the towns and from the collapse of traditional industries. Greater consumerism, the mobility of workers and the travelling habits of the holiday population all combine to reduce still further the feeling of group economic identity on which regionalism rests. In France in particular this model is attractive: *Paris et le désert français* was the title of a justifiably popular treatment of the economics of France in the twentieth century, and the French centralist attitude of domination over the regions has been characterised as internal colonialism of an extreme kind (eg Calvet 1974). Since European Community priorities will lead inexorably to the imposition of a pan-European language, almost certainly English, before the turn of the century, it is very likely that the opposition of the regions within France to the imposition of French will be paralleled by the opposition of countries such as France to this new form of economic domination from London, Bonn and Paris.

Social psychologists, in analysing attitudes towards language variation, often consider that the values attached to regional accents or languages indicate very clearly the **power relationships** individuals attribute to such factors (see Ryan and Giles 1982). Authoritarian language, the voice characteristics and manner of speaking of the intellectual may thus seem to lend weight and value to what he says, whereas the same message conveyed in slang, in a strong regional accent or in inappropriate or illegitimate ways may defeat the intended purpose. This approach is similar to the view which holds that regional languages are appropriate for jokes, for discussion of rural topics or the weather, but that they do not possess the vocabulary, seriousness or even the syntax with which to communicate on aspects of modern life such as science or technology. Although no serious linguist holds such views, the approach has some face validity and regional movements often go to considerable lengths to modernise and adapt the language to enable it to express modern realities.

During the 1939-45 war, regionalism was confused with collaboration with the occupying forces, since regionalist movements had tended to identify with nationalist fervour, with opposition to other groups, and with the racist ideologies of groups such as the National Socialists or the Italian Fascists. It took until the early 1960s and the end of the French colonial empire before regionalism could again both demand and receive attention, at a time when the creation of the European Communities seemed to make a Europe of the regions, rather than of the nations, possible, and when regionalism could be viewed again as a legitimate aspiration for group **identity** rather than as part of a **conceptual system** based on an ideology which had become unacceptable. The 'freedom' rhetoric associated with the events of May 1968 made it seem that regionalism, as part of the desire for greater freedom of the individual, could again be politically important for thinkers who did not wish to accept closed ideological systems, and the emotional force of the campaign against the expropriation of the Larzac plain for military purposes reinforced this view for a time.

A second aspect of this 'conceptual systems' approach to understanding regionalism adds a social dimension to regional conflict. During the seventeenth and eighteenth centuries French came to be used more and more in the cultural and social worlds surrounding the French king; as aristocrats were attracted to Paris and then to Versailles, patois such as Gascon were decried and ridiculed, and the idea of correctness, of *bon usage* and of the associated rules of social behaviour was widely adopted. The literature, music and art of Versailles came to be regarded as the summit of French artistic perfection. In the eighteenth century French was regarded throughout Europe as the vehicle of reason: in the nineteenth and twentieth as that of thought, art and culture. In recent years, scientific and technological progress in certain (restricted) domains such as mathematics or transport, and in the commercial world, have strengthened the symbolic value of standard French as a superior repository of humanistic cultural values: a pre-eminent cultural and intellectual vehicle for Paris. The **cultural assumptions** of the French population have increasingly been to value French as a cultural symbol, while the regions, by contrast, have little to offer as models of high culture: their cultural traditions are all too easily ignored, and their cultural manifestations marginalised.

Politicians and other leaders of society select their language use with care. Their task is to present their ideas, to ensure their acceptance and to provoke collective action in support of their policies and ideologies. They must set the agenda of discussion, decide the framework of consideration, and determine the **discourse**, the vocabulary and significance of terms, in which matters will be discussed. It is no accident that terms like *nous, la France* and *Paris*, and more and more *l'Europe,* are closely associated in French political discourse, nor that linguistic analysis of the speech of de Gaulle can show his equation of *je, la gloire, l'Etat* and *la France.* The discourse of society's leaders can be analysed through the techniques of **discourse analysis** to show how the communicative practices of the Parisian centre have established and maintained the prestige of standard French over peripheral regional forms.

The manners of speaking, or **communicative practices,** of ethnic groups can likewise be denigrated. Many descriptions of the speech styles of regional groups point out how 'unFrench' their linguistic liberty, freedom of creation of new terms, range of diminutives or colourful vocabulary is, and how far the severe discipline of standard, codified French has ensured accuracy, precision, clarity and other desirable qualities as opposed to these childlike characteristics. The same approach applies to creole, to popular French or to other differences from standard French. Similarly, the **legitimacy** of regional languages is contested by their relegation to defined functions, usually those associated with private, domestic purposes, intimacy, or aspects of commercial or public life which are less dignified or less significant than the official domains for which standard French alone is regarded as sufficiently prestigious. Diglossia itself can thus be interpreted as a sociolinguistic process in which the different communicative practices of situations, rather than of groups, is the domain of conflict, and in which language is the central dimension of the opposition.

Language presents a problem for regionalist movements: in many cases the debate between those who wish to preserve the regional language in its past condition, as an historic monument or as an object of veneration, a product of the people, and those who wish it to be an effective vehicle of present-day communication, with all that that implies in terms of codification, standardisation, and terminological innovation, has not been resolved. Its purpose and the social and economic domains in which it should be used in the future are not clear: the need to communicate with the outside world restricts its effectiveness and yet its value in internal economic circuits has been destroyed. Local open-air peasant markets have been replaced by impersonal out-of-town supermarkets often supplied from some distance. In some regions, such as Alsace or the Catalan-speaking South-West, the choice of which language to teach, and in which language to teach, causes major problems: using standard German or standardised Catalan as against the local dialects marginalises the local variety, and hence the very symbol of regionalism may be destroyed by regionalism.

Regionalism, and regional movements, are for some merely the creation of the intelligentsia, an irrelevance to today's problems. The communicative practices of the remaining groups of 'native' regional language speakers, usually rural, poorly educated, isolated groups, are not such as to permit a full range of discourse functions to be natural, and hence a certain artificiality is involved in re-creating levels of language, and terminology, in which contemporary life, social practices and technological developments can be discussed.

The creation of the association *Défense et Promotion des Langues de France* in 1962, grouping representatives from the seven regional language areas, and considerable regional action after 1968 and throughout the 1970s, culminating in the start of the economic crisis in 1974 and 1975, led gradually to more public demands for bilingual education, the recognition of public uses of the relevant languages, and eventually to demands for recognition presented to the European Parliament, based on a report produced in 1981, for a Charter for Minority Languages and Cultures, which was agreed by the Parliament on 16 October 1981. Most action at European level since has been directed towards languages in countries other than France.

The 1982 Giordan report to the French Minister of Culture, on French cultural minorities, represents a high point in the recent consideration of the role of the French State and the regions. It proposed a policy of 'reparations for the historic damage which had been caused to the regional language communities': suggesting the reversal of specific controls which still apply, such as the rule that regional newspapers must contain no more than 25 per cent of their text in a regional language, or the rule that regional languages may not be used in official documents, including cheques, or in law court statements or legal contracts. President Mitterrand, coming to power in 1981, had included '*le droit à la différence*' among his manifesto statements, noting that attacking a people in its culture and its language constituted the deepest wound it was possible to inflict. The Giordan report reflected this view:

Repressing, devaluing, marginalising languages different from one's own forms part of an inhuman logic of élitism and cultural imposition, contradicting the right to be different and to enjoy a democratic social and cultural way of life.

The position of the French political Right, however, was expressed at about the same time by Michel Debré, commenting on the report:

Giordan tries to contradict those many generations who have created France through their intermingling...the secular and republican belief which created French citizenship...the great achievements of French education. The author confuses the respect due to provincial traditions with a deliberate attack on the unity of the Republic. His report expresses the deliberate wish to dismember the French nation (Dossier, 1983, 52).

By 1990 the net effect of the pressure to recognise regional languages within France has been some moves in the educational field to permit teaching of the languages up to university level, and within pre-school classes and in some primary schools, mainly for dedicated groups of parents; there is some teaching in and through the language, but in general the French educational system has remained strongly dominated by standard French. In the media, some television, radio and Press channels are available to regional languages, but again to a very restricted extent. In other aspects of French life the regional languages and dialects play little formal or official role, and if anything the public pressure to recognise and support regional movements has decreased in visibility since the Socialist governments have been in office. Whether increased awareness of ethnic origin and language from areas such as Eastern and Central Europe will rekindle this pressure is uncertain.

Further reading

Baetens Beardsmore, H. 1971. *Le Français régional de Bruxelles.*
Brun, A. 1923. *Essai historique sur l'introduction du français dans les provinces du Midi de la France.*
Calvet, L.-J. 1974. *Linguistique et colonialisme.*
Carton, F., Rossi, M., Autesserre, D., and Léon, P. 1983. *Les Accents des Français.*
Chambers, J. K., and Trudgill, P. 1980. *Dialectology.*
Chaurand, J. 1972. *Introduction à la dialectologie française.*
Giordan, H. 1982. *Démocratie culturelle et droit à la différence.*
Grau, R. 1985. *Les Langues et les cultures minoritaires en France.*
Grillo, R.D. 1989. *Dominant Languages.*
Guiraud, P. 1978b. *Patois et dialectes français.*

Lafont, R. (ed). 1982. *Langue dominante, langues dominées.*
Nouvel, A. 1978. *Le Français parlé en Occitanie.*
Tozzi, M. 1984. *Apprendre et vivre sa langue.*
Vermes, G. (ed). 1988. *Vingt-cinq communautés linguistiques de la France.* (2 vols)
Vermes, G., and Boutet, J. (eds) 1987. *France, pays multilingue* . (2 vols)
Walter, H. 1988. *Le Français dans tous les sens.*
Wolf, L. 1983. *Le Français régional d'Alsace.*
1984. *Par les langues de France.* 2 vols

3 Occitan

3.1 Occitan: history

MOST specialists refer to the language of the south of France as '*occitan*', a term which dates from the fourteenth century. This language used generally to be called '*limousin*' in the Middle Ages, when the *troubadours* spread its fame as a literary vehicle, and '*provençal*' in the nineteenth century, when a major revival of its literary renown was last attempted. The area, almost a third of metropolitan France, lacks any one large centre which could rival Paris, avoided early invasion by the Franks and retained a mixture of Roman and feudal administration until quite late in its history. For Occitan nationalists three dates are significant: 1228, when northern France conquered the South in the Albigensian Crusade; 1793, when federalism was crushed by centralisation as the fundamental policy of the Revolution; and 1907, when peasants and workers rose in revolt against economic domination.

After the Roman Empire collapsed in the fifth century, and despite its replacement by feudalism, the South retained both Roman law, thus avoiding the imposition of the customary law which had been introduced by the Franks, and, through the Church, the administrative organisation of the Roman Empire. Although fragmented, much of the area was controlled from the ninth century by the counts or dukes of Provence, of Toulouse, and of Aquitaine, while in the thirteenth century it became part of the 'Angevin Empire', to be finally attached to France in the fifteenth. Part of the South-West was united with part of northern Spain in the kingdom of Navarre, whose king Henri became French king in 1589, although the French part of Navarre had been a French possession since 1284.

Only in the eleventh and twelfth centuries did the life of the region become gradually more civilised and less troubled by feudal battles, allowing the *troubadours* to create poetry and songs and spread them by travel from castle to great house. This short period of flowering of a specifically southern culture came to a brutal end as the Crusades led by

Simon de Montfort against the Albigensian heresy (the Cathares) brought not merely the military strength of the North to bear on the disorganised South in 1209-29, but also the more sinister and thorough religious might of the Inquisition, tracking down any form of resistance and imposing a tightly controlled regime. The main economic benefit of the Crusade came to the kings of France, who took over the domains of the Count of Toulouse, while the independent towns of the area also sought their protection. Even today the severity with which northern rule was imposed is used by supporters of greater autonomy as an example of what is to be expected of repressive Parisian attitudes.

The speed with which French became imposed as the language of administrative and official matters after the Albigensian Crusades has been documented (Brun 1923) and parallels the speed of the takeover of power. But the Grégoire report of 1794 had noted that most of the population of the south still did not speak French. Some bilinguals, particularly lawyers or educated town-dwellers, clearly acted as interpreters after the Edict of Villers-Cotterets of 1539, and contrasted strongly with a mainly rural population speaking only Occitan. Despite the magnificent tradition of written poetry of the Middle Ages, Occitan was not to become a written language with a full range of expressive possibilities, and was also to lack the centralising, refining impulse which a central power base or town could have provided. Any written forms of Occitan were therefore as diverse as were the different spoken dialects.

In the nineteenth and twentieth centuries the southern problem has been that of an economically dependent region whose wealth, in the form of capital, is exported, placed into foreign loans and state bonds. Its principal agricultural product has been wine, usually of poor quality: the area of vine cultivation increased from 238,000 hectares in 1828 to 450,000 in 1870, and overproduction, together with increasing unemployment in mines and the textile trade, was a cause of peasant and worker riots in 1907 (Keating 1986, 27). In the 1970s, too, the intention of the military to create a nuclear test site in the Cévennes, at Larzac, was seen as further indication that Paris had no regard for the South, and that all the South could do was lobby for yet more subsidies, while the financial and political élite of France consistently ignored the needs of the region.

The increased population from immigration and a higher birth-rate, accompanied by the move from country to town - Montpellier doubled its population between 1962 and 1975 - worsened problems of unemployment. Through the 1960s, 70s and early 80s Occitan nationalism benefited from these worsening conditions, although separatism and independence were never really serious political options. The intellectuals and writers who formed the core of the Occitan movement were themselves divided, partly through a history of language-based split between the east and the west of the region, between the supporters of the *Félibrige* and those of *occitanisme*.

In the nineteenth century Frédéric Mistral, poet and man of letters, attempted together with a group of six friends to resurrect the power and prestige of his native *provençal* as a literary language. The intention was to restore the written language, and in so doing to restore the racial identity and pride of the South. Mistral published his long poem 'Mireille' in *provençal* and French in 1859, and capitalised on its success in pursuing his aim. First it was necessary to devise adequate methods of transcribing and recording the grammar and lexis of the language, of rationalising and codifying spelling, and of carrying out the work which had been done for French itself by the *Académie*, the sixteenth and seventeenth century writers and their accompanying salons. The friends, who called themselves the '*Félibrige*', had an immense task, and although the literary reputation of Mistral enabled him to gain and hold the interest and enthusiasm of the cultivated public throughout France, the effort and dedication required to complete the detailed scholarly work in his lifetime was too much. He produced '*Lou Trésor dou Félibrige*' as an encyclopedic dictionary and grammar, but the problems of dialect fragmentation, of the lack of a large concentrated number of *provençal* speakers, and the fact that his own dialect (that of Maillane, in the region near Arles) was not the best basis for a rationalised language for the whole of the south of France, meant that although the *Félibrige* movement continued after his death and continues today, his work was insufficient to resist the encroachments of French, and certainly insufficient to re-establish *provençal* as a major literary or prestige language.

For three reasons therefore the *Félibrige* reforms did not succeed: Mistral himself was too imposing and singular a figure to carry the full burden; the rhodanien dialect of the Avignon/Arles/Nîmes area is incapable of providing a sufficiently generalisable form of the language to act as the basis for the whole South; and the particular area, not having suffered so much political or religious oppression as the more western parts, and not possessing as important an economic centre as Marseille or Toulouse, did not have the power, the prestige or enthusiasm with which to oppose French.

Nonetheless the orthographic system, based on French spelling conventions, and the numerous linguistic choices Mistral made and illustrated in his works, meant that the *Félibrige* movement provided a basis: 'before then it was total anarchy and no one thought it possible that Occitan could survive' (Bec 1978, 105). The impulse given by the *Félibrige* movement was followed by a number of conferences, meetings and publications in which people from all over the South attempted to find better solutions to the language problems. In 1876 a conference decided to re-examine the spelling problem, and in 1935 a different system was proposed, based on the Languedoc dialects, establishing a generalisable grammar and description of the linguistic system, and using a more traditional approach than the 'phonetic' and French-based orthography of the *Félibrige*.

The association between Occitan nationalism, literature, politics, economics, education and the liberty of the individual should not be underemphasised. A 1936 manifesto, quoted in Lafont 1974, 247-8, demonstrates sentiments of opposition to central power and the desire to establish autonomy quite clearly:

> 1) We recognise no other homeland than (Auvergne) - Béarn - Catalogne - Languedoc - (Limousin) - Gascogne - Provence, provinces of Occitania, the ideal union of our countries.
> 2) We accept France as a fact, the French State as a useful organism which we must reform on the federalist model which we consider a means for giving full and complete life to our countries.
> 3) We consider our countries as the basic cells for the future organisation of Europe, in which imperialisms will cease exploiting small peoples and bringing about fratricidal struggle.
> 4) We consider liberty as the foremost possession of mankind and are ready to oppose any regime which would reduce the liberty of the individual, as long as this liberty does not interfere with others.

The *Félibrige* movement, like other regional movements between the two world wars, became associated with right-wing nationalist politics, and conducted discussions with Pétain during the 1939-45 war. Fierce opposition to the *Félibrige*, and to its programme including linguistic reform based on *provençal* developed among the left-wing resistance groups and intellectuals from 1943. Currently the leaders in movements to inspire linguistic, literary, cultural and indeed economic revival of the specificity of the South are based on the Institut d'Etudes Occitanes (Institut d'Estudis Occitans) at Toulouse, founded within the wartime Resistance, whose view on linguistic matters is that the dialects of that area form a better linguistic basis for rationalisation, and who wish to see a greater effort in education and the media for using the language, greater publication opportunities and the revival of Occitan cultural events, associated with greater political freedom, against a general background of opposition to what is seen as imperialism and centralised control.

The language dispute continues to be of importance. Those who are faithful to the *Félibrige* tradition consider that the *Occitanistes* have created a learned, conservative, even archaic language, whereas the Félibrige tried at least to update and modernise; *Occitanistes* are prepared agressively to counter this and to attack any attempt to divide the unity of their view:

> the awareness of fragmentation inherited from the patois situation, a result of the cutlural oppression of the 18th and 19th centuries, has left active traces particularly in Provence and Auvergne. The 1976 circular from the Minister of Education, in talking of 'languages of *oc*' in the plural, tried to play on this feeling of fragmentation to place obstacles in the path of a unified feeling for occitan culture; in particular it tried to close off Provence from opening towards the occitan whole, and, by orienting its perception of the literary inheritance on the 'great classics of the Mistral movement', to approve the fossilisation of occitan feeling (*Par les langues de France* 1984, 62).

This approach, seeing attempts at political domination in every ministerial circular, is echoed by opposition to economic domination:

> the economic imperialism of the dominating State. The struggle for ethnic languages becomes part of the workers' and peasants' struggle (Bec 1978, 124)

although the attempt to underline the positive cultural identity of Occitan speakers also occurs:

> Culture is not just a matter a books and theatre, of higher education and research, but also of habitat, of cuisine, of leisure, of festivals, of exchanges, of the pleasure of living together, of the common wish to arise from misery, to plan for a different future (*Pour l'Occitan et pour l'Occitanie* 1981, 106).

3.2   Occitan: politics

SINCE the war, the South has normally voted Republican and anti-clerical, with occasional moves towards right-wing extremism. The wine-growers of the Hérault and the Var, and the fruit- and vegetable-growers of the Var, traditionally block the motorways on 1 August to demonstrate their desire for yet more subsidies and yet more favourable treatment from Brussels, a habit which goes back to the traditional patronage system of local politicians (*notables*) whose political strength came from their ability to intercede with the State. In 1984 the violence of the wine-growers was particularly strong. Although *Le Monde* characterised the demonstrations as *le petit jeu traditionnel,* the burning down of a Centre Leclerc supermarket in Carcassonne together with attacks on Spanish and Italian lorries containing food produce demonstrated the ready availability of high tempers, as did an attack by a cultural performer on the mayor of Montpellier in November 1984 for not taking sufficient notice of the Occitan movement. Such minor incidents are however rare and are not comparable with actions against the State in Brittany or Corsica.

Occitan movements supporting autonomy or a federal State have not been so active, so violent or so widespread as those of some other French regions, partly because of the size of the area. Since the Second World War a number of organisations have nonetheless been established, leading protest in turn: the *Institut d' Etudes Occitanes (Institut d' Estudis occitans)* in 1945, created with both an academic and cultural, as well as a political, role to develop studies of Occitan language and culture, the *Parti Nationaliste Occitan* in 1959, the *Comité Occitan d' Etudes et d'Action* in 1962, *Volem Viure al Pais* in 1974. Leaders such as Yves Rouquette of *COEA*, Pierre Maclouf of *Volem Viure al Pais*, and Pierre Bec of the *IEO* until 1980, have presented demands ranging from increased support for viticulture to recreation of the Toulouse county domain, a federal France based on independent regions, and more extreme revolutionary solutions. During the period of socialist presidency from 1981 most of these demands have been considerably moderated, although campaigns for agricultural support have continued unabated.

Keating (1986) analyses Occitan nationalism as based on political demands such as those outlined in the 1962 programme of the *Comité Occitan d'Etudes et d'Action:* a regional assembly, an economic and social council and an Occitan University (ie education system). Such demands were however based on an analysis of the situation as internal colonialism:

an instrument of capitalism: regional industries are taken over by external interests...products of extractive industries are exported for finishing elsewhere; internal distribution circuits are broken up; since the State has been taken over by new managerial classes allied with capitalism, nationalisation compounds the problem, and technocracy, neo-capitalism and the State choose the great options without any intervention by the citizens (Keating 1986, 29 (adapted)).

He sees four themes as interlinked: the peasant struggle against dispossession and depopulation, the opposition to militarism, the ecological dimension, and the Occitan struggle for identity, although the slogan *Volem Viure al Païs* was regarded by some as more tied to conservative peasant values themselves destined for extinction.

In essence therefore Occitan nationalism confronts inner tensions, is divided and comparatively leaderless, although the major figure of Robert Lafont has consistently been present. The main contradiction is that between the backward-looking protectionists, 'linked above all to the defence of viticulture', and those who understand the need for modernisation and transformation. The contradiction between 'a nostalgic veneration for the past...and the defence of the language' and 'the political implications: defence of the territory and the economy' has led to a sad sequence of excessive claims, rejection and emotional despair: '*revendication* and *lamentation*: strident demands followed by a sense of grievance' (Keating 1986, 31).

3.3 Occitan: language and the sociolinguistic situation

THE number of native speakers of Occitan is unknown, and estimations (cf Sauzet in Vermes 1988, 215) vary from twelve million who either speak the language, understand the language, or 'could relearn it', to 'a few hundred thousand'. It seems unlikely that exact figures can be obtained, for a number of reasons. There is of course always a problem in language surveys in defining the amount of knowledge of a language which is necessary in order to classify an individual as a speaker; this is particularly true in a dynamic situation in which for example children may have been brought up in a bilingual home but themselves no longer use the language at all. An additional problem is the definition of the language involved, particularly important in sociolinguistic surveys where there are significant shades of difference between French, French spoken with a regional accent, regional French, language mixture between Occitan and French, dialect of Occitan or Occitan learnt at school. Sociolinguistic surveys of Occitan have been carried out at local level, but no global survey is contemplated as far as we are aware.

The following characteristics are given by Bec (1978) as the main differences which separate Occitan from standard French, and which hence support its claim to be a separate language, a claim which is hardly disputed today:

- few closed vowels;
- no nasalised vowels;
- no diphthongisation (or its consequences in modern French): contrast for example *mel* with French *miel, fel/foi, dever/devoir, dulur/douleur*;
- final vowels are pronounced (*porta/porte, petita/petite, kadena/chaîne*);
- personal pronouns are not normally used (*canti, cantas, canta /je, tu, il chante*);
- there is frequent use of past historic and subjunctive forms;
- the third person plural of verbs, or a reflexive form, is used to indicate the impersonal: where French uses *on dit que, occitan* uses *dison que* or *se ditz que;*
- marked use of poetic and colourful terms;
- richer and more varied vocabulary;
- a less formalised sentence structure than in French, with an apparent lack of logic, a floweriness in style and a delight in word-play contrasting with French disciplined, codified, abstract expression.

The region is divided into three dialect zones: north Occitan, south or middle (*moyen*) Occitan and Gascon. In the North, *limousin, auvergnat* (higher and lower) and *provençal alpin* are distributed from West to East, while the crescent-shaped extension (*croissant*) around Montluçon contains (or used to contain) differences also. In the south Occitan area, *languedocien*, with southern, northern, eastern and western subdialects lies in the West with *provençal* to the East, itself subdivided into *rhodanien* around Arles, Avignon and Nîmes, *provençal maritime* on the Côte d'Azur, and *niçart* around Nice. The Gascon area is similarly subdivided. It will be recalled that these dialects and their subdivisions are themselves yet further subdivided, with different forms attested in individual towns and villages.

There are large differences between the dialects. The main pronunciation differences between Gascon and the rest is the neutralisation of the opposition between [v] and [b], as in Spanish; the main contrast between north and south Occitan the palatalisation of [k] and [g] before [a] in northern forms such as *chanta/canta*. But the differences extend also to lexis, to morphology, and to syntax, and the extent of intercomprehensibility is variable, although written correspondence, and tape-recorded messages, have been successfully sent and received across the Occitan area.

Dialectal fragmentation is felt as a weakness in the attempts to define and codify a standard Occitan, which some say would re-create the medieval situation, before the Albigensian Crusade, when a standardised language was said to be widely used for literary and administrative purposes. For linguists based at the Institut des Etudes Occitanes it appears nonetheless incontrovertible that the Languedocien dialect, the most neutral and conservative, the widest spread geographically, and the only one to have common borders with both Gascon and northern varieties, is best suited to act as the standard.

Today Occitan is used in the home, in the family or between people of the region, in informal situations, while French is used in all formal situations, in the administration, in the schools and colleges and in the courts. One and the same person will use French to speak of intellectual matters, Occitan in bilingual groups when speaking of household matters, of topics associated with local crafts, of basic human needs and desires and for fun. Occitan is spoken, but French is both spoken and written.

Maurand, 1981 and Gardy, 1981 provide two analyses of Occitan diglossia, the latter coming to the conclusion that the diglossic situation, with French as the superior language, will only be corrected by changes in the social situation, so that attempts to tackle the inferior position of Occitan by corpus planning - improving it as a language, codifying or otherwise attempting its renaissance - are doomed to failure without accompanying social and political changes in the conditions of its use, or adequate status planning.

Maurand gives a concrete description of a rural community of 500 people living north-east of Toulouse; 70 per cent are small farmers or stockbreeders, interacting daily in markets, at school and at home:

The main results show that Occitan is linked with agricultural work in which its usage is dominant but not exclusive whereas French is linked with public institutions in which its usage is dominant and exclusive. More generally, French is associated with youth, education, women, with distinction and prestige, with social promotion and the urban world whereas Occitan is associated with old age, lack of education, men, with derision and with the rural world. But in recent years Occitan has become the symbol of Occitan culture and in this respect it may be associated with nostalgia (Maurand 1981, 99).

A striking figure from the paper shows the language used for contacts within the family (see below). The percentages represent the proportions of time devoted to interaction in Occitan, and the difference in usage as between the generations is strikingly indicated. Grandparents communicate mainly in Occitan with each other, while parents spend less than half of their time interacting in Occitan and children (in the late 1970s) do not use the language at all. The potential loss of the language is clear. Furthermore, males retain the use of Occitan, whereas both grandmother talking to her daughter, and mother talking to hers, clearly express the widespread sociolinguistic fact that females generally prefer the prestige variety, or the superior form in diglossic situations: in this case preferring the use of French.

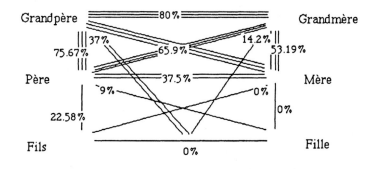

This separation of functions is characteristic of diglossic situations, in which the differential prestige associated with the different linguistic forms is a natural consequence of differential functional utilisation. The Occitan speaker may even go so far as to be ashamed of using Occitan, in particular before strangers or in situations where s/he is unsure of the interlocutor's reactions. Supporters of Occitan use have therefore gone to great lengths both to reassure people that it is acceptable to use Occitan and positively to encourage its use by making people aware that they are not alone in so doing: by poster campaigns ('*As dreit a la paraula!*'), by cultural events, by using the media and by constant pressure on the public authorities to reverse the more damaging of traditional attitudes and practices, for example nominating civil servants, including teachers, into and out of the area.

Occitan/French diglossia is therefore characterised by the functional differentiation of the two languages, by the prestige attached to French in all situations, and by the language shift which appears to be taking place, replacing Occitan by French, either regional French or standard French, in all circumstances. The associations of language and social status - 'the active Occitan speaker is rural, poor, old and male' - are matched by the conditions of its use in language mixing, where it is used 'as a stylistic code, implying irony, malice, emotive flavour' reflecting Occitan speech style, and serving as a sort of audible punctuation with no real meaning even for its users (Sauzet in Vermes 1988, 225).

Throughout the nineteenth century the main efforts of the French education system, universally available after 1830 and free after 1880, were devoted to creating an educated proletariat, able to read and write in French. In order to achieve this, local patois including Occitan were downgraded and systematically ridiculed, with punishments for those caught speaking local languages on the school premises. This long deliberate creation of diglossia is not easily reversed. However, the insertion of Occitan into the present educational system, and its acceptance as an object of education, have two consequences: the re-creation of a language which was dying or dead in certain areas, and the insertion of the language into subject areas outside the rural, cultural and everyday; both aspects which may have some effect on the future.

The future for Occitan is by no means sure. Many commentators expect a complete disappearance of all regional languages; others expect (or hope for) a renaissance and widening of their use and influence while yet others are certain that use of the language will continue, even if only as a symbol of identity rather than a living means of communication. Despite such hopes, and in spite of increased enrolments for the *baccalauréat*, economic, political and cultural pressures are such that complete disappearance seems the most probable outcome. The main factors advanced in support of this belief include:

> continuing loss of political independence;
> the exodus of local élites to Paris;
> the economic backwardness of the South, by contrast with the North;
> the absence of a great unifying political and cultural centre like Paris or Lyons;
> the inability of Occitan to develop a codified common written form;
> divergences between spoken and written Occitan;
> dialectal fragmentation;
> restricted functional utilisation of Occitan: its unavailability for certain types of use particularly in formal and public life;
> the increase in tourism in the area, and particularly in short-time visits of a weekend or so;
> the development of the South as a retirement centre for the elderly from all over France and elsewhere;
> increased immigration: the example of the arrival of *pieds-noirs* from Algeria, and of Arabic-speaking immigrants from the Maghreb, is particularly noted;
> the absence of local Occitan speakers in the administration, and particularly their absence among the teaching force.

By contrast the supporters of Occitan point to a revival of interest in the language in schools: secondary enrolments rose from 6,711 in 1975 to 7,541 in 1981 and to 10,647 in 1986-7 (*Quid*, 1990, 1256) the largest number for any regional language. In Villeneuve-sur-Lot, numbers rose from 2 in 1957 to 1,500 in 1985. In nursery schools (*calandretas*), based on the Catalan and Breton movements, there have also been increased enrolments. Summer schools organised by the Institut d'Estudis Occitans enrolled 1,500 in 1985.

The personal experience of a teacher of Occitan is worth quoting:

> In 1963 I taught young people who already spoke Occitan, although not very well or very much. Really I didn't teach them a language but showed them its geographical extent and relied on the great literary works which illuminate its history. Today (1983) the majority of young people are not speakers of Occitan...I therefore teach the spoken language rather than the functional written. (Joncourt in *Par les langues de France* 1984, 70).

Interest is reviving, also, in the cultural domain: publications in Occitan remain the result of the devoted and unremunerated work of volunteers, but the Institut d'Estudis Occitans notes a catalogue of seventy published works in 1981, with print runs rising from 300 in 1950 to 2,000 in 1980. Theatre and music are said to be rising in popularity, although there is no popular youth culture similar to that of Brittany. FR3, the regional radio, was the constant target of the Institut and other militants, and its programmes in Occitan have increased, but local radio is a better arena, with programmes now available even in the Paris region.

The general conclusion presents an unenviable paradox however. If dialectal fragmentation has led to a lack of status for Occitan, its codification, and hence its insertion onto the **linguistic 'market-place'** as a competitor for French, should lead to bilingualism and hence to an acceptable role for Occitan in both private and public domains. However it would also create diglossia between the codified and normalised form of Occitan on the one hand and local forms on the other, in exactly the same way as now occurs between French and Occitan. Without the status, official character and functional range which can only come about through codification, Occitan is destined to disappear; yet with it, the existing range of forms of native Occitan will disappear.

Further reading

Bec, P. 1967. *La Langue occitane.*

Brun, A. 1923. *Essai historique sur l'introduction du français dans les provinces du Midi de a France.*

Field, T. 1981. Language survival in a European context: the future of Occitan. *Language Problems and Language Planning*, 5: 251-263.

Gardy, P. 1981. La Diglossie comme conflit: l'occitan. *Langages*, 61: 75-91.

Keating, M. 1986. 'Revendication et Lamentation': the failure of regional nationalism in Languedoc. *Journal of Area Studies*, 14: 27-32.

Lafont, R. 1977. *Clefs pour l'Occitanie.*

Maurand, G. 1981. Situation linguistique d'une famille en domaine occitan. *International Journal of the Sociology of Language*, 29: 99-119.

1981. *Pour l'Occitan et pour l'Occitanie.*

4   Regional languages

4.1 Alsatian

4.1.1 Historical situation

Until 1648 Alsace formed part of the Holy Roman Empire and the German
language was used for all purposes. There were, however, two other major
differences from the earlier history of France: during the late Middle Ages,
as a direct consequence of their trading role, the Alsace towns acquired
rather more independence from the feudal past, and hence control of their
own destiny, than was the norm elsewhere; and in the sixteenth century
Protestantism became widespread, as indeed it did in many of the German
regions. The Thirty Years War brought about a transfer of the region to
the French kingdom: after a disastrous and cruel occupation by Swedish
troops, the Alsace towns appealed to France and the Treaty of Westphalia
brought them under French protection in 1648. The Treaty was vague and
diplomatic, but Alsace thought it had retained its economic privileges and
its Protestant religion, and had neither given itself completely to France nor
been wrenched away from a weakened empire by a rapacious France.

After France took control of most of Alsace in 1648, of Lorraine finally
in 1766, and of the Strasbourg area in 1781, the region became part of
France and was slowly assimilated into the French administrative system, a
process in which the *Intendants*, representing the King's justice and his tax
and financial control, played a strong role, and in which the Roman
Catholic Church was supported in its attempts to regain power and
influence. The Revolution of 1789 provoked, as elsewhere in France, a
sharpening of the conflict between centrists and federalists: in Alsace, the
loss of the special status decreed by the Revolutionaries as one of their first
acts led in 1791 to the application of the same *Constitution Civile* governing
the election of priests as elsewhere, a move which shocked the Roman
Catholics, allowing as it did the election of priests by all citizens, including
Protestants and Jews. Two years later the Terror, which banned the use of

German and all German cultural habits, was also felt as an attack on the special situation of Alsace.

In 1870, after the defeat of France, Alsace and Lorraine were annexed by Germany, to become French again in 1918 at the end of the First World War. Germany did not allow regional government until 1911, and it was clear at this time that a movement for autonomy was growing: Alsace felt neither fully French nor completely German. In 1918, however, the returning French did not handle the situation well. Although some aspects of its special situation were safeguarded, for example in retaining the Napoleonic Concordat of 1801, which the rest of France had abandoned long since in order to separate Church and State, and in the better social security system with its sick pay and pension arrangements for state employees, insufficient sensitivity was displayed in education and in language use, and between the wars a different sort of autonomy movement developed, in favour of Alsace Germanness, leading to violence and arrests particularly in 1927 and 1928. As a consequence there was then some French recognition of Alsace *'particularisme'* in education and language use.

From 1940 to 1945 the region was regarded in effect as an integral part of Germany and since then has once again been a part of France. The Nazis bore heavily on Alsace and Lorraine, tearing down inscriptions in French and statues of Frenchmen, teaching only through the medium of German, conscripting 130,000 young men into the *Wehrmacht*, and sending them to the eastern fronts where 40,000 died. But they shot, or sent to concentration camps, those who refused, and banned the use of the Alsace dialects.

The returning French in 1945 again took severe measures, banning the use of German for a time, interning 45,000 people in camps, and imprisoning autonomists. It was difficult for the French to accept that the region did not this time, any more than it did in 1918, wish to surrender its individuality to become completely French, but, as in Brittany, regionalism was for a considerable time associated with anti-French acts such as the brutal massacre of women and children at Oradour, in which troops from Alsace had been involved.

For any Alsatian under the age of forty-five in 1990 therefore Alsace has always been part of France; those over that age remember to a greater or lesser extent the period of intense 'defrancisation' under the Nazis, while those of over 70 have seen four radical changes of government during their lives. These radical changes explain at least in part what has been called *'le particularisme alsacien'*, the identity crisis of those who live in a frontier region dotted with castles, forts and fortified gun emplacements to this day. Contacts with Luxembourg, with Switzerland or with parts of Germany are often much easier than with the rest of France, called 'the interior' by those who live in Alsace, and both the Rhine and the mountainous Vosges are difficult to cross.

Religion has played an important role in underlining the differences with France: the Protestant tradition has remained strong in the only area of contemporary France which avoided the bloody expulsion of Protestants after the Revocation of the Edict of Nantes, and which received many Huguenot immigrants at that time. Lutheran Protestantism is strong in the Strasbourg area, and the Roman Catholic Church, equally, and partly because of this strength, is a powerful voice. Both churches have remained close to their congregations, using French, German and the local dialects in their services.

Alsace is nonetheless without doubt a part of France: 'the nature of the Third Reich, and the Nazi system, did more for the French cause than a century of French monarchic rule' (Klein et al 1982, 70), and the wish today is for recognition and 'semi-autonomy' rather than for complete independence.

4.1.2 Political situation

No one political centre dominates this border region. Strasbourg is the main town, but in the South Basel, in Switzerland, functions as a point of attraction of almost as much importance as nearby Mulhouse, and the proximity of the German frontier means that employment, social and political contacts are nowadays easy: indeed the Rhine is now a symbol of European Community unity. As in other parts of France, the region is artifically divided into administrative departments (for Alsace: Haut-Rhin and Bas-Rhin), while Lorraine 'disappears' into Moselle and looks towards Luxembourg as a main city and centre.

The region votes consistently on the political Right, with for example 51.6% (Bas-Rhin) of votes to Chirac in the 1988 presidential elections, over 52% to right-wing parties, excluding the National Front, in 1986 (first round of the legislatives), 49% of the vote going to the URC in the first round of the legislative elections of June 1988 in the Bas-Rhin, and up to 12% to Le Pen in the 1989 European elections. There is growing support for ecologists, however, with over 9% of votes to Waechter (national average 3.77%) in the first round of the 1988 presidential elections.

A number of administrative arrangements in Alsace are different from those for the rest of France: *Quid* 1990 (757) lists eleven such, of which the most important concern social security, bilingualism, state approval of *notaires*, and the continuation of the Concordat arrangements, with Church primary schools, state payments for priests of the three main religions; and holidays on Boxing Day and Good Friday.

Most of the population of Alsace is too aware of its troubled past actively to seek any further separation from France, although regionalism has grown somewhat since 1980, oriented mainly towards ensuring acceptance of cultural and linguistic difference. The following summary of aims is incorporated in the promotional literature for the René Schickele Club, one of the main organisations expressing Alsatian views:

> an official status for our language;
> use of the dialect in kindergarten schools alongside classes in French;
> early teaching of German to be followed through all age groups and schools;
> more radio broadcasts in dialect and in standard literary German (*Hochdeutsch*);
> more television broadcasts in dialect;
> our cultural identity should be respected in the administration, in the courts, in the naming of streets and areas, in commercial and industrial life and in the schools and colleges, in cultural activities and institutions such as theatres and museums...

4.1.3 Language situation: history, dialects, patterns of usage

Until 1648 Alsace used German for all purposes. From then until 1789, no pressure was exercised for Alsatians to use French. The aristocracy used French as a matter of course but the remainder of the population was in no way obliged to do so, although certain groups, such as the Huguenots, who had arrived in the area as refugees after the Revocation of the Edict of Nantes, members of the bourgeoisie in the legal professions, or those who had commercial links with the rest of France, did. The use of French was imposed at the time of the French Revolution, when German was considered as the language of the enemy, but it was clearly impossible for the whole population to instantly convert, and the area experienced considerable linguistic problems during the Terror. The Revolution's language laws could do no more than mark the beginning of a conversion and educational process, which continued with French becoming the language of education towards the middle of the nineteenth century and the use of French becoming gradually more widespread, without replacing the use of the dialects. From 1871 to 1918 however, German became again the official language, replacing French within the administrative system; French was banned from official use and even the teaching of French in the educational system was stopped. During the 1914-18 war the use of French even in informal situations became a crime.

From 1919 to 1927 German was in its turn banned or restricted; French became once again the only official language. Not until 1927 was the teaching of German re-established in limited fashion as a compulsory subject in the School Certificate; the increase in the number of people understanding and using French was slow but considerable, with over a million speakers, particularly young people, as against 300,000 in 1910, while the normal language in use in all circumstances by the mass of the population remained the dialects. From 1940 to 1945 a vigorous programme of 'defrancisation' was undertaken by the Germans, with German becoming the official language and the use of French, even in informal circumstances, becoming again punishable by fines or worse. In 1945, among the population of those aged from six to ten, French was unknown, while many older children had forgotten it. In 1945, the returning French instituted a vigorous programme of denazification which implied also degermanification: the teaching of German was banned 'to permit French to regain the lost terrain', and was not re-established until 1952, as an optional subject and as a foreign language. German was not included as a regional language under the provisions of the Deixonne Law of 1951, but was treated as a foreign language.

The knowledge of the Alsace dialects by the total population has been monitored by large-scale surveys for a number of years: in 1946, 84% knew the dialect(s), in 1962 87%, and in 1979 75%, although these figures reach over 90% in each case if one considers only those persons originating from Alsace. In 1962 an *INSEE* survey indicated that 80.5% of Alsatians knew French, whereas in 1931 it had been only 50% in the Bas-Rhin, 55% in the Haut-Rhin departments. Knowledge of French is however on the increase, and it is probable that there remain very few monolingual speakers of German or dialect.

In the 1960s and 70s, with the ethnic revival throughout Europe, a new realisation of the special situation of Alsace became evident, as shown by the creation of the René Schickele Club in 1968. The Club set up courses in German and in dialect outside the public school system, while the Holderith method of primary school teaching and of German language teaching was based on the idea of using children's previous knowledge of dialect, and used songs and poems written in dialect. This method was introduced in

1971 and involved nine to eleven-year olds using German for 30 minutes per day on a voluntary basis (*Langues* 1984, 34-8; *Minorités* 1986, 181). Primary school German teaching was supported by ministerial and *recteur* circulars in 1982 and 1985, and reinforced by activities such as school exchanges. It now affects some 75% of children in Bas-Rhin and 65% in Haut-Rhin, although in the towns this drops to less than 50%, and increasingly English is chosen as a foreign language for study in secondary school.

Two main German dialect groups cross the Alsace-Lorraine area: the Franconian (*francique*) and Alemannic (*alémanique*) groups. Sub-dialects of these groups are geographically distributed as follows: *francique mosellan* in north Lorraine, *francique rhénan* in south Lorraine and north Alsace, *haut alémanique* in southern Alsace and *bas-alémanique* in the centre of Alsace. These dialects are the forms used in informal situations. As is the case throughout the German-speaking area, the formal language variety is *Hochdeutsch* or standard written German, used in the Church, in the media, in all writing and in formal circumstances. The region is of course in close contact with German-speaking areas, whether through these dialects and *Hochdeutsch* uses or through the media - German, Swiss, Belgian and Luxembourg television channels can easily be received - and there is therefore no question of a simple diglossic situation in prestige terms: both German and French are equally seen as prestigious languages with a world role, while the dialects are seen in no different way from that in which other areas of Germany view their own forms of German: as forms of language which, while they have a different set of functional uses, are not necessarily to be regarded as inferior. Alsace-Lorraine is hence trilingual rather than bilingual; it could even be considered quadrilingual if note is taken of the strongly marked nature of the regional French outlined in Chapter 2.

Formally, French is the official language as elsewhere in France, although two official French-dialect and French-German interpreters are employed in the Strasbourg courts and dialect or German can be used at the magistrate's discretion. Some municipal councils still debate in dialect, although the official record is taken in French; yet official forms for organisations such as social security, formerly available in both languages are more and more available now only in French.

The 1979 *INSEE* survey on the 'Alsatian Way of Life' remains the most accessible large-scale survey of language use in Alsace. The *INSEE* survey showed that overall Alsace dialects were spoken by 79% of those over fifteen, a drop from 90% in 1962. The same survey showed that dialect is more spoken in country than town; by older rather than younger inhabitants; by males more than females, and at the work-place rather than in contacts with the administration or while shopping. The following sample tables extracted from the survey show the percentages of the total population using dialect.

In communes by size of commune:

Rural	<10,000	10,000-50,000	Strasbourg	Alsace total
88	77	69	62	79

According to age:

<15 years old	16-34 years old	>64 years old
65 (estimated)	67	88

According to the situation of use:

At home	Shops	Work	Necessary for work	Contacts with the administration
60	52	72	33	37

Language-switching or code-switching between languages is particularly important in the language use of Alsace, and a specific study of the practice in the Strasbourg area (Gardner-Chloros 1985) concludes that it is widespread, with triggers for the use of dialect as opposed to French being related to such factors as

the degree of familiarity of the two interlocutors (strangers are addressed mainly in French);
stereotypical expectations, such as the social categories or scale of values: 'lower' social classes being more frequently addressed in dialect than 'upper' socio-economic groups;
physical surroundings: the more luxurious the shopping centre, the more likely French was to be used by salespeople and clients alike. Likewise, in public discussion in a primary school, it proved difficult to get children to 'own up' to using the dialect at home;
the subject of the conversation: technical conversations predisposed towards the use of French, while social intercourse on family, house,

friends, visits and holidays were more frequently conducted in
dialect;

the degree of formality: in formal interviews French was used
whereas in normal working relationships dialect was more frequent.

Other surveys have also found frequent use of language-switching, and
discovered that the use of the dialect is triggered for example in young
males by the desire to affirm one's Alsace identity, or express the feeling of
belonging to the local community, while girls are more inclined to use
French. Such extensive code-switching appears again to indicate a dynamic
situation in which the dialect is giving way to French. One indication of this
is the difference in the use of dialect as between the generations: while 88%
of parents use dialect in talking to grandparents, 63% use it in talking to
parents and 34% of children use it in talking to each other (1979 figures:
Hartweg in Vermes 1988, 50). As an indication of the underlying reasons
why this should be, Gardner-Chloros also lists the mental associations her
sample gave for the use of the three languages:

- *dialect*

    men, older people, country dwellers ('it's a peasant language'),
    nostalgia for the past, symbol of Alsatian identity, childhood, guilt
    (ie guilt similar to the German sense of guilt for wartime atrocities);

- *French*

    women, younger people, city dwellers, Parisian refinement,
    prestige at the national but not the international level (where English
    or German are mentioned), official and administrative ('language of
    the police'), correctness ('essential to speak correct French');

- *German*

    economic advantages, written form of the dialect, reminders of
    wartime among the population aged over fifty (there were very
    negative feelings among this age-group, and a 'near-pathological
    rejection of one or other of the languages involved' (p. 252).

Klein (1984, 42) considered that while French is making progress, the use
of the German dialects is still active. 50-60% of the population watch
German television; there is constant movement across the frontier, with
some 40,000 Alsace workers crossing daily to Germany or Switzerland. But
he agrees that the future will see greater use of French: it is the main TV
and radio language, and monolingual French Press is gaining ground: the
bilingual edition of the *Dernières Nouvelles d'Alsace*, the main local

newspaper, produced 37.2% of total sales in 1975 but this had fallen to 23.4% by 1985, with the French edition making up the ground lost. French is taught throughout the region, and although since 1982 there has been some development in the use of German and dialect as vehicular languages, this is not widespread. French is the language of the administration, and of all written formal uses, and is now accepted as the prestige language within the area.

The experience of the churches is also of interest, particularly for the Protestants present in Alsace since the sixteenth century, traditionally using German or dialect for their services and using the Lutheran Bible. In 1976 a protest, signed by 108 Roman Catholic and 72 Protestant priests, reminded both churches that Alsace was bilingual and demanded both the continuation of the use of German and an end to the practice of providing services only in French for younger parishioners, reserving German and dialect for the older members. Current practice however is still mixed, and varied across the region, with services in French inexorably growing in number. A significant indicator is a 1976 survey of 104 youth groups, 30% of whose meetings were bilingual while 64% were in French (Lienhard 1981, 159).

Against a background of continued widespread societal and individual bi- or tri-lingualism, the language situation in Alsace and Lorraine can thus be summed up as characterised by:

> the increasing use of French as opposed to German or German-based dialects, in a reflection of the higher prestige and attraction of French;
>
> considerable language-switching, with triggers for the use of French related to public life and situations of greater value or prestige;
>
> the use of French as the official language, and the language of education;
>
> the use of a strongly marked regional French;
>
> the use of dialect at home or for private and 'intimate' uses, together with its use for kindergarten or schools outside the public system (mainly religious schools);
>
> the use of *Hochdeutsch* as a written language, in religious contexts or as a language of the media (Press and TV), together with its use in education as a written form of the dialect and according to personal and family wishes.

Alsace and Lorraine: Germanic dialects

Further reading

Klein, J. P., Philipp, M., Bothorel-Witz, A., Finck, A., Klein, G., Doerflinger, M., and Nonn, H. 1982. *Alsace*.

Kleinschmager, R. 1986. *Géopolitique de l'Alsace*.

Philipps, E. 1975. *Les Luttes linguistiques en Alsace jusqu'en 1945*.

Philipps, E. 1978. *La Crise d'identité: l'Alsace face à son destin*.

4.2 Basque

4.2.1 History

The Basque region covers an area now located both in Spain and France, where the present Department of Pyrénées-Atlantiques contains the three former provinces of Labourd, Navarre and Soule. The Spanish area is made up principally of the Navarra region, but also of the three provinces of Guipuzcoa, Vizcaya and Alava. Navarre itself formerly constituted one of the seven kingdoms created after the death of Charlemagne. It is thought that the Basques may have been the original European inhabitants, pre-dating Celtic and other invasions, although Collins (1986, 3) points out that care must be taken with evidence for this and other matters connected with Basque identity since scholars are not necessarily neutral, and may be concerned with advancing the cause of Basque nationalism by stressing the uniqueness and antiquity of the Basque people.

The Basque region of seven provinces or states resisted assimilation by Romans, Arabs and Goths alike, and it is thought that there was a considerable degree of independence as between the Basque provinces. Until 1876, Spanish rulers had accepted the *fueros*, or local customs, whose three basic tenets were that direct participative democracy should control the major part of life, with region or State intervening only for interregional matters; that individual liberty should take precedence; that groups, rather than States, should guarantee liberty. This strong tradition, together with the lack of invasion by others, means that self-reliance and autonomy are strong and continuing factors in the Basque personality.

The French part of Euskadi, the *pays basque,* had been partly ruled by the English rulers of Aquitaine in medieval times: the province of Labourd was under English domination from 1193 to 1451 and Soule from 1193 to 1306. In its chequered history the Spanish kings of Castile have also ruled, and the region was split between Spain and France from 1598, when Henri IV, King of Navarre - which had itself been split into a Spanish and a non-Spanish half in 1512 - became King of France.

Basque law and customs were in general protected in the French provinces until 1789 and in Spain until 1876. As inheritance followed primogeniture, Basque second and subsequent sons were obliged to seek their fortunes abroad, and there are established settlements in North and South America, the Philippines, Australia and elsewhere.

4.2.2 Politics

The first Basque Nationalist Party was founded in 1893 as a left-wing group which, in later times, supported the French *Front populaire* in 1934 and the Spanish Republic in 1936. As a consequence, the Spanish Basque region was opposed to Franco who returned the compliment by bombing Guernica in 1937 and with a consistent history of repression until his death. The Spanish connection is continued today by the presence of three French members of the central committee of *Euskal Alkartasona*, founded in 1986 as a Basque party. In the French *pays basque*, *Enbata*, dissolved in 1974 but still publishing its journal, was founded in 1963; *EMA*, 'movement of the patriotic Basque left', and *GOIZ-ARGI* (founded 1985), present election candidates, and there are a number of cultural, economic and administrative associations favouring at least the creation of a *pays basque* department..

Iparretarrak, founded in 1963, was active in violent acts, particularly in burning tourist houses and attacking the French police; its leader, Philippe Bédart, who participated in the first wave of violence in 1972 and 1973, killed two members of the CRS (French riot police) in 1982 and a gendarme in 1987 at a road block, was himself arrested in 1988. The *Groupement Antiterroriste de la Libération (GAL)* has also been involved in violent acts of counter-terrorism on French soil.

The degree of support for these extremist organisations is now decreasing, both in Spain and France. The assembly of Basque mayors condemned *Iparretarrak* in December 1984 as a *'unique mouvement séparatiste local clandestin, sans aucune assise populaire'*, while greatly increased Spanish regional autonomy after the death of Franco, particularly in police and security matters, has led to much less public support for the murder of Basque policemen: while the police were national, and came mainly from outside the region, there was a degree of public tolerance.

There are also differences between the Spanish and French views of the political problem: for the Spanish Basques, now in control of their own destiny, problems of a declining industrial base and of immigration from other regions of Spain and from elsewhere lead to concern at the disappearance of Basque identity and cultural distinctiveness. The French Basques consider that there is inadequate government funding from Paris for the development of the economy, and that Paris considers the area suitable only for tourism and exploitation; the core-periphery analysis of economic domination, associated with cultural domination through insistence on education in and through the medium of French, is hence felt to be appropriate.

Mitterrand's speech of 13 October 1984 left no doubt that the traditional French government opposition to autonomy for the French *pays basque* contined and continues:

> what you are will be preserved and served so that future generations will find intact the heritage you have yourselves received...If it comes to talk of autonomy, of independence, I say clearly, and frankly that, with me, no. I shall not allow the substance [*tissu*] of France to be destroyed (*Le Monde* 10.10.84).

The effects of terrorist attacks on tourist trade have been serious, leading to loss of a third of visitors between 1983 and 1985. But the region has generally been regarded as underdeveloped, by contrast to the wealthier Spanish Basque country, and economic deprivation is reflected in an ageing population and a principal town, Bayonne, with a mere 43,000 inhabitants.

4.2.3 Language

The earliest surviving texts in Basque (*Euskera*) date only from the late Middle Ages. Basque is a unique language, which it is impossible to insert in language classification schemes, although certain structural similarities with Asian languages have been noted (Ruhlen 1987). A number of widely divergent dialects exist, although identifiable groupings distinguish each of the three northern provinces. The Basque Language Academy, founded in 1918, and others have effected some rationalisation and other aspects of language corpus planning, and Spanish Basque is now standardised. Inevitably, Basque has borrowed heavily from Spanish and French for technical and abstract terminology.

Basque is the official language of the autonomous Basque region of Spain, although it is spoken by only 30 per cent of the population south of the Bidassoa and 45 per cent north. The total population of Basque speakers in Spain is about 600,000. Following particularly the example of the Catalans, but for its own purposes also, the government of the autonomous Spanish Basque region has invested considerable resources in language, including eleven hours of daily broadcasting and TV in the language.

In France there are said to be between 80,000 and 100,000 speakers of Basque, approximately 40 per cent of the population of the Pyrénées Atlantiques, mainly located in rural areas. Despite the appearance of periodicals and weekly magazines, with a circulation of approximately 2-3,000 copies (*Minorités* 1986, 189), Wardhaugh (1987, 117) considers that there remain few Basque speakers, except among the elderly. Traditional

French centralisation policy had been followed in education, and at the beginning of the century the *Préfet* commented, on opening a new college, that it would be a good means for 'making the Basques more French: they are too backward in their customs, habits, civilisation and particularly language' (quoted in Lafont 1982, 98). Nonetheless, there is evidence of a desire to re-establish Basque identity and consciousness, notably by improving provision for language maintenance, and particularly because the strong Basque identity of the Spanish provinces is a powerful influence. The Deixonne Law of 1951 had permitted some teaching of Basque, and there have been other developments since.

In primary education itinerant Basque language teaching, established since 1969, is offered by about 30 teachers in some 140 schools to about 4,000 children; there are one or two experimental bilingual classes or schools, offering teaching of other subjects through Basque, and at secondary level 13 of the 18 *collèges* provide Basque language teaching. In 1986-7 enrolments in both public and private education at secondary level totalled 1,867 pupils. One of the most interesting developments is the *Ikastolak*, private Basque-language schools which receive about 27 per cent of their budget from the French State, but which are financially desperate (*Le Monde Dossiers* 1988), and which are gradually building from the kindergarten (about 400 children) through to the secondary level (currently about 100 children). A Chair of Basque Language and Literature has been established in Bordeaux III since 1948 and university-level diplomas are taught through the University Institute in Bayonne, at Pau and Toulouse.

Sociolinguistically the Basque region is in a situation of language maintenance, with heavy pressure from French leading most probably to its eventual disappearance, although this possibility is countered both by growing regional interest and particularly by the strong Basque region in Spain and its regional autonomy.

Further reading

Collins, R. 1986. *The Basques*.
Ruhlen, M. 1987. *A Guide to the World's Languages*.
1988. Le Pays Basque. *Le Monde Dossiers et Documents*, 154.

4.3 Breton

4.3.1 Historical situation

The Armorican peninsula was colonised during the fourth and fifth centuries AD by emigrants fleeing from the Anglo-Saxon invasions then threatening Wales and Cornwall. The Celts who arrived from the British Islands had already been converted to Christianity, and appear to have been organised in tribes with a military chief and a priest; these groups called themselves *plebs* (Latin for 'people') and this word survives in many Breton place-names under the form *plous*. They sought not merely to escape the Angles and Saxons but also to find land and settlement, and gradually moved towards the East in search of both, coming into contact with the Romanised inhabitants, so that Brittany eventually divided into two, the western part speaking the Celtic tongue(s) the invaders had brought and the eastern part retaining the Gallo-Romance language that was to become a *langue d'oïl* dialect called *'gallo'*.

The invasion was not peaceful, and the wars with the original inhabitants were followed by skirmishes with the invading Franks and Vikings. Conquered by Charlemagne, the Bretons became independent in 845, to be in effect subjugated again by the Vikings who attacked their coasts and eventually settled, although mostly in Normandy. Independence came again after 938, and was to last until 1532. The 'dukes' of Brittany were adept at playing the Franks against the Normans, and the Duchy of Brittany eventually controlled territory up to Nantes and Rennes, with economic, cultural and political independence until the Duke was defeated in fighting the King of France in 1488. Marriages of convenience between Anne of Brittany, the last duchess, and two successive kings of France led to a treaty of union in 1532. The terms of the treaty guaranteed rights and privileges to the Bretons, and shortly after Mitterrand's election in 1981 these were considered again by the French courts. The judgement was that the French Revolution had swept away all such agreements and treaties.

During the sixteenth, seventeenth and eighteenth centuries the Bretons established their maritime tradition, with fishing expeditions as far as Newfoundland and piratical attacks on the British fleet. Jacques Cartier discovered Canada in 1534 although settlement did not start until later; Bretons have been numerous among the settlers in the New World.

Before the Revolution Brittany had retained its own form of government, with a *Parlement* responsible for discussing and approving laws and a meeting of the *Etats* responsible for raising taxes. Both bodies were jealous of their rights and privileges, principally financial. At the time of the French Revolution the Bretons supported federalism with the Girondins, rather than the Jacobine centralist view of organisation for the new State. They revolted against the new ideas from Paris in the uprising of the Chouans, which lasted ten years, and which brought together strands of royalist feeling together with 'national' sentiment in favour of the Breton 'nation' and support for the parish priest (and hence opposition to the anticlericalism of the Revolution). These emotive strands were to recur later and even in the 1980s the feeling was expressed that the Breton nation had been illegally suppressed by the laws of the 1789 Revolution. On the Restoration of 1815 Brittany was not occupied by the British and German troops who had defeated Napoleon, in recognition of its history of opposition to all that had happened since 1789.

Both the centralisation and the industrialisation of the nineteenth century caused difficulties for the peninsula: demographic problems with increased emigration towards Paris but also out of France, and economic problems related to the lack of raw materials and power sources, since Breton wealth was essentially derived from agriculture or fishing. During the nineteenth century, too, the centralisation policy of the Paris government was at its strongest in dealing with education: to make the nation, it was felt, regional languages had to disappear along with regional autonomy and sentiment. The most striking example of this was the severity of school punishments for those caught talking Breton at school: they wore the equivalent of the dunce's cap, were beaten and taught that their language was both inferior and barbaric. Similarly severe punishment - withdrawal of the State salary paid during the period of the Concordat - was meted out to parish priests who used Breton in sermons.

In 1898 the *Union Régionaliste Bretonne* was founded to defend Breton rights. It split in 1911 to create the *Fédération Régionaliste Bretonne*, which, like the *URB*, did not seek independence: the *Parti Nationaliste Breton*, also founded in 1911, did. Nonetheless the *URB* demanded at the Versailles Peace Conference of 1918 the recognition of the right to use their language and political freedom 'because Brittany forms, within the French nation, a distinct nation and people'. The request was refused.

Between the two wars separatist and autonomist demands continued: the *Parti Autonomiste Breton* demanded political and administrative independence 'within the French framework' on the model that Alsatian independence movements used at the same time. In 1932, in Vannes, the celebrations of the fourth centenary of the union between Brittany and

France were disturbed by a monument being blown up; in the same year the *Parti National Breton* was founded, and other (right-wing) organisations prepared for armed revolt; the French police started actively seeking out and imprisoning political activists.

In 1939 on the outbreak of war the *Parti National Breton* was officially dissolved. Two of its leaders went nonetheless to Germany after the defeat of France in an attempt to convince the Germans of the necessity of Breton independence, and appealed to all Bretons to consider themselves relieved of all obligations towards France. They went as far as making tours of prisoner-of-war camps with German approval in attempts to recruit volunteers for a Breton 'army' of support, although the creation of the Vichy government and its policy of collaboration with the occupying Germans led to the collapse of this initiative.

But the *Parti National Breton* was recreated in 1940, disseminating pro-Breton propaganda with German approval until 1944. Alongside this political organisation the Nazis, with Vichy, agreed to the establishment of a *Comité Consultatif de la Bretagne*, presided over by the *Préfet*; this was the first Breton representative group since the *Etats* had been dismissed in 1790, even though it only 'represented' the four departments and excluded the Loire Inférieure (now Loire Atlantique), in which Nantes lies. In the schools a programme of Breton education was set up, with compulsory tests of Breton history and geography, optional language teaching, and Breton accepted as an examination subject. More drastic still, the *PNB* recruited volunteers to join a Breton batallion as part of the Nazi army; this batallion continued operating until August 1944.

Not surprisingly, on the Liberation revenge was swift: more than a thousand arrests, including all members of the *Comité Consultatif*; prison sentences, exile (to Ireland or Wales!), death sentences on 20 and 8 officially shot as traitors. The *PNB* was banned, all cultural and educational measures stopped, and the Breton-language Press closed.

4.3.2 Political situation

Political action did not reappear until 1950, with the creation of the *Comité d'Etudes et de Liaisons des Intérêts Bretons (CELIB)*, which included and includes the Members of Parliament from the four departments and local notables,and pursues matters of Breton interest with the authorities.

Organisations with political aims include the *Union Démocratique Bretonne* ('social and national liberation of the Breton people'), the only party with elected representatives, and one which signed a cooperation pact in 1974 with the IRA and various movements in Spain and Wales. The *UDB* may also congratulate itself on successful political pressure: in August 1985 Mitterrand created the *Conseil National des Langues et Cultures Régionales de France* and instituted a *Certificat d'Aptitude au Professorat de l'Enseignement Secondaire (CAPES)* in Breton, although only as part of a more general language-teaching qualification, after the 1984 *UDB* congress voted to reinforce its autonomy policies. The 1984 congress had reacted, not merely to the lack of a teaching qualification but also to the supreme court's refusal of a request by the *Conseil Régional* to reunite the Loire Atlantique, and Nantes in particular, with the four other Breton departments, a consistent demand of Breton nationalists.

Emgann (1982: 'creation of a free, socialist and self-governing Brittany'), *POBL* ('organisation of a free Brittany'), created in 1982 by transformation from its previous reincarnations (*SAV* and *MOB*); *B5* ('for the inclusion of the Loire Atlantique in the Breton region'), *CUAB* (1976: *Comité pour l'Union Administrative de la Bretagne*) and one or two others are the more visible of a range of groupings, working for political aims and covering the spectrum of political views from Right to Left. The main national parties are generally careful to reject any autonomist or federalist aims at local level, and this applies particularly to the parties of the Left, although these had strongly supported the ideas of regional recognition and dignity inherent in Mitterrand's *'droit à la différence'* policy, which had considerable impact on the Socialist Party from 1974 until 1986.

Some organisations support Breton culture and the wider use of its language, although the political implications of their support is not central. *Stourm ar Brezhoneg*, actively supporting public bilingualism; *Ar Falz*, with its three themes of Brittany, socialism and 'laïcité', publishing teaching material; and organisations for dancers and players of the *cornemuse* and the *bombarde* show the range of interests.

Peasant revolts, provoked by a mixture of nationalist and economic sentiment, took place in 1960, 1961 and 1962, with a degree of *CELIB* support, but their violence and the violent suppression by the *CRS* reawoke many French suspicions. Direct 'terrorist' action in support of independence continues today, despite a truce from 1981 to 1983. Incidents have occurred against state offices, radio stations, the *ANPE* (*Agence Nationale Pour l'Emploi* - job centres), education offices and law courts, with a hotel attacked in May 1989. Organisations supporting direct action include the *Front de Libération de la Bretagne*, founded in 1966, with the aim of pursuing the 'progressive and revolutionary combat which each generation of Bretons has undertaken for the freedom of Brittany and for the right of Bretons to reject colonial status'. The *FLB* created a military wing in 1968: the *Armée Républicaine Bretonne,* which became the *Armée Révolutionnaire Bretonne* in 1971. After trials in 1972 before the State Security Court, the *FLB-ARB* was banned in 1974, but further trials took place with sentences of up to fifteen years.

To judge by the region's voting habits, the extremist, and indeed autonomist, parties in Brittany are marginal, although Le Pen received considerable support in the first round of the 1988 Presidentials, and the ecology vote was comparatively high in the 1988 Legislatives. Voting is not consistent, although the power of the Church remains high: the four departments remained split in 1988, with Côtes du Nord and Finistère voting marginally on the Left and Morbihan and Ile et Vilaine on the Right. The main characteristic of the autonomist and nationalist parties and groupings is their fragmentation and dependence on individuals.

The political situation should be understood against two major Breton problems: demography and economics. Brittany's population in 1988 was 2,763,800, while it had been only a little under two million in 1911. The comparatively stable population figure is not the result of a low birth-rate, but rather of the opposite: the high Breton birth-rate has been accompanied by massive emigration from the region, reaching 6% of the population from 1911 to 1946. Departures totalled 8,700 per year from 1850 to 1960, rising to up to 18,000 per year from 1946 to 1954 (*Le Monde Dossiers et Documents* 1984, 2). Breton immigrants now form 3% of the Paris population, and traditionally occupied low status jobs (30% of Paris domestic workers or cleaners in 1954 were Bretons). The departure of young active workers, leaving behind older agricultural workers to work small parcels of land at a subsistence level, is thus a first problem. But Breton land is productive, and the fishing industry grew throughout the nineteenth century, although it has declined in the twentieth. The departure of the élites is a second problem: it happened before, in the ninth and tenth centuries, when nobles and monks fled the Viking invasions, and returned speaking French after 938; and again at the Revolution.

Today 54% of the population lives mainly in towns, although this is less than the French average of 73%. The urban population has doubled in twenty years, while Brittany has still retained its position as the foremost agricultural region (for total production). The nature of agricultural production has changed, however: in the past small parcels of land producing enough for subsistence (hence the emigration), while today semi-industrial agri-business establishments produce vast quantities of certain products. Milk and milk products, pork and pork-meat products, and poultry are main items: in meat and milk Brittany's production is equal to that of Holland or Denmark, while the region exports as much poultry meat (mainly to the Middle East) as does the United States.

Similarly fishing provides half French fishing production, although only 1% of the population of Brittany is involved. Service industries and activities are accounting for a growing proportion of the population, some 54%, while only 18% are involved in industry, which may explain the near-average unemployment rate of 11% as against the French average of 10.6% in the mid 1980s. Brittany has therefore moved rapidly from an agricultural to an industrial (agri-business) economy needing investment, infrastructure and outlets for its products. The impact on the way of life of its peasant (small-farmer) population has been dramatic: small farmers have either been unable to compete, joined producer cooperatives but still found themselves unable to raise the necessary finance, or become embroiled in a cycle of linked high-cost foodstuff purchases and low-price meat sales to Paris-based marketing organisations. Brittany has been particularly subject to Common Market rules assisting large producers and penalising small ones, but also to transport problems (it is often easier to export cauliflowers, onions or flowers to the UK than to Paris), not eased by the necessity to use railways which are themselves more and more obliged to charge near-economic prices for their little-used rural services.

Small farmers are located mainly in the westerly parts of the peninsula which are also the main Breton-speaking areas, those without industrial investment and those with the worst transport problems. Economic and demographic problems hence exacerbate the cultural and linguistic ones, and it is sometimes difficult to identify whether the complaints and violent action are caused by regional attitudes or purely by economic difficulties.

4.3.3 Language and culture

Breton is a Celtic language similar to Welsh and Scottish or Irish Gaelic. Two main dialect groups exist: KLT (Cornouaille, Léon, Trégor) and Vannetais, with considerable differentiation between them. A unified orthography was finally adopted in 1941 (called the 'zh' type because of the use of this representation, and widely known because of the use of the car sticker *Breizh* which combines the -z of the KLT with the -h of the Vannetais dialect), but a different one was adopted by the Ministry of Education in 1955, and a third, known as the 'interdialectal' version, was set up in 1975. Despite these problems, a number of magazines are produced in Breton and between sixty and eighty books are published annually in the language.

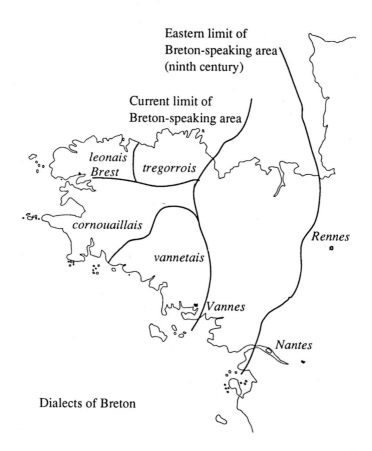

Eastern limit of
Breton-speaking area
(ninth century)

Current limit of
Breton-speaking area

leonais
Brest   *tregorrois*

cornouaillais

vannetais

Vannes

Rennes

Nantes

Dialects of Breton

Breton is declining, rapidly, in use. Its frontier with *gallo* and French has been moving quickly westward over the 19th and 20th centuries, and the total number of people speaking Breton has dropped from about 1,322,300 in 1886 to about 500,000 to 700,000 now: these figures come from a study (LeRoy, 1983) which estimates the number of those actively using Breton in everyday life at 300,000. An 'official' best guess puts the figure at 500,000 speakers (*France Informations*, 1983), and another study (Delsol, 1985) puts the figure of those using Breton on a daily basis at 350,000, with 600,000 being capable of speaking and a total of one million having some knowledge. The EEC report on linguistic minorities (*Minorités*, 1986, 194) notes that 'certain administrations consider even the most pessimistic estimates seriously overestimate the number of Breton speakers'.

These figures reflect the success of the nineteenth century government policy, particularly in education and the Church, against the use of regional languages. In 1925 Anatole de Monzie, Education Minister, was still saying openly that for the unity of France the Breton language should be made to disappear. This policy continued through to 1951, when the Deixonne Law was passed, enabling a limited use of Breton and some other regional languages within the educational system. Other, less deliberately planned influences have had an effect: the First World War was responsible both for massive movements of Breton-speaking conscripts out of the region and for the use of French within the region for administrative purposes ranging from food distribution to the payment of pensions. Today television, life-style changes and the economic situation are particularly powerful agents of continuing linguistic, and indeed political, centralisation.

Only the Church among the organs of the establishment, in its services, parish work and educational services, for long consistently defended the use of patois and regional languages, although its influence is subject to present-day decline, as *Minorités*, 1986, notes. In Church schools courses in Breton language, history and culture had been offered since 1930.

There is however a strong and growing 'Breton movement' supporting and fostering the use of the language. One of the successes is the review *Al Liamm* and its associated publishing activities, although this is not the only such periodical; another important one is the *Emgleo Breiz* movement and its *Brud Nevez* publications. A major manifestation of this movement is the growth of Breton language learning and teaching, particularly the creation of the *Diwan* schools in 1977. These are essentially private kindergartens in which Breton is taught and used as medium of instruction, although they also go through to primary stage and now have a degree of public funding (approximately 15 per cent). Nineteen kindergarten schools and four elementary schools have thus been established. At university level it is now possible to take a degree in Breton at Rennes, together with a teaching qualification (*CAPES* in Breton plus another subject) - the latter reform dating however only from 1985.

In 1984 the *Diwan* schools had 300 children in kindergartens and 5 primary classes, while in the same year state bilingual classes had 200 enrolments. In 1981 2,931 children were taking Breton language classes (3,756 in 1986-7). In 1982, 324 students were following the degree course at Rennes, while a further 60 were doing Master's courses; 72 students were doing Breton courses at Brest. These figures are nonetheless small compared with the 5,383,265 language 'choices' taken up in 1986-7, and the success is relative; state financing for the *Diwan* initiative is constantly under question.

In recent years a number of local organisations have been established which support Breton culture, many of them doing so without necessarily including direct support for the language. To a certain extent this development indicates how few Breton speakers are left; it also shows the degree of interest in aspects of the culture - music, dance, sport - which can act as reminders and symbols of a different way of life and can form powerful identity markers. Media broadcasts, by (local) radio and television, have increased the possibilities for dissemination greatly, and international Celtic contacts also help to establish pride in the importance of Breton.

The Breton sociolinguistic situation is thus complex: the region has a distinctive character, traditions and history, but is, and its population feels it to be, crushed by the political, economic, cultural and intellectual power and attractiveness of Paris. Its language, the symbol of its ethnic identity, suffers: it is no longer used for all functions and is limited to intimate family situations, apart from some remains of commercial and economic exchanges, in selling fish in the large and well-organised markets for example. It is in a clear diglossic situation, lacks prestige, has lost its role as key to social mobility and is hence little used by mothers and daughters. Elegoët (1973) describes its characteristics thus:

> It is the language of daily agricultural labour...in the café, at the market. For adults, Breton is pre-eminent in daily life, but its use by the young is declining. Above the age of twenty, Breton is the language of the men; those who are younger use Breton or French, and the switching is a complex affair. The 'sex' variable is

important: the father speaks to his son in Breton, the daughter uses French to her mother at home. On Sunday after Church, in town, it is inconceivable and even incorrect for a young man to talk to the girls in Breton. Outside intimate and family groups, only French is used, while in the family parents address their parents in Breton and their children in French.

Further reading

Fouere, Y. 1977. *Histoire résumée du mouvement breton.*
Gwegen, J. 1975. *La langue bretonne face à ses oppresseurs.*
LeRoy, M. 1983. La langue bretonne: aperçu historique. *Les Langues Modernes* , 4: 381-388.
Nicolas, M. 1986. *Le Séparatisme en Bretagne.*
1983. La Bretagne. *France Informations*, 120
1984. La Bretagne. *Le Monde Dossiers et Documents*, 107

4.4 Catalan

4.4.1 History

The comparatively small area of France now contained within the Department of Pyrénées Orientales, with Perpignan at its centre and known as Roussillon, houses 3.16 per cent of the total of Catalan speakers, speaking the north Catalan dialect. As with the Basques, the majority of Catalan speakers is in Spain, in the province (*Generalitat*) of Catalunya, and the language is spoken along the coast to Alicante, in the Balearics and also in Andorra (0.2 per cent of speakers). The capital of Catalunya is Barcelona, whose counts established their power in the twelfth century, becoming kings of Aragon in 1137. The region's inhabitants spread over the Mediterranean until the fourteenth century; after that time its powers decreased and its rulers were absorbed into the wider Castilian and Aragon dynasties. In the Treaty of the Pyrenees in 1659 Catalonia was cut in two, with Louis XIV commencing the process of 'francisation' of the northern part which has continued since.

In more recent times Catalunya has formed one of the major Spanish provinces, and during the Civil War of 1936-9 was a centre of Republican support against Franco. Following the latter's death, the autonomy of the *Generalitat* was reestablished in 1978, together with recognition of Catalan as one of its official languages. A systematic policy of Catalan preference is followed by the regional government, particularly in education, where Castilian and Catalan are taught side by side, with all children receiving four hours weekly in Catalan and some 30,000 being taught wholly in Catalan (*Le Monde*, 7.11.85).

French Catalonia is not independent, and has recently been subjected both to massive tourism, in which the major part of the population is now engaged, and to extensive immigration from other parts of France, from Algeria and from Spanish Catalunya. These population movements have evident linguistic consequences.

4.4.2 Politics
Catalan militants in France are divided between two policies, one being an attempt to re-create a common Catalonia as an independent State, with a capital in Barcelona; the other leading to greater autonomy within France. The dangers of the first for the usually left-wing north Catalonian French, with wealthy industrialists and financiers in the South opposing the peasants of the North, make for caution. There are nonetheless strong regional feelings, with Barcelona the effective capital.

Regionalist organisations include *GREC* (*Grup Rossellonès d'Estudis Catalans*), *CREA* (*Comitat Rossellonès d'Estudis i d'Animació*) and others. In terms of French politics, the region votes normally on the Left, but follows the swings of political movements as they occur without a strong continuing tradition.

4.4.3 Language
Catalan is spoken 'by 60 or 70% of the 300,000 inhabitants of the Pyrénées Orientales' (Gauthier in Lafont 1982, 102), 'by 200,000 inhabitants' (*Quid*, 1990, 793). By contrast to Occitan, the work of linguistic codification and normalisation of Catalan has been completed, principally by Pompéu Fabra during the early 1900s, and the existence of this official language in Catalunya means that there exists, for the French also, a prestige variety of the language with the full range of functions and uses, public and private. Any dialectal variation is regarded and accepted as such. In Catalunya itself, there is very strong support for the language, a developed literature, and practical uses in all aspects of public and private life, although competition with Castilian continues. In public signs, documents and in other official uses, a preference for Catalan often still acts as a symbol of the desire for autonomy and identification. Although in public road signs, signs for parking limits and similar street furniture Castilian has generally been replaced by Catalan, remaining Castilian signs are sometimes defaced.

Despite the dialectal differences between north and south Catalan, Catalan speakers in France can therefore refer to a recognised and politically accepted language, and draw both spiritual and material help for the maintenance and development of the language in France itself. In 1986-7 a total of 2,576 students (1981: 1,300) were following courses in Catalan in both public and private secondary education. Kindergarten schools (*Bressola* and *Arrels*) to teach Catalan were founded in 1976 and in 1981 on a voluntary basis, with some support from the French State. From 1951 (Deixonne Law) Catalan teaching was permitted in schools, and courses are now offered to university level in the University of Perpignan, and also in Paris IV.

Sociolinguistically, despite the diglossic situation in which Catalan found itself during most of the nineteenth century, particularly evident in the French-language education policy of the time, there has been a degree of language loyalty and language maintenance affected mainly by the strong Catalan renaissance in Spain, and hence some restoration of Catalan in 'official' functions. As a consequence, Catalan is now more used in public life than before, and the success of the strong movements in education, where Catalan is used both as an object of teaching and a vehicle for learning other subjects, have had a major effect on its prestige and acceptability. Likewise, Catalan usage in the media and in economic life, where the Catalunya authorities use Catalan in trade and administration between the two countries, has led to rather more equality of prestige between the two languages than heretofore. The situation is hence dynamic and somewhat fluid, and the future is less clear than in most other French regions.

Further reading

Bastadas-Boada, A. 1985. La crise de la langue standard dans la zone catalane. In J. Maurais. (ed). 1985. *La Crise des langues.*
Lafont, R. 1982. *Langue dominante, langues dominées.*
Vermes, G. (ed). 1988. *Vingt-cinq communautés linguistiques.* Vol 1, 133-49

4.5 Corsican

4.5.1 History

The island of Corsica had been conquered and ruled by a variety of Mediterranean peoples before the arrival of the Romans in 260 BC. Occupied by the Arabs from the ninth to the eleventh centuries AD,

Corsica was ruled by Genoese, the kings of Aragon, and (in part) by the Banque de St-Georges until Pascal Paoli was elected General in 1755, conducting resistance which continued until the French took over in 1768. After the Revolution, Paoli attempted a secession in 1793-6, with a brief English occupation. Napoleon Bonaparte, the most distinguished politician to come from the island, did not ensure its prosperity, and emigration increased greatly throughout the nineteenth and twentieth centuries, with the result that today there are about 400,000 Corsicans living outside the island: Marseille has about 200,000 (207,250 in 1981), while the population of the island itself was 249,593 in 1988. Settlement is increasingly deserting the interior and half the population now lives in the two main coastal towns of Ajaccio and Bastia.

In 1922 Italy claimed the island, strongly encouraging the autonomist movement, and occupied it in 1942. After the Liberation, Corsican autonomists were tried for treason. The population increased through the movement of officials and businessmen from the mainland, immigration from Sardinia, and from Algeria after 1962, and the current population contains only 50 per cent native Corsicans.

Culturally, Corsican tradition has been based on 'clans', with family honour a principal value, and *vendettas*, followed by taking to the *maquis* and becoming a *bandit*, as the consequence of attacks on it.

4.5.2 Politics

Its history associates Corsica with Italy, and the growth of autonomist movements during the 1920s was encouraged from abroad. During and after the 1939-45 war, however, pressure to establish political independence from France was low, and anti-German resistance took the lives of a number of Corsicans.   The island voted on the Right in 1988 (Presidentials), with 57.4% (Corse du Sud) and 51.8% (Haute-Corse)

With 40 per cent of Corsicans who have emigrated to France remaining on the electoral registers of their *communes*, the way is open for fraud and for Sicilian-type vendettas.   In recent elections strong efforts have been made to remove dead, duplicated and incapable electors from the lists: in 1981, this led to 13,020 voters being removed from the lists, although the 1986 local assembly elections were still annulled for fraud and re-run in 1987.

A new political organisation in 1982 led to the creation of an independent Assembly on the island, with the right of voting its own budget and proposing to the Prime Minister changes or adaptations of French administrative law or arrangements to suit Corsican circumstances. Within limits, Corsican internal independence is hence now achieved, although the President of the Corsican Assembly must consult two Councils (Economic and Social, and Culture, Education, and Environment) and state functions are still exercised by a state representative.   Elections to this Assembly in March 1987 were based on Corsican parties with links to the main French parties, although autonomists (*Union di u populu corsu - UPC*) and independentists (*Mouvement Corse pour l'Autodétermination - MCA*) achieved a significant if small percentage of the vote (8.45 per cent). The autonomist, independent, and separatist parties have formed and reformed: the *Action Régionaliste Corse* (*ARC*) was formed by the brothers Siméoni in 1967, renamed the *Azzione per a Renascita Corsa* in 1973, conducted a number of bomb attacks and was dissolved in 1975 to be reborn as the *Associu di Patrioti Corsi* (*APC*) in 1976, renamed in 1977 as the *Union di u populu corsu* (*UPC*).

Political violence has been a feature of Corsican internal politics since the mid-1960s, with 100 incidents over the period from 1964 to 1970 growing to 715 in 1982, and still frequent (542 in 1986, 499 in 1987, and continuing incidents in 1988 and 1989). Many of these have been attributed to the *Front Nationaliste de Libération Corse* (*FNLC*), which was founded in 1976 and banned in 1982, although it was still responsible for murders in 1983 and indeed since. Likewise the *MCA* was banned in 1987. In 1983 the *Association pour la Corse Française et Républicaine* (*CFR*) was formed to counter the *FNLC*, with a mass demonstration in 1984 against continuing *FNLC* violence.

The violence has been directed particularly against representatives of the French State: policemen and gendarmes in particular, tax offices, and, more recently, teachers and civil servants. It can hence be generally regarded as violence in pursuit of the autonomist aim, although connections with crime and the settling of scores cloud the issue.

4.5.3 Language

Corsican is a dialect of Italian with similarities to central and southern Italian dialects: it has evolved independently but with considerable influence from Tuscan and from Genoese dialects during the five centuries of control from that region.   The language has many dialectal subgroups which are undergoing a unifying process, particularly since 1970 with improved communications (Tozzi 1984, 55-7).

A survey conducted in 1979 by *INSEE* (Gauthier 1980) reported that 79% of heads of family, 69% of their wives and 59% of their children said they spoke Corsican. Biétry (1985) repeats the estimated number of speakers of Corsican as between 80,000 and 100,000, but considers the figure to be an overestimate, notes that Corsican is no longer the working language *(la langue du pain)* and expects its use to diminish.

The language is used as a banner and symbol by autonomists, particularly by the *FNLC*, so its use in public life is often tantamount to a political and ideological statement. Nonetheless Corsican is widely used in local councils, which reserve French for official written documents. A programme of official bilingualism was approved by the Assembly in 1983 (by 37 to nil, with 7 absentions), although it was then vetoed by the Mauroy government.

In the same year, the Ministry of Education reported that there had been a total of 825 students of Corsican in 1981 (2,982 in 1986-7). The language was not included in the provisions of the Deixonne Law of 1951, although teaching of Corsican became possible after 1974 and was strengthened in 1981. The problem with teaching Corsican in the educational system is that Italian is regarded officially as the correct, standard, educational and written version of the language, in the same way that *Hochdeutsch* is the educational and written version of the language(s) spoken in Alsace-Lorraine and Dutch that of the Flemish area. Logically, therefore, Italian should be taught in the schools, whereas what is locally demanded is the living Corsican of families and the village. Nonetheless Corsican is taught in 88% of primary and 80% of secondary schools (*Minorités* 1986, 213), although other sources indicate a maximum of 65% of primary children and 17% of secondary children receiving instruction.

In the media, a bilingual edition of the main newspaper (*Nice Matin*) has been published for over fifty years, although with very little in Corsican. Small circulation journals also appear: one monthly (*Kyrn*) claims sales of 40,000. Likewise FR3 and local radios broadcast in Corsican (*Minorités*, 1986, 216).

The sociolinguistic situation is therefore apparently classic diglossia between French and Corsican in terms of French being the official language for all administrative purposes, with Corsican still a living spoken form for intimate and domestic uses, although this position is somewhat confused with the use of spoken Corsican in some aspects of public life, and its acceptance in the educational sphere. Since the use of Corsican is seen as a symbol of and for autonomists wishing to establish (more) regional autonomy, language attitudes are associated with political attitudes and aspirations, themselves often based on economic problems.

Actual language usage on the island however shows a high degree of language mixing, with both French and Corsican heavily influenced by each other. The regional French is heavily accented, with considerable lexical borrowing and uncertainty over genders (*des ciseaux belles*), while Corsican itself has necessarily been greatly influenced. Standard Italian (ie the formal written variety) is also a linguistic fact, and the influence of large numbers of Italian tourists and the easy reception of Italian television affects the total scene.

Further reading
Gauthier, G. 1982. La Corse. In R Lafont (ed) 1982. *Langue dominante, langues dominées.*

4.6 Flemish

4.6.1 History
The Flanders area in the north of France is about one fifth of the former Flanders county, established in 883 and confirmed in 1056 as under the dominion of the French king and also partly within the Holy Roman Empire. The region was fought over in the thirteenth and fourteenth centuries, but remained mainly under French control until 1555, from when, until 1658, it was part of the Spanish domains, although ruled independently. The present frontiers were not established until 1712.

Historically the term *Flandres* was applied to a large area of the north of France: in the tenth century the term covered all of present-day France north of the Somme, East and West Flanders (now in Belgium) and Zealand-Flanders, now in Holland. Westhoek, the name of the French sub-region close to the Belgian border where Flemish is now spoken, is but a small portion of this area.

4.6.2 Politics
There is little autonomy or federalist political feeling in the region, although a number of associations and groups based on the language problem are active. The first to be formed, the *Comité Flamand de France* has remained a learned society without political ambitions, but concerned to establish the use of standard Dutch. In the 1920s, with the growth of regionalist and autonomy movements, the *Vlamsch Verbond van Frankryk*

was founded, to move towards collaboration with the Nazis during the Second World War. During and after the last war, right-wing Flemish groups in Belgium and Holland also had dealings with the Nazi Party in Germany, and right-wing nationalist sentiment has remained a widespread political attitude for a considerable time.

Local language associations exist, with the *Cercle Michel de Swaen* the best-known and most right-wing. Generally speaking the region is politically right-wing, although the industrial areas oppose this.

4.6.3 Language

The language frontier with French has varied over the centuries, with Flemish in general giving way to pressure from French in the South and West. In the twelfth century, Flemish was thus spoken north of a line from Boulogne to Armentières, but is limited today to the Westhoek region around Dunkirk. In France, the number of speakers has declined from 250,000 in the nineteenth century to 150,000 in 1940 and between 40 and 50,000 today (Tozzi 1984, 43).

The language spoken in Westhoek (*vlaemsch*) differs from that spoken in Belgium (*flamand*), which was adapted and officially approved by the Belgian king in 1830 on behalf of the new kingdom, as a 'language created in the nineteenth century by linguists in order to oppose the penetration of French into Belgian Flanders' (Tozzi 1984, 43). Standard Dutch (*néerlandais*) differs yet again. The exact degree of difference between these different forms is disputed, with the differences being essentially dialectal. For the Dutch, the forms are known as *westvlaams* (in France), *oostvlaams*, *brabants* (in North Belgium), *limburgs* (in both southern Belgium and Dutch Limburg), *saksisch* (in Saxony), *zeeuws* (in Zealand) and *hollands* (in the main part of the Netherlands).

French Flemish is now seen as a rural, somewhat archaic variety, spoken by between 40,000 and 100,000 rural dwellers near the Belgian border. Since standard Dutch is the prestige language of Holland, with a full range of abstract and technical terminology and a codified grammar and lexicon, the Westhoek dialect suffers both from prestigious French and also from prestigious Dutch, and hence remains an inferior and little-prized variety, as is evidenced by the support local language associations offer for standard Dutch in public life. One reason for its survival may be the *kermesses* and similar social gatherings, called *chambres de rhétorique*, although they take the form of friendly gatherings, literary clubs, popular schools and amateur theatres, at which its use is still normal. Radio Uylenspiegel, a local station, broadcasts in Flemish and is widely listened to, although only about 10 per cent of its broadcasts are now in Flemish.

Like all regional languages in France, its use was forbidden in school: the school wall in Berthen carried the instruction *Défense de parler flamand* until 1961. It was taught after 1982, and 300 students were recruited in 1983 (593 in 1986) when it was officially recognised for teaching in the schools, but today it is realised that no children in France have Flemish as their mother tongue. Wardhaugh (1987, 113) considers its extinction in France 'imminent'.

Further reading
Vandeputte, O. 1981. *Dutch.*

5 French abroad

5.1 Historical situation

FROM the sixteenth century, after the disappearance of Latin and despite the competition from Italian and Spanish, French was widely used throughout Europe among the aristocracy and for diplomatic contact. Over the next two centuries it strengthened this role as a 'universal' language, and the central importance of France and the French language in disseminating ideas reached its climax in the eighteenth century and with the Revolution. In the nineteenth century the European powers including France were hungry for colonial expansion, for the movement of people and goods, for raw materials for their industries and for markets for their products; France participated eagerly in the rush to extend influence world-wide. The present-day situation, in which French is one of the few languages used in all continents, is a direct consequence of military, economic, cultural and political expansion; significantly, it is not a consequence of mass emigration such as that of Spanish-speaking peoples to South America or English-speaking peoples to North America or Australia.

After the establishment and consolidation of France's European territory, a slow process mainly of military and diplomatic conquest from Paris, and which was not completed until 1860 with the attachment of Nice and Savoy, France's first overseas empire began in the sixteenth and seventeenth centuries with settlements in Canada and Louisiana, in the West Indies and across the Pacific, including continental India. First landings were made by Jacques Cartier in 1534 on the St Laurent, and French Canada was established from 1604 with fur trappers and trading posts. Other trading posts were established in India, and African territories were also seen primarily as channels through which French goods and supplies could be transmitted. In North America fairly small settlements took place in Louisiana and along the Mississipi.

This empire was greatly reduced in 1763, through the Treaty of Paris. Most overseas territories were ceded to Britain, leaving mainly small islands and trading outlets. Only in Canada did the emigrants who had established themselves, mainly from the maritime provinces and the west of France, remain in significant numbers despite deportations by the English and voluntary movements towards Louisiana and the north-eastern United States. France at this time lost Dominica, Saint-Vincent, Tobago, Grenada and the Grenadines in the West Indies, the left bank of the Mississipi, Senegal and all the Indian territories except for Mahé and Pondichéri. She retained Mauritius, the island of Réunion, Guadeloupe and the western half of Santo Domingo, which she was to lose in 1804 when it became Haiti, while Louisiana was sold to the United States in 1803.

It is noteworthy that this first empire was only rarely the creation of free-trading and colonising expansionists. More frequently French installation in a new territory came about because of persecution at home, for example of Protestants fleeing after the Revocation of the Edict of Nantes in 1685, or the taking of La Rochelle, although the French king deliberately prevented Protestants from settling in the New World, thus ensuring that the future USA spoke English rather than French. Dispossessed or desperate peasants, particularly from the West and Brittany, or, after 1763, fleeing or deported by the British from Canada, took their regional language or their patois with them. In the slave-using territories in the West Indies and in the Pacific, **pidgin** languages developed, derived from mixtures of French and the African languages and used at first as means of communication between master and slave or as a general lingua franca, later to become a native, first language as a **creole**. Everywhere French or a version of French was in essence the language of the dispossessed or the underprivileged, and in some cases was spoken by settlers who had no great love of France nor wish to support its interests. In the case of Canada, after 1763 French speakers felt betrayed and unsupported by France itself, which had failed to send troops or supplies in their hour of need.

The empire was rebuilt in the nineteenth century, from 1830 on. France established herself in Indochina in 1863, in Oceania - French Polynesia in 1847 and New Caledonia in 1854 - but particularly in Africa. The three Maghreb countries, Algeria (1830), Tunisia (1881) and Morocco (1912) were taken over in the North, and a variety of countries in West and Central Africa were also conquered, although in some French-speaking Belgium was the colonial power, rather than France itself. Using their present names these countries were: Mauretania, Senegal, Mali, Guinea, Ivory Coast, Burkina-Fasso, Togo, Benin, Niger in the West; the Central

African Republic, Chad, French Cameroon, Gabon, Zaïre, Rwanda, Burundi in the centre. Madagascar, off the coast, was taken over in 1896. In the Near East, too, Syria and the Lebanon became protectorates after the First World War. This empire was not complete until 1918 and in this second period of expansion French was the language of the conqueror, of the ruler and of the administrative official: it was the language of the élite.

Many of the links between France and French-speaking areas abroad became loosened during the decolonisation process, accelerated since the end of the Second World War. While the French empire reached its largest in 1939, with a total population of forty-eight million, this had reduced to one and half million by 1960. Nonetheless the total population of French speakers across the world is estimated at 105,886,000, of whom the greatest concentration (56 million) is in France including the overseas departments and territories, known as *DOM-TOM* (*Département* or *Territoire d'Outre-Mer*). Even though French is a second rather than maternal language for 34 per cent of the 100 million total, it is widely spread throughout the world, with different roles and status in different countries: **official**, used as the tool of government and education; **vehicular**, used for specific purposes such as commerce or diplomacy; or **vernacular**, the mother tongue; and rarely all three together as in France.

The French spoken in Luxembourg, Belgium and Switzerland, and in parts of some other countries bordering on France, has developed in the same way as the language of France itself - directly from the Latin spoken by the soldiers and administrators of Rome. Everywhere else in the world where French is spoken it is the language of Paris, adapted and changed over time, which has been retained or imposed as a result of emigration or military force. Hence it is possible to classify French outside France as falling into one of three types: the French of the **borderlands**, the French of **emigration** or the French of **expansion**. In sociolinguistic terms, the attitudes of speakers could be summarised as those of potential internal inferiority (in relation to the French of Paris) in the first case, external inferiority (of a creole or marked regional variety in relation to 'standard' French) in the second, and of superiority (in relation to local languages) in the last: the use of French carries very different values in different parts of the world.

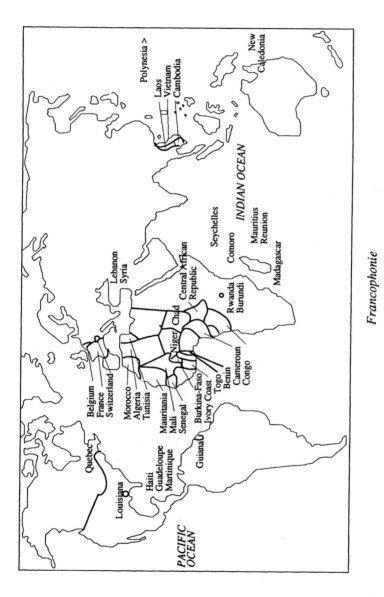

Francophonie

5.2 Countries, regions and territories

IN the following survey, the figures of French speakers given are those of 1985, published in a report (Farandjis 1986c) to the High Francophone Council (*Haut Conseil de la Francophonie*). These were modified later (Farandjis 1987 & 1989), and the statistics quoted are due for correction, on a rolling basis, to accompany the scheduled meetings of Heads of Francophone States. The modifications up to 1989 have been included here. The first figure given is for speakers of French as a mother tongue (*français langue maternelle*) and the second for those who have received an education in French for a period of at least four years at secondary level. The survey is necessarily brief and factual.

5.2.1 Europe

Over eight million people outside France, in Luxembourg, Belgium, Switzerland and the Aosta valley, fall within this definition of the French speaker, some 5,510,000 of them as mother tongue users. In <u>Luxembourg</u> (50,000 + 250,000), French is used in education and generally throughout the administration as one of the three languages in common use (French, German, and the Luxembourg dialect of German), with German being more widespread in the rural areas. The towns are multilingual without apparent conflict, and many of the population are normally trilingual.

<u>Switzerland</u> (1,300,000 + 1,200,000) likewise enjoys an unproblematic situation, with French one of the three main official languages (French, German (about 4,000,000 speakers) and Italian (about 300,000 speakers)). The fourth official language, Romansh, is spoken by a very small proportion of the population, about 1 per cent or 50,700 people, and is very likely to disappear because of its lack of an adequate number of speakers. True bi- or trilingualism is not common, and the population of the cantons of Geneva, Vaud, Neuchâtel and Jura use French more or less exclusively, with Fribourg and the Valais in a more mixed linguistic situation. Despite the imbalance of population and geography, with most of Switzerland and the Swiss being 'German', French coexists peacefully with German and is widely used as a lingua franca. Interestingly, German-speaking Swiss are proud of *Schwyzertütsch*, the Swiss dialect of German, and although they use standard German in education, the media and official life, Swiss German is normal in both domestic and many semi-official situations. By contrast, Swiss French is not so highly regarded, and the French of Paris is considered the prestige variety and the form to be quoted as correct.

In the <u>Aosta</u> valley in Italy (10,000) French retains an official status, but in reality is giving way to Italian, used by economic immigrants from the south of Italy and by the growing population of commuters working in Turin rather than in agriculture in the valley itself.

In <u>Belgium</u> (4,150,000 + 1,300,000), despite the continued existence of one Parliament and government, a long-standing conflict between French and Flemish speakers has led to more or less complete partition of the country, extending even to separate ministries, schools and universities, educational and social provision. The administrative division of the country has left some points of linguistic conflict, where French is spoken in Flemish areas or vice-versa: Comines/Koemen, the Fourons/Voeren, and particularly Brussels, a French-speaking enclave in Flemish Belgium, and there remain difficulties with the small German-speaking area in the east of the country. Language, and language loyalties 'override all other questions that form part of the body politic' (Baetens Beardsmore 1980, 145).

Belgium was created as a modern State in 1830, with French as the official language. For much of its history French served as the language of the court and of the administration, and after 1839 an almost classic diglossia prevailed, with Flemish limited to its use by native speakers in subsidiary, non-official and domestic functions, although it was permitted in the courts even under Napoleon's administration. The first census (1846) showed a population of 2.4 million Flemish speakers and 1.8 million French, and the initial domination by the French in political and administrative life was certain to have repercussions. The subsequent history of Belgium is based on the Flemish slowly extending their power: in 1883 - bilingual schools in the north of the country; in 1898 - Flemish as one of the two official languages of the State; in 1921 - monolingual Flemish administration in certain areas (see also Wardhaugh 1987, 206).

The agricultural wealth of the French-speaking area, in the south of the country, and the resulting economic, added to intellectual and cultural, domination, had produced serious grievances among the Flemish community by the 1930s. The phenomenon of language shift became an interesting indicator of relativities: one sixth of children born into Flemish families had replaced their mother tongue by French before adulthood (Meillet quoted in Swing 1980, 17) and most bilingual schools taught in Dutch just long enough for Flemish children to learn adequate French. Reaction against this state of affairs, strengthened by religious separatism and Flemish nationalism, grew and the language law of 1939 instituted unilingual schools. The process continued after the 1939-45 war, and the

1963 law set up completely different educational systems at all levels, while the new Constitution of 1971 confirmed this separation and created four semi-autonomous regions: French-, Flemish-, and German-speaking, together with Brussels itself as a bilingual area. Belgium is hence now a federal State, with independent assemblies in Flanders, Wallonia and Brussels, separate cultural councils for each of the three linguistic communities, and rules for linguistic parity in a range of matters including for example the constitution of the Cabinet. Anti-French feelings among the Flemish community, and anti-Flemish sentiments by the French speakers, have been exacerbated in the past by religious differences and by occupation in two world wars, in which the German occupants favoured the Flemish, and after which the French exacted revenge on Flemish nationalists.

Because of the sensitive nature of the language situation, precise figures on the proportion of the population that speaks each of these languages is not available: the last census to ask the question took place in 1947. Wardhaugh (1987, 204) estimates that 56% of the Belgian population resides in the Flemish area, 32% in the French part, and 11% in Brussels. Brussels itself is notionally bilingual, but in reality French is spoken by an estimated 75-85% of the population, although the capital is located in the Flemish-speaking area. Practical solutions to the increasing dominance of French have included deliberate refusal to increase the bilingual Brussels administrative area beyond the present nineteen communes, although French speakers now living in the immediately surrounding areas have also gained some rights. The real hot-spots of language-based political trouble in Belgium are the small pockets of French speakers surrounded by Flemish speakers and the similar groups of Flemish close to the French-speaking border (see Poole 1985).

Language attitudes in Belgium are complex, with both communities suffering similar linguistic insecurity. The French speakers speak a variety of the language which does not have high prestige: the standard grammar of French, *Le Bon Usage*, by Grévisse, was originally written to correct '*belgicismes*', and Belgian pronunciation is commonly regarded by the French as unlovely. Belgian French speakers tend to look to Parisian French (*français*, as opposed to *wallon*) as a high prestige standard form. Similarly, Flemish speakers in Belgium use a low prestige variety of the language, and also look towards a standard high prestige form (*nederlands* or Dutch, as opposed to *vlaams* or Flemish) as spoken in Holland. Our own use of 'Flemish' in this section is open to misinterpretation, but is not intended to be offensive, nor to 'support' the 'French' point of view.

5.2.2 Near East

In <u>Lebanon</u> (25,000 + 600,000) and <u>Syria</u> (5,000 + 10,000) contacts with French, which go back to the time of the Crusades, were strengthened during the League of Nations protectorate after the First World War. It is in the educational field that French remains notable, but the role of French as a language of privilege, together with the acute political situation in the Lebanon has reduced its role considerably there. Nonetheless, in 1984 it was claimed that 15 per cent of Lebanese 'often' and a further 15 per cent 'rarely' spoke French at home.

Arabic is the official language for both countries, with French competing with English for second place. In the Lebanon bi- and multilingualism is the norm; there is a multilingual Press and active contact with other Mediterranean countries. Syria has a growing political role in the region, but effectively much less contact with European and French-speaking persons, and the situation is further complicated by religious conflict: France still has strong emotional ties with the Beirut Christians, as evidenced by its political and military support for them during 1989.

5.2.3 North Africa

The three North African 'Maghreb' countries - <u>Algeria</u> (150,000 + 6,500,000), <u>Tunisia</u> (70,000 + 2,200,000) and <u>Morocco</u> (130,000 + 4,000,000) have retained a French-based educational system despite the role that Arabic plays at primary level, and the clear wish and intention of all three that Arabic language and culture should become the norm in secondary and Higher Education. Thus 6,735,000 of the 9,667,000 school population (69.7 per cent) learn French, and French becomes the language of instruction after the fourth primary year (Farandjis 1987, 65). Algeria, conquered over the period from 1830 to 1847, underwent a bloody war of independence which ended in 1962, while both the other countries achieved independence in less vicious and bitter ways. The forced emigration of French-speaking settlers, known as *'pieds-noirs'* from Algeria to Mediterranean France and French colonies abroad (for example to New Caledonia) has left bad memories, as have the terrorist methods used by both sides in what was seen as a classic struggle between imperialist and colonial, as opposed to nationalist and religious motivations.

In all three countries French plays a part in a complex sociolinguistic situation. The role of Arabic is mixed: at once the language of freedom and pan-Arabism, of revolutionary and forward-looking social progress, the language of the poor and the dispossessed, it is also that of religious bigotry and Islamic fundamentalism. It is also the normal and the official language of all three States. Its use often contrasts however with that of the local languages (for example Berber in Algeria) in the domestic or commercial situation. French is the language of past prestige, of the educated élite, of oppression, of conservatism and of the past; yet it is at the same time the forward-looking means of accessing the wider world of science, technology and diplomacy, although English is rising in importance in this role.

After 132 years of colonial control of Algeria by the French, when the war ended in 1962 very few schools had been established for the Arab population. All instruction was in French, and the élites who were educated went to France. Commerce, too, was geared towards interaction with France, so that all types of élite were cut off from their Arab roots. The Arabic language itself needed modernising to act as a vehicle for scientific and technological developments. The Arabisation process was decided on, both as an emotional rejection of French after the war of independence, and also as a unifying factor, and in schools classes were taught in Arabic as soon as was practical. Thus by 1974 all arts subjects were taught in Arabic in primary and secondary schooling: at higher level, economics, engineering and medecine were taught in Arabic while other subjects still used French. Language attitudes are therefore still ambiguous: French is useful as a window on the world, and the links with France are strengthened by emigration, by commercial links, and by history; but French is still regarded as the language of military and cultural oppression.

In Morocco a thorough study (Bentahila 1983) has been made of language attitudes before and after independence, examining the attitudes of present-day Moroccans to the complex linguistic situation in a country in which colloquial Arabic, classical Arabic, Berber and French are all in common use. After independence in 1956 'one of the major concerns for Morocco is to return to its original culture by establishing an education that is Moroccan in its thinking, Arabic in its language and Muslim in its spirit' (King's speech, 1958). French colonial education policy had left Morocco with practically no native élite: 36 Moroccan doctors (19 Muslims and 17 Jews) as against 875 French; 30 engineers (15 Muslim and 15 Jews) as against 2,500 French, and the post-independence investment in education, which involved Arabisation, was vast. The school population went from 330,000 pupils in 1955 to 1,450,000 in 1974. However, Arabisation is a slow process, and French continues to play a large role in the day-to-day running of the country and in the lives of large numbers of its people. Attitudes in Morocco can be briefly summarised as characterising French as practical, modern, and of value in commerce, education and administration; Moroccan Arabic as easiest to use and the most valuable for everyday life; and Classical Arabic as essential for the religious and spiritual life and for aesthetic purposes. Bentahila claims (165) that the two languages (Arabic and French) 'complement each other...it would be difficult to persuade the Moroccan bilingual to abandon one of his languages, because this would inevitably be felt as a loss'.

Tunisia has had a less conflictual experience of French colonialism than Algeria, and the consequential reaction against the use of French has been less fierce. Arabic instruction had continued in the schools, and Arabic culture had not disappeared from the élite, so independence did not mark such a brutal rupture. The Tunisian educational system remains a faithful copy of the French, and the process of Arabisation has not been taken so far.

5.2.4 Sub-Saharan Africa

For twenty-two countries situated south of the Sahara (630,000 + 13,585,000) French is an official language. It is sometimes used as the language of education - and hence the difference between the small number of native speakers and the large numbers of those who have undergone a French-language education - and often as a vehicular language at national or international level. These countries are former French or Belgian colonies, and French is seen as the language of social advancement, a minority and élitist acquisition, nonetheless necessary for scientific and technical, and often commercial, exchanges. Most countries have very complex multilingual situations, with constant switching between languages and unclear, but recognisable, functional differentiation between them in the local situation. Thus for example a recent study of language use in Ziguinchor, in <u>Senegal</u>, found that only 11 of the 115 questionnaire respondents were monolingual: 30 were bilingual, 34 trilingual, and 40 used more than three languages (Descamps-Hocquet 1988). The history of the use of Swahili, Arabic and other vehicular languages, of their relationship with the many vernacular languages and the few official languages varies from country to country in a continent in which the development of national identity and national sentiment from previous tribal allegiances is itself a recent and uncertain growth. Contrasts between town and village life, between ancient traditions and the march of progress, are common, and the development of an urban proletariat is sometimes accompanied by the development as a vernacular of an African popular French.

Tabi-Manga (1982) gives some indications of how French is adapted to local conditions in <u>Cameroon</u>. He quotes lexical examples showing three types of development: parasynonyms, borrowings and calques. These linguistic developments sometimes originate in interference with local languages, sometimes in interference with other European languages, mainly English, and sometimes result from the necessary adaptation of French to local circumstances.

> Parasynonyms:
> - *aviation* for *aéroport*: *déposez-moi à l'aviation;*
> - *étrangers* for *invités*: *je ne peux pas venir chez toi, j'ai des étrangers à la maison;*
> - *connaître* for *savoir*: *je connais qui a tort dans le conflit Cameroun-Nigeria.*
>
> Borrowings from English or native languages:
> - *motor-boy* for *contrôleur d'autocar de brousse;*
> - *le bayam-sellam* for a small pedlar;
> - *njoh* = free: *Essomba ne paie pas le taxi, il voyage njoh.*
>
> Calques:
> - *prendre quelqu'un par le pied* = to admire someone: *tu danses très bien, je te prends par le pied;*
> - *mettre la tête à* = to apply oneself: *ma fille, mets ta tête à tes études.*

Detailed and professional analyses of the language situation in individual countries are rare, although Dumas et al (eds) 1986 present brief surveys of many sub-Saharan African countries, examining both the problems of language planning for education and the existing language mix.

5.2.5 West Indies

The French presence in the West Indies goes back to 1635, and many of the islands have changed colonial masters among the French, Spanish and English. The original inhabitants were slaughtered or died out before the end of the seventeenth century, and the import of slave labour from Africa started in the middle of that century. The number of French colonists has never been high, and the population of black origin soon outnumbered them; as the original colonists however, wealth and domination generally remained with them and there has been considerable unrest ranging from the revolt which enabled Haiti to become independent in 1804 to subsequent waves of strikes in 1870, 1900, 1950 and 1967.

Haiti (50,000 + 700,000) has been independent since 1804. The country is for all practical purposes administered in Haitian French-based creole and there is a developed creole literature, although standard French is viewed as the 'correct' form to use, and is the official language. The Republic of Haiti is the largest creole-speaking community, providing about half the total speakers (Green in Ager and French 1986, 160), and following considerable emigration over a period of time, there are large groups of Haitians in the Bahamas, Cuba, Canada and New York, where the numbers are in excess of 200,000. The sociolinguistic situation is that of classic diglossia, with standard French, spoken by less than 10 per cent of the total population, in a superior position to creole, although the status of creole is periodically raised (Bourhis 1982).

In the other countries of the West Indies (Dominica, Grenada, Santa-Lucia, Saint Vincent, Trinity and Tobago) very few French speakers remain (10,000), while the overseas departments still directly administered from France (Guadeloupe, Martinique and French Guyana) are treated by France as integral parts of the country, with directly elected members of Parliament, although a Minister has responsibility also for these *DOM-TOM*. In these other West Indian countries and *DOM-TOM* creole is the normal language of communication while standard French is the only officially recognised language in the *DOM-TOM*. The French educational system is becoming more open to the mass of the population, which is thus becoming more aware of the diglossic situation as between standard French and creole.

There is some evidence, too, that creole is used as a symbol by the independence movements, which retain some activity, particularly in Guadeloupe, where they have used violence as a political tool, with bombs placed at irregular intervals. The *Alliance Révolutionnaire Caraïbe* was dissolved by the Paris government in May 1984. Local political parties make at least token acknowledgement of such independence movements: the Communist Party for example supports 'democratic and popular autonomy as a stage towards socialist independence'. But the relationship between such movements and the language question is tenuous.

5.2.6 Pacific and Indian Oceans

French influence and indeed presence throughout the Pacific is currently strongly contested, particularly by New Zealand and Australia, whose objections to French nuclear, commercial and colonial policy have been strengthened by apparent French disregard for the norms of diplomatic behaviour (for example in the *Rainbow Warrior* affair, when French secret-service personnel sank a Greenpeace vessel in a New Zealand harbour). The visit by the French Prime Minister Rocard in August 1989 acknowledged the necessity to improve this situation. The nature of the French presence is very varied: from independent countries like Vanuatu (1,000 + 30,000), the Comore Islamic Republic (3,000 + 20,000) to *DOM* ((Réunion) and *TOM* (Mayotte, New Caledonia, French Polynesia) and former colonies (Madagascar (30,000 + 1,000,000), Seychelles (2,000 + 10,000) and Mauritius (40,000 + 300,000). Again the presence of a creole alongside standard French has allocated the élitist role to the latter, and the cross influence of both local languages and English, together with English-based pidgins and creoles, renders the individual situations complex.

Thus in Madagascar, which was colonised for a short period in the seventeenth century and again from 1895 to 1960, French policies of assimilation in education have had mixed results. The local language, Malgache, had a written form only in the nineteenth century, and is still not standardised. French, having been the only language approved for education until 1951, is still widely available as a second language, with Malgache as the vehicle, despite considerable difficulties with materials and teacher supply. Although French is used for administration and among the intellectual élite, 80 per cent of the population manages quite happily without it, and it is very likely that the role of the language will decrease, particularly in view of the strenuous '*malgachisation*' policy that was followed immediately after independence.

In Réunion, which was colonised from 1665 together with Mauritius and Rodriguez (the three islands are collectively known as the Mascarenes (*Mascareignes*)), no original local inhabitants were discovered. The island's first role was that of staging post, and immigration since has produced a very complex ethnic mix, although Réunion has not received so many Indian immigrants as Mauritius. All the Mascarenes, and the Seychelles, have therefore a complex linguistic system, with creole and French in diglossic relation in Réunion, and English added to the picture in Mauritius as official language. Standard French is little used in Réunion, and the overall position there is best described as a French-creole continuum, with

French used more for official and formal purposes and creole for intimate and informal occasions, although there is a tendency to associate creole usage with blacks and Indians rather than with ethnic whites (Chaudenson in Valdman 1979).

French Polynesia is slowly gaining independence from France, and the linguistic situation presents conflicts and competition with English and with Polynesian languages themselves. Thus immigration to Tahiti of Chinese and English speakers has rendered the local situation complex, with four recognisable groups: French, 'half-breeds' (*métis*) who are becoming the new middle class, Chinese speakers, who are usually trilingual (Chinese/French/Tahitian) or bilingual (Chinese/French), and speakers of Polynesian languages. Tahitian is used as the vehicular language, with French reserved for administrative and official uses, and recent educational developments allowing secondary and further education in French may have the effect of supporting the role of French as language of the élite. Nonetheless Tahitian is since 1980 an official language, along with French, and educational policy is to expand its teaching (Barret in *Prospective*, 1982, 222).

The case of New Caledonia is somewhat special. The present population is made up of French settlers, many from Algeria, who are strongly opposed to independence, and who form under 40 per cent of the total. The Melanesians, about 45 per cent of the population, generally look forward to independence. Politically the schism is absolute, with the formation of the *Front de Libération Kanak et Socialiste* (*FLKS*) aiming for separation and keen to ensure that referenda for independence are not subject to electoral manipulation, that the original inhabitants are not outvoted by settlers and that the enormous mineral wealth of the islands is not used by French interests as a reason for delaying political settlements. The Rocard solution, agreed in 1989, which delays the final transfer of power to the end of the century, nonetheless appears to have taken the heat out of the situation. Sociolinguistically, the French language is clearly the main vehicle used by both sides in the political infighting, while the role of French is similar to that elsewhere: it is the official language, used in all administrative and formal contexts, and the other languages are all in an inferior position from the point of view of power relationships.

5.2.7 Indochina

Following the war of independence from 1945 to 1954 when, at Dien Bien Phu, the French were finally defeated, and the consequential American involvement in Vietnam, and despite the continuing diplomatic contacts, the role of French in the area seems set to decline. Cambodia and Laos are both members, together with Vietnam (10,000 + 500,000), of the group of Francophone States, but the troubled political situation in the area means that the sociolinguistic situation is unlikely to provide any serious practical internal role for French.

5.2.8 North America

Canada will be treated separately in 5.3 below. There are 1,300,000 French speakers in the United States, of whom most live in New England or Louisiana as a result of both original settlement and resettlement after the English conquest of Quebec.

Louisiana, named after Louis XIV, was colonised from France, with New Orleans having in 1750 a population of about 5,000 whites and 2,000 black slaves. Immigration from Acadia (eastern Canada) after forced deportation by the English in 1755 and after 1763 increased this population, but the territory was nonetheless sold to the United States in 1803. French remained an official language until 1865, and could then still be understood and spoken by up to a million people. In the 1880s however, communications were improved. In the 1920s industrialisation and oil discoveries, added to a 1921 law preventing French language education, opened up the backwoods and the swamps and many Cajuns - the word is adapted from *Acadiens*, those who left *Acadie* or French Canada - abandoned their French inheritance to gain economic advancement in English. Today 500,000 people, 15 per cent of Louisiana's population, are said to be francophone (Henry 1984), although the authoritative 1985 report on the state of *Francophonie* gives 200,000 native speakers and a further 50,000 who have had French language education. In 1968 Louisiana declared itself to be officially bilingual in English and French.

Phillips (in Valdman 1979) identified three varieties of French currently still used in Louisiana: standard French, a creolised version of French spoken mainly by the black community, called gombo, and *acadien* (cajun). Neither of the latter two have written versions. Despite the efforts of the Council for the Development of French in Louisiana (CODOFIL) and the employment, with French help, of additional foreign-language teachers, French is poorly placed to resist English. The general language situation in the United States is difficult for all non-English-speaking communities due partly to the overwhelming pressure to conform to the norms of American society, to belong and to participate in the English-speaking culture. Hispanophones, however, whether original inhabitants or more recent immigrants living in the towns, and who have adopted the role of an urban proletariat, are demonstrating growing linguistic power, particularly in the South. Language loyalty in the United States is the subject of many sociolinguistic studies (Fishman et al 1966), and the retention of language as a symbol seems most effective in isolated rural communities or where there is a foreseeable new role for the community as such.

French is spoken elsewhere in the United States, particularly in the northern parts of New England and in the States bordering on Canada. French here is suffering from the general decrease in status and prestige of all languages apart from English, and it seems unlikely that it will continue for many more generations to be a normal spoken and written language in frequent use.

5.3 Canada

5.3.1 Historical situation

Jacques Cartier, a native of St Malo, started exploring the banks of the St Laurent river in 1534. It was not until 1608 however that the town of Quebec was founded, followed by Trois Rivières in 1634 and Montreal in 1642. Settlement was fairly slow, particularly by comparison with that of the English at the same time: 2,500 French *habitants* by 1663 as against 85,000 English. By the time the English conquered Quebec in 1759, 65,000 French had obtained control of the interior of the country, setting up treaties with the Red Indians and preventing the 1,610,000 English from moving inland (Brunet 1979). The 1763 Treaty of Paris officially recognised this numerical contrast and the French defeat at Quebec and ceded the area to England. The English had no intention of allowing French to continue to be used as a language in the area and officially banned its use, coupling this repressive measure with the forced or greatly encouraged displacement of many of the *Acadiens* to other areas, particularly to Louisiana and to the north-eastern areas of what would become the independent United States after the war of independence in 1776 and the creation of the United States in 1783. The abandonment of the Canadian settlers by Paris, and their feeling that they were entirely on their own against a hostile environment, contributed greatly to their attitude towards their Frenchness and to the later developments in community solidarity against English domination.

Problems between Canadians and *Canadiens* existed therefore from the beginning of settlement. Local assemblies had to be established to aid local administration, from 1792 onwards, and the 1839 Durham Commission noted the continued problems between the two 'races' or 'nations', caused not by conflict between government and people, but rather by conflict among religions, styles of life, languages and attitudes as between conqueror and vanquished. The British North America Act of 1867 instituted the present federal system and in effect created Canada as an independent State. In so doing it allowed a measure of self-government by the province of Quebec, including the use of French as well as English in its administrative and judicial system. The French thought the same practice was to be maintained as settlers moved westward, but Manitoba for example decreed in 1870 that English alone would be used in its administration. The province of Quebec did not become officially bilingual until 1910, and the French-speaking population remained essentially rural and dominated by the Roman Catholic Church, leaving city life, economic and trade activities to be dominated by English speakers. Officially the system did not prevent Francophone representation: there was always French representation on the Supreme Court; Quebec government had guaranteed French representation, and many Federal Prime Ministers came also from the French-speaking minority (Wardhaugh 1987, 222).

After the Second World War the rapid economic growth of Canada provoked a 'Quiet Revolution' in Quebec, during which the French Canadian population reacted against its rural existence and Church domination, developing an urban proletariat and a conscious desire to have its political way, maintaining its language and cultural identity. A main factor in this move was opposition to the growing weight of economic domination by the United States, which owned the majority of large businesses located in Quebec, and which invested constantly north of the border. Some 80% of the French population of Canada lived in Quebec, while the proportion of the Canadian population that was of French origin was 30%, a proportion that was to continue falling - to 26.8% in 1981 - as immigration increased and the French birth-rate decreased. Outside Quebec, French was disappearing fast. Finally, immigration to Quebec, and particularly to Montreal, brought in those, not necessarily themselves English-speaking, who preferred to educate their children in English.

After a Royal Commission on Bilingualism and Biculturalism, Canada became officially bilingual in 1969 through the Official Languages Act, which guaranteed rights to French-speaking minorities outside Quebec similar to those the English-speaking minority possessed within that state. The *Parti Québecois* took power in Quebec in 1976, on a platform that included separatism, and passed Law 101 (the Charter of the French Language) in 1977. Despite the fact that in 1980 only 40 per cent of Quebeckers went so far as voting for the *Parti Québecois* plan for a degree of independence from Canada (*souveraineté-association*), the signals were clear and were associated with a series of minor terrorist acts to underline the potential for separation which still existed.

When the Canadian Constitution was 'repatriated' from London in 1982, certain language rights were incorporated for all Canadians. These did not satisfy Quebec, and a compromise, agreed at Lake Meech between the nine provincial and the federal Prime Ministers, and due for ratification in June 1990, formally accepting Canada's linguistic duality and Quebec's distinct character, was necessary before Quebec could formally adopt the Constitution. Opposition from anglophones was intense in early 1990, and dispute over Quebec's language laws and the concept of a *société distincte* was particularly strong, with some municipalities declaring themselves monolingual in English.

Indeed the Supreme Court had ruled in 1984 that Quebec educational provision for anglophones was too restricted, and the *Parti Québecois* had lost power there in 1985. The report to Parliament, also in 1985, of the Commissioner of Official Languages, based on the 1981 census returns, concluded that there was some danger of linguistic territorialism on the Belgian model, with French being in practice confined to Quebec and English only being used elsewhere in Canada. In December 1988 the Supreme Court ruled again on Quebec's language laws, decreeing that some parts of the 1977 Law 101 were unconstitutional, while Quebec's response was to pass Law 178 in the same month to ensure that only French-language signs appeared outside shops and buildings.

5.3.2 Quebec: corpus and status planning

Quebec is now officially monolingual in French, while the rest of Canada is officially bilingual. Four reasons lie behind the move towards this differentiation: the decrease in the number of French speakers outside Quebec; the decline in the birth-rate of French speakers in Quebec; massive immigration into Quebec of those who speak neither English nor French;

and the domination of political and economic life by Anglophones (d'Anglejan in Bourhis 1984).

From 1901 to 1961 there was comparative stability in the relative positions of English and French speakers in Canada: approximately 30-32 per cent of the population spoke French. But the 1971 census revealed that this proportion had dropped between 1961 and 1971, and that this decline was likely to continue to a level of 23 per cent French speakers by 2000. The likely consequences were felt to include increased linguistic separation on territorial lines, with a monoglot - 80 per cent French-speaking - Quebec and a monoglot rest of Canada, increased pressure on French speakers living outside Quebec to drop their French and adopt English, and, eventually, the disappearance of French.

Until 1960 the Quebec birth-rate had been very high by comparison with the English-speaking provinces: the influence of the Roman Catholic Church was evident in this 'revenge of the cradle'. But changes in life-styles, increased Anglophone immigration to the west of Quebec and the progressive urbanisation resulted in the 1980s in a rate of 1.99 live births per thousand of the population as against a figure of 2.2 in the rest of Canada. In addition, the majority of immigrants, whether Anglophone or not, moved towards Montreal, enrolling their children in English-language schools: the Italians, for example, whom the French-speaking Canadians might logically have expected to count among their allies and 52 per cent of whom in 1943 had indeed been enrolling their children in French language schools, had reduced this proportion to 9 per cent by 1972. The educational system was also divided on religious lines, with the French-language schools available only for Roman Catholics: Jewish or other denominational immigrants were automatically directed towards English language education.

By 1970, too, economic domination of Quebec business life by English speakers was almost absolute: French speakers occupied lower-paid jobs, while the average salary of English speakers was notably higher. The working language in office and civil service was English, while French dominated among labourers and domestics; a good level of English was essential for social advancement.

French in Quebec was not prestigious. Hardly surprisingly, the first attempt to impose its use, in 1974, was unsuccessful, and it was necessary to wait for the arrival of the *Parti Québecois* in power to ensure passage of Law 101, which imposed the use of French alone in the State's administration, in employment and in the educational system. In order to ensure adequate recognition of their identity, French Canadians set about language planning on two lines: correcting the status of French, and, secondly, ensuring that the language itself could withstand the conflict in which it was placed by modernisation and linguistic change. Both status planning and corpus planning formed part of Law 101, and indeed had been involved before.

The *Office de la Langue Française* had been set up in 1961 in order to study Quebec French, to create and to recommend appropriate terms for use in the province, and to attempt to resist over-use of Anglicisms. Its first duties were thus oriented towards correcting errors and establishing norms of usage, and it recommended that European Standard French should be adopted as the ideal. After 1972 the *Office* turned its attention towards the creation of scientific and technological terms and towards a policy of equality between the languages. This technical work allowed French terms to be accepted for use in the work-place, and there followed a notable increase in the proportions of French speakers among managers: from 18% in 1964 to 30% in 1979 overall, with a rise from 22% to 45% among the lower and middle executives.

Law 101 was adopted in 1977. It replaced a 1974 law which had made French the province's official language, but which had retained a number of 'linguistic privileges' for the Anglophone minority, particularly in education. Law 101 mentions languages other than French, but makes no special arrangements for English: it was more than linguistic legislation and made a deliberate attempt to shift the debate towards a positive Quebec outlook rather than merely negative anti-English moves. Like various language-planning instruments used in new African States, Law 101 was seen as a mechanism for the creation of a nation; its intention was to raise the status of French and change the previously accepted prestige relationships of languages. These attempts to establish a new domination by French had consequences for linguistic minorities - Asians, Africans and indeed the native Esquimo (Inouit) population, although 79 per cent of these stated their continuing use of English in the 1981 census returns.

The mechanisms created by the legislation included a role for the *Office de la Langue Française* in supervising the application of the law and in defining and conducting relevant research; a *Commission de la Langue Française*, whose responsibility it is to pursue offenders and ensure that punishments are carried out; a *Conseil de la Langue Française*, with the role of advising the Minister and providing opinions on regulations drafted by the *Office*. The 'linguistic police' had been established.

The results of the legislation have generally been positive in improving the status of French:

> Most French-speaking Quebeckers can now live and work entirely in French, and French is gaining strength in the upper levels of the business world (d'Anglejan in Bourhis 1984, 45),

although Bibeau (in Vandenthorpe 1984, 29) is not so sure:

> English remains a real second language for French-speaking Quebeckers: that is, they cannot avoid its use in certain sectors of activity...while English speakers find French a politically second language, which is in effect foreign and which they can do without.

The linguistic battle within Quebec is by no means over. The Quebec Liberal Party, in government in 1990, is debating a revision of Law 101 to permit optional and conditional bilingualism, and there is continuing opposition particularly to the laws on signs, commercial contact, and the use of French in the work-place, all of which have been the subject of High Court judgements.

5.3.3 Quebec: French regional and social varieties

The origin of Quebec French is the regional dialects of west France in particular, modified by the long period of contact with English and by adaptation to North American conditions. Direct contacts with France were poor for a considerable time, but are now again close, and immigration has continued. Hence three major types of Canadian French can be recognised: standard European French, Canadian French, and (several varieties of) popular French - rural, urban and regional.

The popular level (baptised '*joual*' from its pronunciation of the French *cheval*) is characterised by its wide use of 'religious' swearwords (*criss, câlice, tabarnak, ostie*) and, in contrast to standard French, a 'drawling' pronunciation, longer vowels, diphthongs, loss of consonants and final syllables, and a different intonation pattern, which pose considerable problems for standard French speakers. Borrowing from American English is frequent, with words like *watcher* and *mouver* (as verbs), *fun, truck, canne* (as a can - *une canne de beans*), *dompe* (dump), *bécosse* (back-house). Likewise meanings have developed differently from those common in standard French, with *chambre* where standard French would use *pièce, gaz* for *carburant, agenda* for *ordre du jour*. French Canadian lexis also includes items which sound archaic to French ears - *pinte, accoutumance;*

and words which have been created in French ways but which either do not exist in French or which have been created differently: *barbouillette* (*gant de toilette*), *bordages* (*bords de rivière gelés*). Suffixes are particularly common, and different from standard French: *téléphonable, allable, démolissage, espaçage*. Genders are sometimes different: *une été*; as are the forms of verbs or adjectives: *vous disez, avarde*; or syntactic forms: *dis-moi le pas* for standard French *ne me le dis pas* (Hartley 1981).

Corpus planning is difficult in the sense that politicians and linguists may agree on desirable developments, for example in establishing the norm, but it is effectively the choice by speakers in all walks of life which will ensure acceptance or otherwise of the proposals made. Dugas (in Bédard and Maurais 1983, 645) notes that principles which might help in the process include the retention of words now regarded as archaic (*claque* for galoshes); words of local importance (*pruche*), words which have changed sense in standard French (*peinturer*), words which have a different frequency of use in standard French from that of Canadian use (*débarbouillette*), and a collection of 'anti-Anglicisms' such as *magasinage* for French *shopping* or *annonceur* for French *speaker*. The larger danger for Canadian French remains the constant pressure from Anglo-American, and particularly the pressure to adopt lexical borrowings. Examples include direct borrowings such as *tire, clutch, dash, boss, break, shift*; English senses for 'French' words: *record* in the sense of *dossier, altération* in the sense of *réparation, franchise* in the sense of *concession, graduation* in the sense of *remise des diplômes*. Naturalised borrowings which have entered the language and have a long history of usage include *lousse* for loose, *scrigne* for screen, *paparmane* for peppermint; and anglicised structuralisms such as *tapis mur à mur* for wall to wall carpeting, *bureau chef* for head office, *centre d'achat* for shopping centre, and many more (cf Bibeau in Vandenthorpe 1984, 28).

5.3.4 Quebec: attitudes of speech communities

Classic research studies (Gardner R C and Lambert E W 1959) on the attitudes of French- and English-speaking Canadians tended to show the high prestige value accorded to English and the low value placed on French speakers. These studies are felt now to have lost validity, but changes in attitudes in Quebec since the passage of linguistic legislation show continuing confusion, particularly on the prestige value to be placed on Canadian French as opposed to the Paris standard. Television and Press have made the clear choice for the European standard, but French Canadian is intimately linked to local pride and to the economic advantages of local forms.

As French has been more widely used, pride in its use has grown. Bourhis (1982, 58) points out that the early efforts of language planners probably contributed to denigration of the Canadian educated standard in the attempt to replace it by European (or 'Central') French, and that most studies up to 1975 reflected this view.   Bourhis' view is that Quebec has the possibility of developing its own middle-class French to become an acceptable standard and a prestige variety within the province.   He considers that the apparent success of language planning in raising attitudes towards French by comparison with those towards English could be reflected in further movements within French, but points out that as yet there is little or no research proof of this.

Further reading
Bourhis, Y. 1984. *Language Conflict and Language Planning in Quebec.*
Bouthillier, G. and Meynaud, J. 1972. *Le Choc des langues au Québec.*
Hartley, A. 1981. French, Québec, Francophonie. *Bradford Occasional Papers*, 2: 60-86
Termote, M. and Gauvreau, D. 1988. *La Situation démolinguistique du Québec.*
Vandenthorpe, C. (ed) 1984. *Découvrir le Québec.*
Wardhaugh, R. 1983. *Language and Nationhood.*

5.4 Attitudes and policies in France

THE underlying fear colouring French governmental attitudes and policies towards the international role and status of France is clearly expressed in the 1985 report on the state of *Francophonie* world-wide:

> The challenge before *Francophonie* is the same as that which faces all languages and cultural communities: that of a total uniformity of the planet, coupled with a lowering of our humanity to the level of mediocrity...linguistic uniformity   through the use of   Anglo-American and leading to a reduction of language (and thus intellectual and spiritual) resources by the utilisation of some form of basic English, a jargon, a language mix, a pidgin. (Farandjis 1986, 341).

France therefore fears the disappearance of the French language from education, science, technology and commerce, and from the domains of diplomacy and cultural expression where it feels there should be an important international role for the language to play.   Presentations of this attitude and policy are, at least in recent years, careful to avoid implications of neo-colonialism or attempts to reimpose a French political, financial and diplomatic hegemony; nor is the policy based on a simple anti-American reflex. Rather it is felt that other world languages, including Anglo-American, would suffer if the whole world were reduced to using a utilitarian 'code, universally valid, a simplified international lingua franca'. Hence the French government laid out in 1983 (*Projet*, 1983, 5) precise objectives for the presentation of France's international presence, with the aim of ensuring a continuing major role for the country and the language, seen as inseparable:

- a new priority: ensuring France's place in world communication and audio-visual networks;
- promoting the French language and the pluralism of international communication;
- a policy for French publishing: close links between the cultural and the commercial aspects;
- development of technical and scientific cooperation;
- the humanities and social sciences: knowledge of the contemporary world and the cultural dimension of development;
- international management of world resources and creativity;
- a double purpose for French educational establishments abroad following French educational curricula and syllabuses.

Policies follow from the attitudes and beliefs of politicians, which are themselves coloured by generally accepted views in the population at large. A 1986 *IPSOS* survey of public views on *Francophonie* gave some indication of these wider views; the results were debated at the meeting of the High Francophone Council in 1986:

- knowledge both of the meaning of the word '*Francophonie*' and of the contribution of French writers was 'catastrophically low';
- the élite did not believe in the defence of French as such nor in its future;
- the word '*Francophonie*' was felt by many to be frightening;
- feelings of belonging to a Francophone community were less well developed in France than those of belonging to Europe;
- *Francophonie* should not be limited to linguistic and literary specialists;
- *Francophonie* was felt to be a French-centred concept with imperialist overtones;

- political figures, and Members of Parliament were interested, but not as a point of main concern, in matters associated with *Francophonie*.

These conclusions indicate the degree of public confusion still existing in France on the whole *Francophonie* concept. Although the Press follows the work of the High Francophone Council and its meetings with interest, chaired as they are by the President working with the full support of the Prime Minister, considerable scepticism is expressed as to whether its work will lead to success in any of its domains of interest.

Recent summit meetings of the Heads of State of Francophone countries, held in Paris in 1986, Quebec in 1987 and Dakar in 1989, and the practical projects arising from them, have done something to change this attitude. The correct title, carefully worded to enable representatives from Quebec, Belgium, Switzerland and other parts of countries to attend, is a 'summit of Heads of State and of Government of countries having in common the use of French'. Projects and themes of discussion and action have included agriculture, energy, communication, and information technology, and the domains of interest which have emerged are those of language, education, communication, culture, economics, science and technology.

These meetings are slowly establishing the credibility of the Francophone States as a world force despite their late start and the power of other groupings such as the Arab League and the Organisation of American States. The model of the British Commonwealth is particularly interesting and provided a pointed contrast of economic power, wealth and global influence in 1987-8 when the Francophone States met in Quebec and the Commonwealth in Vancouver.

The main point of interest is the fact that the French language is seen as the unifying symbol around which the community of French nations can group, as a defensive measure against the growing power and influence of the Anglophone countries, but also as a positive meeting point for countries wishing to play a world role. Certainly this political aim has been seen as important by successive French governments: after the defeat of the Socialists in 1986, Chirac instituted a Minister for *Francophonie* (Mme Lucette Michaux-Chevry from Guadeloupe) to counter the strong presidential interest in the topic, and since 1988, and the return of a Socialist government under Rocard, a number of ministries have clear interests in this area, with Alain Decaux appointed as the official Minister in charge and given significant political as well as cultural tasks, as for instance in Lebanon in August 1989.

What are the bases of French attitudes towards the use of French in the world? They include the general feeling that French has certain intrinsic qualities which make it a preferable means of expression: clarity, logic, precision, subtlety, stability and rationality. Such qualities have been endlessly analysed - for a recent example see de Broglie 1986 - and it is by no means clear that all unbiased linguists would necessarily agree that these are anything but rationalisations of prejudice; they nonetheless form part of the French psyche. Similarly, self-perceptions of French culture identify intellectual rigour, reliance on judgement and development of the skill of decision-making (*'il faut trancher'*), the ability to analyse and present textual material, and, again, rational and measured analyses of the human situation, as being major contributions to the human spirit.

Beliefs such as these do not lead to modest statements of helpfulness towards other peoples and other cultures, but have rather led in the past to accusations by these other peoples of cultural and intellectual dominance, and to conflict rather than cooperation. The civilising mission of France in her colonial period, and since, has been seen as an attempt to impose her own views because they are necessarily better; and although a refusal to accept a spirit of compromise or accommodation in any domain, including the political as well as the cultural or linguistic, can be regarded as either a strength or a weakness (see Zeldin 1983, 352), it is rarely seen as a mark of tolerance and understanding of others.

The traditional French attitude towards geographical variation can thus be summarised as one of condescension: any regional language variety or alternative formulation which did not reflect the forms approved in Paris was *ipso facto* inferior. The assumption also was that French was a language used for the higher manifestations of the human spirit, in literature, philosophy and the arts, and that the practices and interests of cultural élites were necessarily those which should be spread, as benefits, to all. Above all the assumption was that the French language was a central benefit to mankind which it would be essential to impart in its purest form. Any aid which France could provide for the world would enable the world to share in the benefits of the superior culture of France itself, which could only be done with the same linguistic instrument as that used by Paris.

This attitude was reflected in linguistic policies carried out by France up till about 1970. Thereafter, two Gaullist-inspired views have predominated: that France should support national identities, particularly those created through French influence and even more so those using French; and secondly that the sometimes grandiose philosophical and cultural aim should be supported by pragmatic assistance and technical aid, particularly towards Third World countries: the *politique* should give way to the *économique*. The French language could then be seen as a practical and effective means of communication, valid not merely in cultural but also in scientific and technical domains. The intention became to share rather than to impose, to offer benefits for a practical and working élite rather than a leisured and aristocratic one, although French interests were still paramount.

This approach has been strengthened in recent years as French governments have come to understand the necessity to identify and gain the support of a significant French-speaking world community. The task is Herculean: French is spoken by only about 70-100 million people world-wide, of whom half live in France itself, whereas of the other European languages English is spoken by at least 300 million, Spanish by 250 million, and Russian by 150 million.

Languages spoken world-wide (in millions of speakers)

Mother-tongue speakers		Official language populations	
Chinese	1,000	English	1,400
English	350	Chinese	1,000
Spanish	250	Hindi	700
Hindi	200	Spanish	280
Arabic	150	Russian	270
Bengali	150	French	220
Russian	150	Arabic	170
Portuguese	135	Portuguese	160
Japanese	120	Malay	160
German	100	Bengali	150
French	70	Japanese	120

Crystal 1987, 287

The Francophone community is economically split, too: its wealthy members, particularly France and Canada, are wealthier than the average of developed countries, while its underdeveloped members are economically backward and politically weak countries (Guillou and Littardi 1988). If French is to be a significant world language in a world in which the economic and political importance of Asia, rather than Africa, is increasing, the Francophone States will need to provide economic aid and encourage considerable private investment in African Francophone countries for some time to come. The prospects are for a hard future in this area.

A third phase has been entered upon in the 1980s: the belief that French is under threat, but that other languages and cultures are also under threat from widespread and uniform economic imperialism using English as a lingua franca to impose its own views. While recognising the value of other cultures, this view defends a diversity of approaches and maintains that uniformity is the great danger to mankind at large.

These three policies (see also Muller, 1985, 28), reflecting three different approaches to language variation as well as to international relations, demonstrate nonetheless the underlying conflictual role in which French is placed on the world scene. Whether French attempts to impose itself as the language of the élite, to advance itself as a preferred means of economic and administrative progress, or to defend itself as part of mankind's inheritance, it will necessarily find itself in competition with other languages and other ways of thinking.

5.5 Attitudes and policies abroad

OUTSIDE Europe, excepting Quebec, French in the world is normally the mode of expression of an élite: there are few countries in which French is the native language of the masses, and even in those the language concerned is a creole or other major adaptation. French hence has no 'roots' abroad, in the same way that Portuguese has roots among all classes of society in Brazil, Spanish has developed its own forms in South America and Mexico, or English has adapted to the needs of Australia or the United States while still remaining essentially the same. Typically therefore French is a language of power and of a minority, causing resentment rather than support, and conflict rather than cooperation; this reaction has also been strengthened by the cultural hegemony of Paris and the stress on 'correctness' of usage supported by the *Académie Française* and by the movement for the 'defence' of French, which resists any change to cope with recent developments and any concession to local circumstances.

In Morocco, a bilingual society, language-switching and the choice of language for particular purposes are clear indicators of attitudes towards languages on the part of those who are bilingual. Thus French is associated with education, sophistication, modernisation and social progress. French gives an impression of vivacity and openness towards the Western world; it is the key to modern intellectual developments and knowledge. By contrast, (Moroccan) Arabic is associated with domestic situations, with simple straightforwardness and with intimate feelings. The situation is rendered more complex by the presence of Classical Arabic, a language valued for its functions in religion and in literature (Bentahila 1983).

By contrast in the West Indies political and linguistic opposition form part of the same attitude. Bebel-Gisler (1981) summarises the situation for someone from Guadeloupe, where the creole is a 'strangled force' and French a 'dominating force'. For her, the denigration of creole is 'only one specific case of French linguistic and cultural imperialism'. She considers the problem of attitudes towards creole, both language and speakers, as having its roots in the racist prejudice of linguists, who consider creole to be 'a childlike form of French', equivalent to French baby-talk. Green (in Ager and French 1986, 177) similarly points out how difficult it is, 'even for well-intentioned French listeners', not to consider the use of an expression like *planter* to mean *placer* or *mettre* as having 'a certain lack of sophistication', as would English speakers hearing the English creole '*bagarap*' used to mean 'spoil/destroy'. Similar prejudice, according to Bebel-Gisler, is expressed by politicians, who have 'banned creole from the classroom, repressed and censured its use in the civil service, forbidden it in all those circumstances where Power and Authority are represented'. The middle classes act in the same way when they use standard French for its social and political legitimising power, for the advantages its use confers in commercial, employment and financial activities, and when they use the French-language-based educational system as a means of selection. Such a set of attitudes is reminiscent again of those of metropolitan France towards its own regional languages: in essence, standard French is highly prized and all other varieties are regarded as inferior.

5.6 French in international organisations

THE 1985 report on the world situation of French (Farandjis 1986c) records that in spite of the generally favourable legal position concerning the use of French in international organisations, growing use and power of English is causing serious problems, to the point that French today occupies the second place in most of them. The same report identifies the following factors as contributing to this situation.

- the relatively small numbers of French-speaking personnel: underrepresentation is flagrant in certain departments, such as the political departments in organisations dependent on UNO;
- the linguistic environment: French speakers are more evident and make their presence and language known to a greater extent in organisations physically located in French-speaking countries (European Communities, International Labour Office);
- increases in the cost of translation services: in the EC, interpreters and translators account for half the A grade staff;
- the weight and power of the United States: overwhelming in military organisations such as NATO or financial ones such as the IMF;
- the necessity of participating in international scientific activity: scientists must disseminate their work as rapidly as possible, and writing in English is the only practical method of doing this;
- the decrease in the teaching of French in countries which nonetheless have a strong French tradition, such as Greece or Portugal, whose diplomats now frequently use English in international meetings.

Such factors have helped to create the present situation in which French is practically unused in certain organisations (IMF, International Bank), tends to reduce in others (WHO, NATO), is falling back in yet others (UNO, where 23 per cent of delegations use French as against 32 per cent which use English), but retains its strength in others, particularly in the EEC and its institutions.

Further reading

Ager, D. E. 1989. La Francophonie. *ACTIF 1989:* 19-33

Ager, D. E.. 1990. La Francophonie: quels progrès? *ACTIF 1990.* 64-72

Ager, D. E. and French, R. (eds) 1986. *La Francophonie.*

Baetens Beardsmore, H. 1980. Bilingualism in Belgium. *Journal of Multilingual and Multicultural Development*, 1: 145-154

Bebel-Gisler, H. 1981. *La Langue créole, force jugulée.*

Bentahila, A. 1983. *Language Attitudes among Arabic-French Blinguals in Morocco.*

Bourhis, Y. 1982. Language policies and language attitudes: le monde de la francophonie.

Chaudenson, R. 1979. *Les Créoles français.*

Broglie, G. de 1986. *Le Français pour qu'il vive.*

Deniau, X. 1983. *La Francophonie.*

Farandjis, S. 1986c. *Etat de la Francophonie dans le monde: Rapport 1985.*

Farandjis, S. 1987. *Etat de la francophonie dans le monde: Rapport 1986-87.*

Farandjis, S. 1989. *Etat de la Francophonie dans le monde: Rapport 1989.*

Fosty, A. 1985. *La Langue française dans les institutions communautaires de l'Europe.*

François, P. 1985. Francophonie d'hier et d'aujourd'hui. *Regards sur l'actualité* ,108: 27-42

Guillou, M. and Littardi, A. 1988. *La Francophonie s'éveille.*

Manessy, G. and Wald, P. *Le Français en Afrique Noire.*

Maugey, A. 1987. *La Francophonie en direct.*

Maurais, J. (ed), 1985. *La Crise des Langues.*

Muller, B. 1985. *Le Français d'aujourd'hui.*

Poole, A. 1985. The Fourons: a microcosm of Belgium's linguistic problems. *Journal of Area Studies*, 11: 22-5

Schläpfer, R. (ed) 1985. *La Suisse aux quatre langues.*

Swing, E. S. 1980. *Bilingualism and Linguistic Segregation in the Schools of Brussels.*

Tétu, M. 1987. *La Francophonie.*

Wardhaugh, R. 1987. *Languages in Competition.*

Valdman, A. (ed) 1979. *Le Français hors de France.*

Veltman, C. 1987. *L'Avenir du français aux Etats-Unis.*

Viatte, A. 1969. *La Francophonie.*

6 Social variation: age and sex

6.1 Age

IT would be logical to expect differences in life-style, employment, or political interests as between the generations to be matched by a difference in language use. The exact nature of language variation by generation varies with the passage of years, so the specific linguistic points noted in 1915 or 1945 as characteristic of the French 'younger generation' will be quite different from those observed in 1990. Some of the linguistic differences will correlate, not merely with differences of age, but with the different social realities facing the generations: relations between parents and children are not what they were forty years ago, and social change and economic realities have an effect on the nature of language even if it is only in the interpretation to be given to individual words such as *chômage* or *cohabitation*.

Sociologists generally feel that the intergenerational conflict which marked the 1960s in France has not continued: 'All the surveys carried out among those aged below twenty show that young French people have in general few problems with their parents' (Mermet 1985, 111). The need to establish one's own identity, to be different from one's parents, is perhaps therefore not so marked in the late 1980s and early 1990s as it was in the 1950s and 1960s.

For many purposes in the social sciences two types of generations can be distinguished: the long (thirty years) and the short (fifteen). Linguistically, however, the three generations of interest are probably best defined as the period of schooling; the period of economic activity; and the period of retirement, roughly definable as three unequal groups of people aged up to 19, from 20 to 59, and those over 60, although there are obviously no clear-cut divisions at such ages.

It is worth noting that in 1900 only 13 per cent of the French population was aged over 60, while currently one third of all adults is over 60, and that the proportion of the old is increasing, partly because of the declining birth-rate and partly because the old live longer. Conversely the 'baby boom' of 1945 is reflected in a continuing surge of births in 1967, although the effect in 1987 was modified by the birth control pill. The future net effect of these changes is likely to be similar to that in other European countries: proportionately fewer people in the economically active group, and a declining population overall.

The changes in the proportions of French people in these three long generations over the past forty years can be seen from the following table (figures are percentages of the total population):

As at	0-19	20-59	60+
1.1.47	29.6	54.3	16.1
1.1.67	34.1	48.2	17.7
1.1.87	28.5	53	18.5

France is very aware of the pattern of its population distribution, partly because of the widespread awareness of the *'années creuses'* caused by the deaths of young men in the 1914-18 war, and partly because of governmental publicity given to the twice-repeated problem of the replacement of generations: in the thirties, when birthrate fell, and the period since 1971, when the same phenomenon has occurred to a more marked extent. Thus on 1 January 1987 there were approximately 575,000 Frenchmen and women who were born in 1926, aged 61; more than 850,000 who had been born in 1946, the year of the post-war baby boom, aged 41; a similar figure born in 1966, aged 21, while live births had dropped in 1976 to 720,000. There have been slight increases more recently (805,000 in 1981, but 760,000 in 1984), but the figures of average births per woman have shown a drop from 2.64 for women born in 1930 to 2.09 (estimated) for those born in 1950. The birth-rate figure (average births for all women) shows an even more dramatic drop, from 2.9 in 1964 to 1.83 in 1976 and 1983 (Roncière 1987, *Cahiers Français* 1985).

6.1.1 Children's language

As babies and children grow they develop language in a recognised sequence from sounds to words: at first one 'element', then two and more until by the age of 4, the grammar of the language is more or less complete. Further development continues until by 15 or so the child possesses full grammatical and social knowledge, knowing not merely words and expressions but their meaning in terms of conveying intentions and their value in terms of the social effect of their use (Romaine 1984, Cellard

1984). In this process they come successively under the influence of three groups - the mother and the immediate family; the peer group; and the school, which provide in turn three models of language: that of the maternal influence, that of friends and acquaintances, and that of the State, or at least of official and formal induction into society. It is easy in the case of French to see a parallel between these age-based differences and three recognisable varieties of language: the maternal (?regional) language or dialect; spoken, informal and popular French; and the written, formal and public usage of the norm.

Analyses of child usage have tended to concentrate on matters such as the age at which certain grammatical concepts or other formal aspects of language are acquired. One can see this process either as the gradual elimination of 'errors', or as movement from what is at any one time a coherent system or **interlanguage**, discarded and replaced by another coherent system as the child moves towards mastery. The different approaches to understanding child language have implications for education as well as child psychology, and find application in all aspects of first language teaching. A survey of French child language conducted by the research organisation *CREDIF* in the late 1960s for example noted 'incorrect' forms, and provided a wealth of recordings, analyses and transcripts illustrating typical child usage patterns. A sample list of such 'incorrect' forms found in the speech of six-year olds, taken from Maresse-Palaert (1969), reads as follows:

- use of the plural: in the third person of verbs, for example: *i z atterit devant; des monsieurs qui conduit un avion*;
- agreements between subject and verb: *les petit oiseaux; il a rentré, les autres*;
- confusion between *son* and *leur*;
- incorrect verb forms: *qui z ont* (for *qui ont*);
- lack of masculine/feminine agreement in adjectives;
- misuse of *'charnières'* such as *que*
- lack of adequate vocabulary: the notion of time exists, but there is ignorance of forms such as *avant que;* words like *assez* are used in approximations of quantities, while precise terms are not known; forms expressing judgement are limited and *trouver que* or *se demander si* are unknown.

The same source provides a brief example of the continuous speech of a child of the same age (in a 'common-sense' transcription, with the words of the adult 'interviewer' in brackets):

> *alors y a un chasseur qui a venu pis il l'a tué pis on a repris la grandmère. on lui a ouvert le ventre pis on l'a repris (morte?) il l'avait pas croquée, il l'avait avalée comme ça. et pis alors le chasseur il a tué le loup pis alors il lui a ouvert pis alors il l'a repris pis après on lui a recousu pis après on lui a mis du plastique pis on l'a recousu (pourquoi faire?) pour comme ça i reconnaître pas que c'est la grandmère, pis après il l'a recousu pis alors après il l'a pas vu, alors il est parti tout triste, tout triste dans la forêt comme ça on l'a plus jamais revu.*

The main characteristics of this style are evident: repetition, the use of simple temporal indicators (*puis, alors*), often as pause markers, non-standard syntax (*il a venu*), a limited vocabulary and lack of explanatory forms.

More recent studies of the 'quality of language' used by young people, reported in Gueunier (1985, 16-19), conclude that the linguistic competence of the young is lower than that of their predecessors, and provide particular examples of poor command of spelling. Thus 65% of elementary children have knowledge of the subjunctive of *faire* (*fasse*), but only 45.7% can spell it correctly; only 9.8% can spell the full agreements involved in groups such as *les cerises rouges* or *les voitures roulent.* At secondary level 83.7% of children can manipulate *que* correctly, 49.7% *dont.*

These results need to be moderated, both for the fact that approximately 10% of the population is estimated to be illiterate anyway (Espérandieu et al 1984), and for ideological reasons quoted in Prost (1983). Prost suggests that no valid measure exists for long-term comparisons; that school populations have changed greatly in social composition; and that educational priorities have shifted towards scientific disciplines. Social class and social inequality will also directly affect the language usage of children (Espéret 1979). Furthermore, a specific study of spelling, comparing results obtained on a dictation in 1873 with the same test in 1986-7, seems to demonstrate conclusively the advantage of twentieth century education (Chervel and Manesse 1989).

Other approaches to the study of child language examine the development of 'communicative' strategies, analysing for example how children move in story-telling from presenting a sequence of scenes (*y avait le vilain petit canard; y avaient des enfants qui l'attrapaient Et puis y avait quelqu'un qui lançait de la galette...*) to understanding and using a full range of narrative techniques (François et al 1984).

Studies of adolescents are less concerned with correctness or with language acquisition and more with the characteristics of language associated with interests, practices and behaviour. Thus surveys can identify the 'words which count' for adolescents: *Famille, travail, amour, voyages, droits de l'homme, sport, argent, musique, sexualité,* and those areas which are of least interest to them: *Patrie, religion, armée, politique, révolution* and last of all *syndicalisme* (Mermet 1985, 104). In a similar approach Muller (1985, 179) draws attention to juveniles' awareness of the vocabulary of areas such as sport, transport, leisure, drugs, or music. Studies of the leisure practices of young people show that they are interested in group and external activites, while persons over 40 direct their attention towards the home. A particularly significant generation gap was found in surveys of 1974 and 1981, indicating that the events of May 1968 had created wide divisions between those aged below 24 and those aged over 40, while those aged up to 39 had generally drawn together, with fewer notable distinctions between the 20-24-year olds and those aged from 25 to 39. Nonetheless, these wide distinctions in cultural practices are obscured when social-class differences are taken into account, and students for example were more likely than non-students to listen to records, listen to rock music, go out in the evening, read news or magazines, and less likely to watch TV or listen to songs (Roncière 1987, 98-108).

Adolescents are hence likely to have a wide active vocabulary, relating to the spread of their interests, to develop new terms and expressions and thus be open to linguistic innovation, and to be users of slang and special languages relating to particular interests (school-based slang, computers). The main characteristic of these is their ephemeral nature, although certain types of slang formation recur, such as *verlan* (words inverted: *femme* becomes *meuf, mec* becomes *cem*; see Section 8.5.2).

The dispute in Anglo-Saxon countries about educational sociolinguistics, deriving particularly from the work of Bernstein and opposing a deficit and a difference theory, and educational policies of compensation for the one and acceptance of diversity for the other, have found little echo in France, where educational policies are dictated from the Ministry Inspectorate and where there has been a long history of planning for correctness and for the 'purity' of French.

6.1.2 Adults and the old

Older speakers are likely to be more conservative, pedantic, and linguistically defensive than younger ones. In a country where the population is ageing, such attitudes are likely to become more pronounced. Characteristic of linguistic purism is the belief that the language of one's own generation is better than that of the younger, and often, that the language of one's parents or grandparents represents some golden age of purity. There exist nonetheless forms and styles which are characteristic of older generations, most referring to the social reality of those times.

Many words in the active vocabulary of older generations, referring to objects, events or attitudes of the past, also belong to the passive vocabulary of those born more recently: Muller (1985, 179) instances words such as *aéroplane, tramway, poilu, canotier*. Likewise Martinet (1945) divides his corpus of prisoners of war into three generations according to their pronunciation characteristics, although the data is now, more than forty years later, superseded. Among other features, Martinet noted particularly the retention of differences in vowel duration in pairs such as *bêle/belle* and *mâle/malle* as characteristic of the older people in his sample.

6.2 Sex

THREE interacting oppositions are involved in discussion of the role of sex in differences of language use in French: biological sex, and hence a difference in language use by men and women; **grammatical gender**, where the language has an inbuilt system which does not wholly match biological gender; and **social gender**, or language usage or attitudes which are coloured by or correlate with the social roles of women and men or with socially determined views. If, as some suggest, inbuilt or unconscious linguistic sexism exists in the French language, this is likely to reflect such socially determined views and roles, whose consequences have been incorporated into contemporary language usage.

The male/female biological opposition is not always reflected by the masculine/feminine grammatical opposition of French nouns: a number of nouns in French have feminine grammatical gender but refer to males or vice versa, such as

la sentinelle sentinel	*un mannequin* model
la recrue recruit	*un laideron* ugly woman

In the contemporary spoken language the grammatical gender distinctions are not always evident: the past participle does not indicate gender in spoken phrases such as *il est venu* and *elle est venue*. However, even in cases where a distinction of sound should be made, this appears to be becoming less frequent: thus a woman is likely to say *j'étais confus/pris de panique/déjà prêt*, and Durand (1936, 285-6) suggests that, despite the creation of analogical feminine forms in the popular language (*voyou/voyoute, (viande) crute, guéri/guérite*), the distinction may eventually disappear entirely, although this appears to be unlikely for some time.

Gender is a grammatical category which applies to all nouns in French and hence there is no logical reason why speakers should necessarily regard an object as female merely because it has feminine gender: *la table* and *la maison* should hence not be regarded as female. Nonetheless Yaguello (1978) whose work provides a focus for much research work on language and sex, points to some 'sexist' attitudes which can be inferred from gender allocation:

> *l'océan* (m) is larger than *la mer* (f); *le fleuve* (m) is larger than *la rivière* (f); *le ruisseau* (m) is larger than *la source* (f); *le jour* (m) contains a 'male principle' by opposition to *la nuit* (f); likewise *le soleil* (m) and *la lune* (f), and two of the four elements - *le feu* (m) and *l'air* (m) as opposed to *la terre* (f) and *l'eau* (f).

In names of professions, the masculine form is often the only one to exist, and the feminine form signifies 'wife of':

> *ambassadeur ambassadrice,*   *président présidente,*
> *maréchal maréchale,*   *général générale.*

Women following these occupations in their own right are sometimes referred to by the use of the feminine article, or by the addition of *femme*:

> *le/la professeur, ministre, maire;*
> *un avocat/ un avocat-femme, un écrivain-femme, un auteur-femme*
> *un docteur/ une femme-docteur, une femme-chauffeur, une femme-policier, une femme-savant, une femme-chirurgien.*

In some cases the 'lower' profession has both a masculine and feminine form, while the 'higher' activity has a masculine form only:

> *l'instituteur* and *l'institutrice* but *le professeur;*
> *le directeur* and *la directrice* but *le Recteur;*

> *le conseiller* and *la conseillère conjugale* but *le conseiller municipal.*

Similarly, when men enter professions previously undertaken only by women, the title is 'elevated', often by creating a pseudo-scientific neologism from Greek or Latin roots for the male form:

> *la sage-femme* but *le maïeuticien.*

The question of *féminisation des titres* was examined by a terminology commission set up by Mme Yvette Roudy, Minister for Women's Rights under the Socialist Government in 1984. Claude Sarraute, *Le Monde* journalist, was a member and noted (*Le Monde* 8.5.84) that 70 per cent of respondents to her request for views on the topic had opposed change on the grounds that grammatical and sexual gender did not coincide, that feminised forms were laughable (*cheftesse* was cited as an example), and that many woman felt more valued by using the masculine form. At very much the same time the League for Women's Rights published a striking advertisement (a man dressed as a Playboy Club bunny girl) to incite the government to pass an antisexist law.

In general the French Press received both actions with derision, and the final report of the Terminology Commission was delivered to the Prime Minister in December 1985, and stayed there until a circular was issued on the day of the 1986 election which was to see the government replaced. The circular contained a full list of recommendations for systematising usage, summarised in Evans 1987 as preferring the conservative solution: in effect suggesting only the use of the feminine article (*une médecin, la professeur*). However, Evans also notes that the Commission's report had indicated that only fifteen words had presented problems (of 5,000 studied), and that the difficulties so presented were in 'heads rather than in the words themselves'. The particular words which were proposed in the Commission's report for change, but rejected in the circular, involved those where no accepted feminine form existed for words ending in *-eur*: *professeur, ingénieur, auteur, proviseur.* The Commission tentatively suggested *professeuse, autrice,* noting the Quebec acceptance of the usage of *auteure, professeure,* but pointing out that it would be preferable to follow a standardised rule and create a new feminine form. The Prime Ministerial circular disagreed, and opted for the conservative use of the article *un/une,* as had indeed been proposed as an alternative in the report.

At the moment therefore, the use of such forms as *écrivaine* (as used by the President of the Commission, Benoîte Groult) or *autrice* is highly charged and restricted to dedicated feminists. Such usage would be seen as indicative of social, if not indeed political, attitudes. There appears no intention on the part of governments since to revive the matter nor to pursue the Commission's report.

Yaguello (1978, 57) summarises the results of research on male/female differences in **communicative styles** as follows:

> The stereotype of virile language implies the use of slang and swearwords, word-play and in particular sexually oriented word-play; taste for insults, a richer and wider range of vocabulary, mastery of technical, political, intellectual and sporting registers, quasi-monopoly of public speech, control of mixed conversations, exclusive use of ritual and coded languages, authoritarian and categorial discourse, greater liberty in respect of standard usage, more creativity than women. The female stereotype shows characteristics with negative connotations: purism, non-creativity, taste for hyperbole, mastery of the registers of minor domains, timid and non-assertive speech, chit-chat (*bavardage*), incapacity to manipulate abstract concepts, hypercorrection, fear of (non-standard uses of) words.

Aebischer (1985), noting general agreement on the superior verbal performance of women and their hypercorrection, observes that five hypotheses first outlined by Lakoff in relation to American English held good for French also: women employ a more subtle vocabulary, for example in the description of colours; they use euphemisms instead of swearwords or other taboo forms; they use certain types of adjectives more than men (*charmant, délicieux, sidéré*); they use tags (*n'est-ce-pas*); and a questioning and 'insecure' intonation pattern.

Examples of research relevant to these statements may be found in the further reading recommended at the end of this section. It has been suggested however that much of this correlational research is flawed, and that such simplistic oppositions are themselves indicative of sex bias in the research conducted (Lamothe 1983, 25); and as an instance, that research (West & Zimmerman in Thorne, Kramerae and Henley 1983,111) showing that females are more frequently subjected to interruption than males in mixed conversations can be interpreted not as examples of male dominance but of cooperative and supportive acts in interaction. Indeed Desautels (1983, 34) shows that females interrupt males more than three times as frequently as they interrupt each other in French-speaking Canadian groups.

This is not to say, however, that differences in communicative styles do not exist. Irigaray (1987) demonstrates in a number of contexts both that women and men see the world differently and that their language use is different: in analysing hysterical or obsessive discourse of patients undergoing psychoanalysis, for example, results such as these were obtained:

Linguistic variable	
Subject phrases	Men use *je* more than women (62.5% as against 42.6%); women use *tu* more than men (29.3% as against 0%).
Verbal phrases	Women select 'process' verbs (*aimer, regarder, mettre*), while men use verbs describing utterance (*je me disais, j'ose à peine affirmer*) or verbs describing states (*je me sens libéré*). Women, by contrast with men, use 'incomplete' rather than 'completed' tenses etc (preferring imperfect, present or future tenses, transitive verbs, active forms).
Object phrases	Women refer to concrete and inanimate objects (*robes, appartement*), while men refer to abstractions (*discours, difficultés, désir*).
Circumstancial phrases	Women prefer spatial references (*dans le métro*) with relationship to *tu*, while men use references related to the subject *je*.
Adjectives and adverbs	Women use quantitative and comparative terms (*aussi net, trop, tout*), while men prefer attitude descriptors (*sceptique, nerveux, à peine, encore*).

Irigaray (1987, 122-3) concludes that

Women are conscious of sex in their speech (*sexualisent leur discours*)...In male speech the external world appears as abstract inanimate objects integrated with the subject's universe...Women's speech designates men as subjects...and the world as concrete inanimate objects belonging to the universe of the other. Hence they retain a relationship with the real world but do not perceive it as theirs.

As an indicator of (past) social attitudes, and hence of the inbuilt sexism of the French language, Yaguello (1978, 103) quotes Damourette et Pichon (1911-33) devastatingly in their comment on terminological innovation:

Feminine nouns for machines are particularly revealing; they seem to take as model the idea of egg-laying chickens, whose fundamental fecundity is demonstrated by an indefinitely repeated act. Hence incubators (*la cuveuse mécanique*), and sweepers (*balayeuse*), trimmers (*ébarbeuses*), planing machines (*raboteuses*), reapers (*faucheuses*), harvesters (*moissonneuses*), drilling machines (*perforatrices*), which repeat the same motion when some outside agent rouses them from passivity (*'féconde leur passivité'*) could only be feminine. By contrast, the slide-rule (*curseur*), the sights (of a weapon) (*viseur*), a tug (*remorqueur*), independent objects which carry their own usefulness, had to be masculine.

Most recent creations of machine names of any size and type of action have been feminine, although indeed *la calculatrice* is a hand-held calculator whereas *le calculateur/l'ordinateur,* the larger machines, are masculine.

Sexism, interpreted as denigration of the female sex, is also evident however in the contemporary language, which reveals current French attitudes towards women. For Yaguello, 'denigration of women is omnipresent in the language, in every level and in all registers'. She provides a list of synonyms for 'woman' in a selection of dictionaries, showing that a large proportion are pejorative or have erotic overtones: thus for the letter 'p' the list is as follows:

personne, personne du sexe, pucelle, petite, poison, poufiasse, péronnelle, poule, poulette, poupée, pute, putain

Likewise, the connotations of certain collocations of noun and adjective are striking:

Une femme savante is ridiculous, while *un homme savant* is respected;
Une femme légère is light in her morals, while a man is light in wit;

One loves *petites femmes*, but admires *grands hommes; petits hommes* only exist in Gulliver's Travels and *grandes femmes* are just those who have difficulty in finding clothes to fit.

Yaguello (1978, 142-7) concludes that the problem of denigration is not confined to France and French, but is 'part of a greater whole that I term the language of scorn, an instrument for the systematic denigration of women, which has existed since the beginning of civilisation in all patriarchal societies'.

Social attitudes generally are ambiguous at the present time, despite the increasing role of women in public life and in the professions and occupations generally. Life-styles have changed greatly, and there is now more freedom even than when Yaguello's work was first published. 'Sexism' as such, however, does not appear to be a frequently discussed issue, and overtly discriminatory usages such as those once found in legal language (*la femme X, la fille Y*) have disappeared (Gueunier 1985, 11). It is nonetheless not impossible to discover in both written and spoken French, and in graphic images, portrayals of women which denigrate them, and which treat women as objects, whether consciously as in sex magazines and similar publications or less overtly and consciously, and the interpretation of such language use as a reflection of the relative power roles of the sexes in society can still be made.

Mermet (1987, 63) nonetheless considers that feminism as such has decreased in intensity, and that 'literature is full of sad stories of liberated women who yearn for the "prison"'. He feels that the demands which gave birth to the feminist movement in France led to extremist actions, and have now been largely satisfied; he notes that in many cases career women are not content with a life in which the complementarity of the sexes is not achieved. Women 'no longer contend for equality in general, but for a compromise acceptable to the couple...feminism pure and simple has had its day'. A more thorough study of women's attitudes towards their social rôle (Aebischer 1985), deriving from a study of interviews with women on their attitudes towards small talk or 'chit-chat' (*bavardage*), identified four types of attitude. All the women concerned agreed that conversation on topics of 'minor' interest was characteristic of women's use of language, and Aebischer was able to characterise women's perceptions of attitudes towards a women's language as showing a double contrast: between individual and collective solutions, and between those who valued and those who did not, the specificity of women's language.

Traditional woman accepts her husband's domination and sees her role as being essentially supportive and complementary to his career. Modern woman, by contrast, is either a career woman operating in a 'man's world' or sees her relationships with men as being a matter of her own choice and under her own control.

These individual solutions contrast with the group solutions of the new woman, who adopts a feminist position valuing her difference with men and conscious of the need to affirm this in all aspects of life, while the suffragette fights for economic, political and social equality, abandoning any demand for special privilege and pursuing status and position in the same way as men. Each solution will have its own characteristic preferred language use reflecting these choices, with the suffragette approximating closest to male usage as traditionally defined.

Solutions	individual	collective
valuing women's language	traditional woman	new woman
devaluing women's language	modern woman	suffragette

Further reading

Aebischer, V. 1985. *Les Femmes et le langage.*

Chervel, A. and Manesse, D. 1989. *La Dictée.*

Duneton, C. 1978. *A hurler le soir au fond des collèges.*

Durand, M. 1936. *Le Genre grammatical en français parlé à Paris et dans la région parisienne.*

Evans, H. 1985. A feminine issue in contemporary French usage. *Modern Languages,* 66, 4: 231-6

Evans, H. 1987. The government and linguistic change in France: The case of feminisation. *ASMCF Review,* 31: 20-6

François, F. et al 1977. *La Syntaxe de l'enfant de 5 ans.*

François, F. et al. 1978a. *Syntaxe et mise en mots de l'enfant de 5 ans.*

François, F. et al 1978b. *Eléments de linguistique appliqués à l'étude du langage de l'enfant.*

François, F. et al. 1984. *Conduites linguistiques chez le jeune enfant.*

Irigaray, L. (ed). 1987. Le sexe linguistique. *Langages* 85

Kramerae, C., Schulz, M., and O'Barr, W. M. (eds) 1984. *Language and Power.*

Maresse-Polaert, J. 1969. *Etude sur le langage des enfants de six ans.*

Maurais, J. (ed) *La Crise des langues.*

Prost, A. 1983. *Les Lycéens et leurs études au seuil du XXIe siècle.*

Romaine, S. 1984. *The Language of Children and Adolescents.*

Roncière, M. C. de la (ed). 1987. Jeunes d'aujourd'hui - Regards sur les 13-25 ans en France, *Notes et Etudes Documentaires*

Thorne, B., Kramerae, C., and Henley, A. (eds). 1983. *Language Gender and Society.*

Yaguello, M. 1978. *Les Mots et les femmes.*

7   Social categories

7.1 Models of society

ANY analysis of social variation, or of language variation in social settings,
is dependent on an overt or covert model of society and of social analysis.
Such models are referred to by social scientists, including sociolinguists, in
their work, and ordinary members of society, particularly of French
society, are aware of them, at least in general outline. This awareness,
demonstrated by the popularity of such compilations as Mermet 1985, re-
edited in 1987 and 1989, exists not least because of the political implications
of these socio-economic models. Public perceptions of sociolinguistic
variation may well affect, and be affected by, political viewpoints: both
social scientists and ordinary citizens bring their own values and points of
view to social analysis, and there are few value-free analyses of society, of
linguistic variation in society, or of social attitudes.

Society is made up of **human groups** which engage in interaction;
generally speaking sociologists and political scientists are concerned with
individuals only in so far as they exemplify the group(s) to which they
belong, or play roles in interaction between groups. The groups - a family,
a faith, women, children, the working class - can be identified through their
roles in **social systems:** the legal, educational, religious, political,
economic; while their interaction is revealed through such **social
processes** as the differentiation of functions (in a functional or structural
analysis), the socialisation of children, or the dialectic of the power
struggle (in a Marxian analysis).

Social theories can simply be divided into those which assume
cooperation between social groups and those which assume conflict. One
first approach to social analysis (Weber) defines some groups by socio-
occupational or economic criteria (ie social categories) and regards them as
forming **social strata** which each have a different function and which
remain in a static relationship although individuals may migrate to them or
from them. These social groups can be viewed as cooperating to achieve

common goals, and in the process maintaining **social equilibrium**. A different approach (Marx) assumes that, in a capitalist society, those who possess the means of production and the exchange of goods will necessarily engage in a power struggle with those who do not: there will be a conflict of economically defined classes which are locked into a historical process aimed at achieving equilibrium only in some far-off millennium.

Social groups interact in a number of ways: through political activity, economic domination, and through the exchange of symbols, among them language. Linguistic and attitudinal interaction can conveniently be thought of as falling into one of three types (Nichols in Kramerae et al 1984): the first, based on a stratificational (structural, functional) approach, leads in sociolinguistics to statements of fact about the correlation of linguistic and social variables; the second, based on Marxist approaches, leads to analyses of conflictual power relationships as mediated through language; while the third (interactional), based on 'the informal relationships contracted by the individual' (Milroy 1980,174), may lead for example to the analysis of an individual's linguistic repertoire and its relationship to his social network. Underlying theories hence have a direct effect, not merely on the interpretation of sociolinguistic 'facts', but also on their selection and on the way in which they are presented and analysed. Most sociolinguistic research in France is for example based on the second, conflictual, approach, while most American work is derived from the first, cooperative approach.

7.2 Social class in France

THE French social scene has been much studied: the most relevant wide-ranging surveys of the contemporary scene for English readers are given in Ardagh 1982, Flower 1983, Hantrais 1982, Zeldin 1983, while more detailed contemporary data are provided by such works as Reynaud and Grafmeyer (eds) 1981, the different volumes of the Bloch-Lainé report prepared when the Socialists came to power in 1981 (Bloch-Lainé 1982), an update of the main aspects of this carried out by members of the same team in 1986 (ADA 1986), Mermet 1985, 1987 and 1989, Verdié 1989 and similar compilations. The annual *Données Sociales*, similar to the British HMSO publication 'Social Trends', provide relevant statistical information. Historical treatments on this global level include for example G. Wright 1987, V. Wright 1983, Trotignon 1984 and many others.

French social statisticians working for the *Institut National des Statistiques et Etudes Economiques (INSEE)* and using census returns, provide the most authoritative data on social classes or strata in France. They use a list of **socio-occupational categories** (*catégories socio-professionnelles*) to classify the working population, arguing that other recognised social class markers such as education, income, life-style, cultural and leisure behaviour, and management responsibilities, correlate closely with this single indicator. Walter (1982, 39), among others, has criticised the use of these categories for sociolinguistic research, particularly since they grouped, before the 1982 revision, very disparate professions (primary school teachers lumped in with the *cadres moyens,* or the army, police, clergy and artists in one category), but notes their practical value since all social data in France are based on them.

The socio-occupational categories as defined by *INSEE* for the census returns divide the French population into numbered groups at three levels of detail: aggregate, normal publication level and detailed level (although still more detailed analyses of the data can be made available). The first two of these levels are described below:

> Aggregate level: 8 headings, of which 6 are for the gainfully employed:
> 1. Farmers: owners and tenants
> 2. Self-employed artisans, business people and heads of firms
> 3. Higher intellectual professions and managers
> 4. Intermediate professions
> 5. Employees
> 6. Workers
> 7. Retired
> 8. Others not gainfully employed
>
> Normal publication level: 24 headings of which 19 are for the gainfully employed:
> 10. Farmers: owners and tenants
> 21. Self-employed artisans
> 22. Business people and similar
> 23. Heads of firms of 10 employees or more
> 31. Liberal professions
> 32. Higher Civil Servants, intellectual and artistic professions
> 41. Intermediate professions in education, health, civil service and similar

48. Foremen, line managers
51. Civil Service employees
54. Private enterprise staff
55. Shop employees
56. Domestic employees
61. Qualified workers
66. Non-qualified workers
67. Agricultural workers
71. Former farmers
72. Former self-employed, business and heads of firms
73. Former managers and intermediate professions
76. Former employees and workers
81. Unemployed never having worked
82. Various non-employed

Census data are allocated to this occupational table, and the individual researcher then derives his own interpretation of how French class structure is made up, and how the social categories change over time. One may hence regroup these socio-occupational categories into four and the following distribution of the French working population would emerge:

French socio-occupational groups

	1962	1968	1975	1982
		(millions)		
Owners, liberal professions, higher managers	2.81	2.95	3.17	3.55
Intermediate (executives, employees)	4.46	5.58	7.13	8.43
Workers, domestics	8.87	8.87	9.95	9.80
Agricultural (owners and workers)	3.86	3.04	2.03	1.75
Total working population	19.25	20.90	21.78	23.53
Total population (France itself)	46.46	49.49	52.6	54.27

Source: *Cahiers Français* 219, 1985

Redistributing the figures again to give the division into upper, middle and lower social 'classes' which is often used in American or British social analyses shows a percentage distribution of the working population as 15%, 40% and 45% approximately on the 1981 census.

On any analysis the upper classes include the wealthy *grande bourgeoisie,* not all of whom work; the aristocracy; and a network of Paris-based senior analyses shows a percentage distribution of the working population as 15%, 40% and 45% approximately on the 1981 census.

On any analysis the upper classes include the wealthy *grande bourgeoisie*, not all of whom work; the aristocracy; and a network of Paris-based senior executives, civil servants, bankers and others who wield financial, administrative, political and social power and which reproduces itself in hereditary ways, mainly through the educational system (Zeldin 1983). This 'meritocracy', many of whom have achieved their positions through the system of apparently open competitive entry to the *Grandes Ecoles*, is characteristic of French society, as is its Paris base and its close network of contacts.

The middle executives, teachers, minor civil servants, salaried workers, owners of small businesses and self-employed have traditionally exercised considerable power in France: conservative in politics, prone to social mobility from the top as well as the bottom, not wealthy but devoted to the traditional French sports of tax evasion and the preservation of vested interests, the new middle classes are changing in some respects and some commentators see new openness and cooperation replacing traditionally mistrustful and even selfish attitudes (Ardagh 1982, 645).

The lower classes contain tradesmen and labourers, craft workers (artisans) and agricultural workers, the unemployed, immigrants, the lower-paid such as the old or temporary workers, and the *marginaux* or submerged, also sometimes called the *Quart-Monde* (Fourth World).

Although on such objective criteria any one individual may be allocated to a social class, group or category which is required by the analyst, people's perceptions of their own social group may not coincide, and they may construct a **reference group** to which they feel they belong or wish to belong, and with which they feel in sympathy. Thus according to 1977 survey data published in *L'Expansion*, 68 per cent of the population felt they belonged to a particular social class, although many modestly regarded themselves as lower in the social hierarchy than their occupation by itself would have indicated. The table below demonstrates how many of the population have attitudes and a sense of belonging more appropriate to a class other than that in which the 'objective' measure of occupation places them. In the table, those who were 'objectively' members of the social classes listed on the left felt they belonged or wished to belong to the classes identified on the right. A similar analysis, included in the table, can be done to show how far members of different political parties have class allegeances (figures are percentages of those responding).

Reference group

By occupation (of the head of the family)	Bourgeois	Middle class	Working class	Peasant	Other
Agricultural	0	12	8	70	10
Small shopkeepers, artisans	4	52	23	2	20
Higher managers etc	23	59	9	0	9
Intermediate	9	61	25	0	5
Employees	1	46	44	1	8
Workers	0	19	76	0	5
By political party					
Communists	0	11	82	1	6
Socialists	4	35	47	6	8
Right	10	43	29	19	8
Not stated	2	34	37	19	8
All	5	34	40	13	8

For sociolinguistics, six aspects of the social categories merit further consideration (Downes, 1984). It is particularly interesting to see how categories, and their members, change over time by analysing structural mobility and hence the hierarchy of classes; how class membership changes between the generations, and hence to identify the permanency of classes over time; how individuals move through the categories, and hence the strength of group membership. The physical proximity of category members; the practices which characterise the social class; and the nature and degree of normative pressures within the category are the remaining three, and it is easy to see how each may affect language use within and between the classes.

Structural mobility has radically affected the French social and economic scene during the last thirty years. The principal movements that have occurred have been a dramatic decrease in the number and proportions of agricultural workers, a process that has been going on for more than a century. Some 46% of the working population was directly involved in agriculture in 1866, a proportion which had fallen to 7% in

1985. A similar decrease in 'workers' on the shop floor of industry has been more recent, affecting particularly the period since 1968.

An increase in office work and in the intermediate professions in the tertiary sector has been accompanied by an increase in the number of women at work, particularly in national and local government, where the rise has been from 2,229,000 in 1962 to 4,862,000 in 1985. Over 2 million small shopkeepers have given way to supermarkets, although small business still retains 8% of the working population. Another factor has been the increase, particularly since the mid-1970s in the proportion of unemployed, from 1% of the working population in 1962 to a peak of 10% in 1985.

The table below, taken from Mermet 1987, 251, summarises the main movements in the proportions of the working population in defined socio-occupational categories between 1968 and 1985, movements which have led to considerable changes in the value and prestige of one type of employment against another. Gueunier (1985), noting the same changes in class sizes and proportions, together with the increasing proportions of working women and the decline in rural populations, considers that the growth in the middle classes should have considerable linguistic consequences. She feels that the linguistic insecurity following their recent social rise might lead to increased examples of 'hypercorrection' and a general rise in language 'quality', while the better education and living conditions involved in tertiary employment would likewise increase the use of standard forms and decrease the use of local dialects and 'popular' speech forms.

Structural mobility

	1968	1985
'Owners' etc	5.1	9.1
Artisans & shopkeepers	10.7	8
Intermediate professions	31.6	46
Workers	39.3	29.8
Farm workers	11.5	7.1
Total numbers	19,916,000	21,319,000

Figures are percentages of the working population in each year.

Intergenerational mobility is an indicator of the stability of the composition of a socio-occupational category. In France the general position is that, overall, the proportion of 'stable' men (ie those who occupy the same job as their fathers) aged between 40 and 59 in 1977 was 24%, as opposed to 40% in 1953, so clearly intergenerational mobility is on the increase. These figures must however be modified for the individual professions: increased mobility is more evident for farm workers, workers and those in liberal professions, and less so for employees and middle management (Thélot 1982, 55). Indeed, more detailed analyses show that this increased mobility is greater, in every major employment category, than would be expected by the major changes in structural mobility already mentioned. They also show that the occupational shifts which do occur followed much the same lines in 1977 as in 1953.

The following table shows, for men of working age, both how stable individual occupations are and also the type of employment to which the sons mainly move:

Intergenerational mobility: men (sons) aged 40-59 in 1977

Father's occupation	Percentage of sons in the same occupation	Next most chosen occupation
Farmers	38	Workers: 35
Farm workers	13	Workers: 61
Heads of firms	21	Upper management: 26
Upper management	43	Middle management: 22
Middle management	30	Upper management: 30
Employees	17	Workers: 35
Workers	58	Employees: 14

Source: Thélot 1982, 46

Thélot (1982, 102), when comparing **individual social mobility** by examining the development of individual careers, notes:

> Post-war development has brought about familiar changes: lower middle-class occupations, and employees, have become more fragmented, while management has not. Massive exodus from agricultural employment has increased the number of workers, enabling those who started as workers to become employees or enter lower management roles; finally, [there has been] a general improvement in the career track of those in administration, particularly office workers, but also in middle management.

ADA (1986) note, in further discussing the question of social mobility, that French society is particularly subject to inequalities. Thus although the relationship between the net salary of workers and higher management has dropped from 1:4.7 in 1965 to 1:3.9 in 1975, it has remained at approximately this figure since (1:3.6 in 1984); and the distribution of wealth is likewise unequal, with 8% of households receiving 90% of the country's income. Likewise the impact of unemployment has been very unequal, with an 11% rate in 1985 among workers, 3% among managers and technicians.

The central position of Paris in the development and present-day situation of France is fundamental to any understanding of possible relationships between **physical proximity** and social classes: the élite of French society, almost without exception, make their homes in central Paris and communicate by telephone. The presence of a filled personal book of phone numbers is one proof of membership of this social class, which is hence remarkably coherent and unified. In other classes, for example in working-class situations, the large employers of labourers and manual workers have generally reduced workforces during the last twenty years, and hence the basis for solidarity and fraternal movements and collective action, such as strikes or mass demonstrations, has reduced. It nonetheless happens that groups do assemble in large numbers, whether for peasant protests in the Var, for protests against the 'reform' of church schools, or for student strikes in Paris, and although clearly these crowds are not necessarily all members of the same social class, some such meetings are more homogeneous than others. The annual *Fête de l'Humanité*, assembling families and friends for a Communist day out, is another example, although obviously with the large numbers involved such meetings cannot be anything other than representative of social categories.

Social class practices are difficult to describe in general terms, and Mermet 1985 and 1987 prefers to use the concept of 'Life Styles' to analyse French social attitudes, an approach which tends to cut across class boundaries. According to this analysis, the French can be divided into the following five 'Mentalities', each further subdivided. Thus the 'Materialists' (26.8% of the population) are defined as 'giving priority to the preservation of the quality of life in small groups (eg the family) through joint action for mutual support'; the 'Egocentrics' (22.5%), as 'refusing to recognise the world crisis, and giving priority to corporate defence of acquired advantage in order to preserve life's pleasures'; the 'Rigourists' (20.1%), as 'refusing modernism, and seeking a return to ancestral values to reestablish order and discipline'; the 'Drop-outs' (17.3%), as 'refusing the industrial crisis, giving priority to individual adventure to escape from the decadence of civilisation'; while the 'Activists' (13.3%) 'prioritise innovation and pragmatic efforts to compete, intending to change the world through realism'.

More traditional approaches to social-class practices describe the habits and practices of social groups in terms applicable to tightly knit groups, and it may well be that with socio-economic developments such groups are more difficult to identify in contemporary French society, with the exception of Paris-based higher income groups. One indicator of this might be the increasing length of education and the higher level of certification achieved by children: the pass level at the *baccalauréat* has risen from 12% of the population in 1966 to 20% in 1970 and 30% (estimated) in 1990 (Gueunier 1985, 7).

French society makes a strong point of individualism (see also Zeldin 1983, 50) and hence **normative pressure** - pressure to conform to social norms of speech, in particular - should theoretically be low. In fact French individualism is to a certain extent a myth, and conformity is as strong as in any other Western society. This is particularly so in cultural and linguistic matters, as evidenced by the strong opposition in late 1989 to the wearing of Islamic veils in the state lay schools. Only in the upper classes does there appear to be strong normative pressure within the social class to speak in a similar way, and differently from other citizens, and this is partly due again to the common educational background of the *Grandes Ecoles* system, and of the special *lycée* classes preparing for them, together with the 'old boys' network' of former students (Ardagh 1982, 510). Nonetheless, small primary groups in direct face-to-face contact exercise strong linguistic pressure on their members, as illustrated in a study by Laks (1983) of teenage boys at a leisure centre.

7.3 Upper- and lower-class usage

THESE considerations mean that American and British sociolinguists, used to the subtleties of strong class distinctions, sometimes have difficulty in understanding the nature of the linguistic contrasts which are relevant to French and to France. These, no less real than those correlating with class membership, are based less on class oppositions than on the social situations in which a particular member of society may find himself. The following review of gross linguistic differences between an upper and lower social group should hence be treated with caution, both because the individual variables can rarely if ever be uniquely associated with social category differences - most are also characteristic of other differences such as regional or situational contrasts; and also because the interpretation of social-category differences can be undertaken in a number of ways as we shall see.

7.3.1 Pronunciation

An upper class vowel system of 16 vowels contrasts with a 13-vowel system of the lower social groups:

Upper class			Lower class		
i	y	u	i	y	u
e	ø	o	e	ø	o
ɛ	œ	ɔ	ɛ	œ	ɔ
a	ɑ		a		

plus the central vowel ə
and four nasals: ɑ̃ ɛ̃ œ̃ ɔ̃   and three nasals: ɑ̃ ɛ̃ ɔ̃

The upper classes

- have a general tendency to use open vowels, while the lower classes use closed vowels widely. *Elle* however is often opened to [al] in lower-class speech;
- use front [a] rather than back [ɑ], but generally maintain the distinction;
- often pronounce the nasal [ɑ̃] as [ɔ̃];
- maintain the nasal [œ̃], but often pronounce it as closer to [ɑ̃] than the lower class [ɛ̃];
- maintain liaisons and the use of [ə] ;
- maintain the lengthened vowel in words like *fête* or *mâle*.

The lower classes

- have a tendency to raise [a] to [ɛ] - *Paris Soir* [pari swar] becomes [pɛri swɛr];
- drop liaisons, replace [ə] by one of the central rounded vowels [ø] or [œ], and insert the [ə] into triple consonant clusters - thus *un ours(e) blanc* or *un film(e) d'art*.

The consonant systems are the same, with the possible exception of the absence of [ŋ] in lower-class speech, but the upper classes tend to pronounce double consonants as longer than single ones.

The lower classes

- omit final liquids (*quat'* for *quatre*; *i'* for *il*);
- overemphasise uvular 'r' (*r grasseyé*);
- assimilate consonants: *esplosion* for *explosion*, *ostiné* for *obstiné*; *escayer* and *miyyard* for *escalier* or *milliard*;
- dissimilate consonants: *colidor* for *corridor*, *célébral* for *cérébral*
- use metathesis: *auterfois* for *autrefois*, *sercher* for *chercher*, *lusque* for *luxe*;
- make '*cuirs*' (adding [t]): *il faudra-t-aller;* and '*velours*' (adding [z]) *donnez-moi-z-en, quatre-z-officiers.*

Guiraud (1978a) identifies in addition three types of lower-class 'accent', by which is meant an overall manner of pronouncing: an '*accent veule*' , caused by relaxing muscles; an '*accent crapuleux*' caused by lengthening some vowels; and an '*accent voyou*', caused by a closed mouth, 'spitting' the words from the corner of the mouth.

7.3.2 Lexis

Most research in this area is *ad hoc* and limited, and has been concerned with assessing how far lower-class usage is 'correct' - ie close to the standard, which itself is based on upper-class usage. Danvy in Gardin et al 1980, for example, examines the ways in which children from different social classes form verbal nouns correctly, looking for such pairs indicating process and result as

criblage	*criblure*
abattage	*abattis*
épluchage	*épluchures*
casse	*cassure*
gonflage	*gonflement*
éclatement	*éclat*

He found that the lower class children made many more mistakes than others, particularly in formations with *-age* in process words, and in the use of the four 'normal' suffixes (*-is, -ure, ment, -zero*) in result words, and he concludes both that working-class children are less familiar with the 'normal' forms and that they are both less consistent in their guesses and less aware of how to guess.

The choice of some terms is however recognised as a specific social-class marker, as for example in the use of *des fois* instead of *quelquefois*. Such simple oppositions are rare, and the selection of vocabulary by lower-class as opposed to upper-class speakers depends more on situation, topic of conversation, and purpose or function of the exchange than on class. It is nonetheless clear that lower-class speakers, when placed in situations such as a school classroom or a formal meeting, are generally less able to call on a varied, formal or 'official' vocabulary than upper-class speakers.

7.3.3 Syntax

As with lexis, most research work has been directed to comparing working-class usage with 'correct' forms, and little statistically reliable or quantitative work has been carried out. Nonetheless the standard descriptions indicate that the lower classes

- regularise the formation of gender differences: *avarde* for *avare*;
- regularise verb forms - *mouler* for *moudre*, *romper* for *rompre*, *cuiser* for *cuire, chuter* for *choir*;
- regularise the formation of verbal nouns: *jetage* for *rejet* and *stationnage* for *stationnement*;
- dispense with feminine forms of adjectives: *elle est gros , ma femme est jaloux*;
- reinforce personal pronouns: *moi je pense...*;
- make generalised use of *que* as a link word, particularly in sentences in which the subject/topic is detached, whether to left or right:
  mon mari que je suis toujours sans nouvelles
  tu t'es gouré que je te dis
  où qu'il est?
  c'est moi que je voudrais le voir
  elle est là qu'elle attend
  l'homme qu'il est venu avec
  elle est bête que c'est pas à y croire;
- make generalised use of juxtaposition rather than subordination;
- intensify:
  negatives: *pas un clou, pas un pet, que dalle*
  adjectives, by the use of adverbs: *c'est vachement bon*;
- use a final preposition: *c'est fait pour, il est venu avec*;

- use *à* rather than *de* to indicate possession: *la fille au boulanger*;
- use the *passé surcomposé: j'ai eu vendu des cartes.*

7.3.4 Style

Standard educated French is generally admired for its clarity and precision, associated with a certain dryness and impersonality, lack of imagery and restriction in vocabulary. Many commentators hence assess lower-class speech styles as being 'too' rich and colourful, with wide use of word-play, swearwords, metaphors and exaggeration - full of 'hyperbole, redundancies, tautologies, pleonasm, parasitical derivation, full of images and plays on words' (Guiraud 1978a, 83). Upper class styles, however, are also negatively assessed by Duneton (1978, 189-90):

> At the depths of the French language, behind the throat so to speak, lurks the distant hat-box vision of Marie de Rambutin-Chantal - what I call the duchess effect (*l'effet marquise*): '*Il épouse dimanche au Louvre, avec la permission du Roi, Mademoiselle, Mademoiselle de ... Mademoiselle, devinez le nom? Il épouse Mademoiselle, la Grande Mademoiselle, Mademoiselle fille de feu Monsieur*'. That's the real timbre of our language, such as it has been composed, polished, cadenced for us to use.

Beauvais (1970) also poked fun at the over-elaborate style of the upper classes, echoing Labov's criticism of American 'bourgeois' style as being excessively wordy and vapid by comparison with the sharpness and vivacity of working-class word-play. Both commentators criticise a tendency towards abstraction, towards complex and elaborate presentation of ideas, and a lack of emotion or colour; an excessive, consciously artificial, lightness of tone, and a wordy and didactic flavour. Beauvais (1970, 7-15) was particularly interested in the effect of some lexical choices:

> By calling France 'the hexagon' we operate on the resonance of the word and modify the concept itself. Through the linguistic sleight of hand which moves our country from geography to geometry we affect the traditional view we have of it: refusing its carnal side we reduce its shape, its contours and its very substance to an abstract piece of decor like modern interior design. Marking the passage from a concrete language to a disembodied one, the hexagonal way shows up as a significant reflection of our development, or to speak hexagonal, of our evolution; the more the world progresses, the more we leave real things behind...Each wave of new ideas and

objects reinforces the hermetism, or the extraordinariness, of hexagonal through its import of new words, each more amazing, more learned, more incomprehensible than the preceding. 'Napoleonity' for the bicentenary; 'terminal biological process' for death: these are examples merely.

7.4 Interpretations of social category differences

THROUGHOUT the 1970s two major theories coloured much sociolinguistic research, in France as elsewhere, and had far-reaching consequences in education and in social work: a **'deficit'** theory, erroneously attributed to the work of Bernstein, which held that working-class speech was limited to 'private' situations, and used a defective or **'restricted code'**, while upper-class speech was appropriate to 'public' situations, used an **'elaborated code'** and was hence able to deal with a wider range of circumstances; and a **'difference'** theory, attributed to Labov, which agreed that the two codes were different, but held that each was appropriate for its circumstances and that each was capable of fully expressing the range of human feelings, needs and desires. Sociolinguists, who were themselves educated representatives of the upper classes, had, according to the latter view, to take special care to ensure that they were fully aware of the range of language available to the working class and not to assume that hesitancy or lack of educated vocabulary indicated any deficiency in intellect or verbal ability.

In France the problems associated with the deficit theory were identified as the static definition of 'socio-cultural milieu' arrived at by using measures such as occupation and income, which led merely to the statement of the obvious that socially disadvantaged children were also linguistically and educationally disadvantaged. Researchers hence wished to add variables such as social-class practices (for example leisure practices) and class consciousness (for example political activity) in order to 'permit the entry of the class struggle into sociolinguistic work' (see Marcellesi in Gardin et al 1980, 597). An influence on this work was Bakhtine (eg 1977) and other Soviet linguists and critics.

Much of French sociolinguistics has hence devoted itself to the analysis of language-based attitudes, and in particular to establishing theories of (social-class) opposition and conflict, while little work has been carried out on data-oriented studies. Laks (1984) demonstrates that French research papers over the period 1968-1983 fell into four main categories:

sociolinguistic work with a linguistic orientation, sociolinguistic work with a descriptive orientation, discourse and textual analyses, and lastly critical, theoretical or ideological works: 50% of all publications fell into the last category, while 20% of all publications were in fact concerned with 'what sociolinguistics itself is, what it should be, what its motivations are. The analysis of phenomena only accounts for 19% of publications' (116).

France generally is not a (linguistically) class-ridden society. The process of creating a unified French nation affected not merely regional language differences but also social ones, with the result that although class-based language differences exist, they are not fundamental in the way that a 'posh' accent is fundamental to life chances in Britain. French sociolinguists hence demonstrate a certain impatience with correlational studies, and call attention to distinctions of register or level, maintaining that all Frenchmen of any social class may use speech styles such as the vulgar and the popular in appropriate circumstances.

Bourdieu, however, a leading French sociologist, in a number of works (eg Bourdieu 1982), has pursued the idea that the bourgeoisie, intending to retain social and economic advantage, also retains linguistic advantage on the **linguistic market-place** (ie in any social exchange) by using its ability to manipulate **legitimate language** as though it formed **linguistic capital**: the profit received deriving from the **distinctiveness** achieved by the educational process. 'Legitimate' language is so only for so long as the relevant market-place - ie French society - accepts it as such, and hence the value accorded to a linguistic variable is not static but **dynamic**. Bourdieu notes that 'correct' French (or a popular, vulgar, distinguished, style) is perceived as such only because of relativities: it takes constant work to ensure that legitimate language remains so, through the efforts of grammarians and teachers, for example, who strive to retain class privilege. Styles of pronunciation, of word choice, and of expression must hence change to ensure that distinctiveness remains. Thus although the the new language of the twentieth century intellectual, baptised '*hexagonal*' by Beauvais (1970), becomes a hesitant, interrogative, wordy style, contrasting with the sonorous and dominating tone of the nineteenth century intellectual, it is nonetheless the mark of the intellectual and divides him from the rest of society just as clearly.

Bourdieu notes also that social groups are formed of individuals, and that although there exists a '**habitus**', a set of classifying variables which enable observers to distinguish one 'class' from another, each individual has also his own 'habitus'. In this distinction he rejoins other sociologists who have used by a researcher and a technician outside the group, was to use *et*, the group studied used *puis* (pronounced [pi]). Within the group, however, a dominating sub-group used '*et pi*' three times as frequently as the dominated sub-group, who used '*pi*' by itself.

Further reading

ADA. 1986. *Bilan de la France 1986.*
Ardagh, J. 1982. *France in the 1980s.*
Bakhtine, M. 1977. *Le Marxisme et la philosophie du langage.*
Bauche, H. 1920. *Le Français populaire.*
Beauvais, R. 1970. *L'Hexagonal tel qu'on le parle.*
Bernstein, B. 1971. *Class Codes and Control.*
Bloch-Lainé, F. 1982. *Bilan de la France 1981.*
Bourdieu, P. 1982. *Ce que parler veut dire.*
Deyhime, G. 1967. Enquête sur la phonologie du français contemporain. *La Linguistique,* 1: 97-108 and 2: 57-84
Duneton, C. 1978. *A Hurler le soir au fond des collèges.*
Dupeux, G. 1972. *La Société française 1789-1970.*
Espérandieu, V. et al 1984. *Des Illettrés en France, rapport au Premier Ministre.*
Espéret, E. 1979. *Langage et origine sociale des élèves.*
Flower, J.(ed). 1983. *France Today - Introductory Studies.*
Gardin, B., Marcellesi, J-B., GRECO Rouen. 1980. *Sociolinguistique: Approches, théories, pratiques.*
Gueunier, N. 1985. La crise du français en France. In J., Maurais (ed), *La Crise des langues.*
Guiraud, P. 1978. *Le français populaire.*
Hantrais, L. 1982. *Contemporary French Society.*
Kramerae, C. et al (eds) 1984. *Language and Power.*
Laks, B. 1983. Langage et pratiques sociales. *Actes de la Recherche en Sciences Sociales,* 46: 73-97
Laks, B. 1984. Le champ de la sociolinguistique française de 1963 à 1983, production et fonctionnement. *Langue Française,* 63: 103-28
Martinet, P. 1945. *La Prononciation du français contemporain.*
Mermet, G. 1985. *Francoscopie.*
Mermet, G. 1987. *Francoscopie 1987.*
Mermet, G. 1989. *Francoscopie 1989.*
Mettas, O. 1973. Les réalisations vocaliques d'un sociolecte parisien. *Travaux de l'Institut phonétique de Strasbourg,* 5: 1-11
Milroy, L. 1980. *Language and Social Networks.*
Muller, B. 1985. *Le Français d'aujourd'hui.*
Prost, A. 1983. *Les Lycéens et leurs études au seuil du XXIe siècle.*
Reynaud, J. D. and Grafmeyer, Y. (eds) 1981. *Français, qui êtes-vous?*
Rigault, A. (ed). 1971. *La grammaire du français parlé.*
Thélot, C. 1982. *Tel père, tel fils?*
Thibault, P. (ed) 1979. *Le Français parlé - études sociolinguistques.*
Trotignon ,Y. 1984. *La France au XXe siècle.*
Verdié, M. (ed). 1989. *L'Etat de la France.*
Walter, H. 1982. *Enquête phonologique et variétés du français.*
Wright, G. 1987. *France in Modern Times.*

Trotignon ,Y. 1984. *La France au XXe siècle.*
Verdié, M. (ed). 1989. *L'Etat de la France.*
Walter, H. 1982. *Enquête phonologique et variétés du français.*
Wright, G. 1987. *France in Modern Times.*
Wright, V. 1983. *The Government and Politics of France.*
Zeldin, T. 1983. *The French.*
1985. La population française de A à Z. *Cahiers Français* 219

8 The outsider

OUTSIDERS are defined for the purposes of this chapter as immigrants and social outcasts, the latter limited to criminals with an identifiable linguistic pattern. France has traditionally welcomed immigrants, whether they are political or economic refugees or simply driven by the desire to settle in an attractive country. As in most European countries, the population of France is racially mixed, and has been for generations: contemporary social statistics showing origin by nationality provide a snapshot of a constantly changing scene. For the purposes of this chapter we consider mainly three settled groups of immigrants - Jews, Gypsies and Armenians - principally because these three have been separately identified in the Giordan report (Giordan 1982).

In discussion of immigrants generally, three recurring themes have linguistic as well as social and personal implications: the constant tension between assimilation/integration to the host society and the maintenance of a separate identity; the inevitable differences between the problems of the original immigrants and those of their descendants of the second and third generations; and the problems associated with culture differences, for example in dress, in religious practices, or in the economic role of women.

8.1 Jews

8.1.1 Historical situation

Jews were present in France from the fourth century, and the object of social and religious discrimination from the fifth and sixth, although this did not become severe until the First Crusade in 1095. Theoretically they were completely banned from residence in France from 1394 until the Revolution, although in fact ghettos were tolerated. The consequence of this *clandestinité légale* was the creation of tightly knit communities whose members were responsible for their own survival, their own legal, economic, social and religious practices, and whose elected Rabbis had considerable temporal as well as religious powers. Before the Revolution Sephardic Jews were present in the South-West (originally as refugees from Spain and Portugal), Ashkenazim in Alsace and Lorraine, and in the former Papal domains of Avignon and in Provence; their numbers dropped between 1394 and the Revolution from 100,000 to 40,000.

The Revolution treated Jews as any other citizen, refusing any recognition to groups or communities. Complete legal equality was obtained from 1846, and Jews began to establish themselves more widely throughout France, although they concentrated in Paris. The Dreyfus Affair of 1894-9 raised the positive feelings of the majority of Frenchmen towards Jews, although this was based more on feelings of natural justice than any specific pro- or anti-Jewishness.

Russian and Polish Jews fleeing pogroms came to France particularly between 1882 and 1914, and after the First World War others came from Hungary and Palestine. After 1933 a number came from Nazi Germany. If the influx of 20,000 Russian and Polish Jews had caused some problems for the settled, mainly Sephardic community, the arrival of 100,000, mainly proletarian others between the wars led to population concentrations with their own strong internal links, not integrating well into the existing French Jewish communities, and indeed provoking some negative reactions there.

The 300,000 Jews from this variety of sources faced the Nazi occupation from 1940 to 1945, with deportations from 1942: the '*Rafle du Vel d'Hiv*' of July 1942 rounded up 19,000 for shipment to concentration camps. After the war, 185,000 were left, victims of French police action and the Vichy regime as well as of German policies. The clandestine life necessary for survival, the creation of Jewish resistance armies, and the support offered by both Protestant and Catholic churches led to a decrease in anti-Semitism and to closer integration to French life for some, although others opted for a new life in Israel.

The four decades from 1945 to 1985 were marked by different problems for French Jewry: between 1945 and 1955 mainly Ashkenazim were concentrated in Paris. The baby boom increased their number, as it did for other French citizens: from 185,000 in 1945 to 300,000 in 1955. From 1955 to 1965 a considerable influx of refugees from the Maghreb countries after independence, and of those fleeing Arab-Israeli conflict around the Middle East added 120,000 of the 140,000 Algerian Jews, and these Jews formed 15 per cent of the total number of Algerian refugees entering France at that time. In addition, 10,000 from Egypt, and 90,000 from Morocco and Tunisia greatly increased the proportion of Sephardic Jews in

France, spreading themselves over the whole country and re-creating Jewish communities in towns where none had lived since 1394, and increasing the number of recognised communities from 128 to 300.

From 1965 to 1975 the succession of wars between Israel and the Arab States marked the French Jewish community, which sent financial support, undertook political action in favour of Israel, and shared the increasing pride at the military achievements of the small beleaguered State. Likewise, the growth of ethnic nationalism and feelings of *droit à la différence* accentuated feelings of separateness. From 1975 to 1985, and indeed to the present day, however, while there has been some moderation of support for Israel, increased violence towards Jews in France has developed opposing political attitudes among Jews themselves, some supporting a stronger, more separate identity and others in favour of more complete integration into French society.

8.1.2 Present situation

The current communities of Jews in France retain the differences between Ashkenazim and Sephardim. The Ashkenazim derive from two origins: those originally from and in many cases still living in Alsace/Lorraine number approximately 120,000, while those descended from refugees of the 1930s and before, fleeing persecution in the East, number 240,000. The Sephardim, approximately 300,000 in total, are mainly of more recent refugee origin, are generally more active in community life, and may well consider the Ashkenazim as in some sense traitors to their Jewishness, with a greater wish to assimilate and integrate than they themselves possess. Since many Sephardim are of Maghreb origin, they are often further separated from the mainstream of French life by their appearance and low socio-economic status.

Within Judaism, strands, tendencies and cults abound: quite apart from the Ashkenazim/Sephardim division, there are orthodox, conservative and liberal Jews. The first two have retained the use of Hebrew in religious observance, while the liberal tendency (*Union Libérale Israélite*), centred around the synagogue in the rue Copernic in Paris, socially élitist and progressive, has introduced French together with other innovations such as the presence of both sexes during services.

Jews today are heavily concentrated in the Paris region (54% of the total), with a further 23% in the Midi. There is little of the ghetto mentality however: if Jews constitute 8-10% of the population of central Paris, they do not in general congregate in particular *arrondissements*, except for the quarter in the Marais around the rue Rosier. Nonetheless Maghreb immigrant groups do concentrate in close suburbs such as Sarcelles, Créteil, Enghien and La Courneuve. Outside Paris, Marseille, with 70,000, Lyon, with 25,000 and Strasbourg with 16,000 represent the largest concentrations of Jews.

8.1.3 Linguistic situation

The Talmudic requirement of living in a religious community with ten adult males means that Judaism is by definition a collective activity. Similarly, the long history of persecution and anti-Semitism across Europe and the Middle East means that Jewishness is defined by contrast to a surrounding environment, and the success of Jews in retaining their identity while playing a full part in contemporary society means that linguistically it is to be expected that Jews will be normally bilingual and will attach great importance to language as a sign of their collective. In many countries, Jews are thus trilingual: in Hebrew, in the national language, and in an adaptation of this such as Yiddish (based on German) or Judaeo-Spanish. The most evident indicator of Jewishness is the retention of Hebrew, and Girard considers that the majority of French Jews follow orthodox or conservative religious practices, including the use of Hebrew, although he also notes (Girard 1983, 178) the results of a survey among Jewish movement leaders under the age of forty which indicate an almost complete ignorance of the language, together with a lack of awareness of Jewish history before 1948, of rabbinical writings or of religious observances.

Hebrew, a liturgical language which had dropped out of common use for 2,000 years before it was revived, and which has taken a new life as the official language of Israel, is of course taught within the French educational system, in the context of formal agreements with Israel, as a foreign language. In 1981-2 the numbers of students in *terminales* classes studying Hebrew in this way, whether as a first, second or third language, was however only 285 of a total number of 502,834 such choices (*SIGES* 1983), although the language is available at all levels of the educational system. Ohana in Verbunt 1985 (43) notes however the increase in Hebrew teaching over the decade 1975-85, with fifty-nine schools teaching the subject in 1985 and a teaching staff of eighty-four.

A further linguistic complication arises with those Jews who have arrived from Eastern Europe, where Yiddish is the normal means of communication and identification, and the definition of a Jew is 'someone who speaks Yiddish' - *A Yid iz a mentsch wer redt yiddish*. In many cases this is also a situation which is undergoing change with second- and third-generation descendants of the original refugees losing the use of the language, although it is estimated that between 60,000 and 80,000 people speak Yiddish in France.

Because of recent immigration, part of the general recent inflow of Sephardim into the south-west of France, and particularly from the Maghreb, Judaeo-Spanish (sometimes called Ladino, although strictly speaking Ladino is a liturgical transcription from Hebrew to twelfth-thirteenth century Spanish and not a spoken language), also affects the total linguistic situation of Jews in contemporary France. Judaeo-Spanish is in effect fifteenth century Spanish, still spoken by Jews who were expelled from Spain in 1492 and established themselves around the Mediterranean basin, where the language was affected but not destroyed by the surrounding linguistic environment. Thus those who went to Morocco found Arabic words and speech habits affecting them; on their further emigration from Morocco to France, French loan-words have been introduced: Sephiha in Verbunt, 1985, 48 quotes the example of *dile de venir* (*dis-lui de venir*) replacing *dile que venga*. The language, spoken by some 400,000 across the world, of whom 80,000 live in France (Sephiha in Vermes 1988), is retained in the same tradition as it has been preserved since 1492, and is a further indication that Jewishness is not necessarily or exclusively tied to Hebrew.

There is no widespread recognition of a Jewish 'accent' or form of speaking, such as used to exist in the UK ('the Golders Green accent').

8.2 Gypsies

8.2.1 History and present situation

It is now known that nomadic gypsies originate from northern India, and that they have spread throughout Europe over the centuries, retaining something of their original language and culture and becoming nomads without fixed abode. Their way of life has been kept alive in the most negative circumstances, and even their name is unclear: the *Centre de Recherches Tsiganes* is happy to use the terms *tsiganes, bohémiens, nomades, gitans* interchangeably, and the term *romanichel* is also employed.

The first recorded gypsies in France were noticed in Mâcon in 1419. The lack of written sources for their history means that their spread and location since can be charted mainly through the repressive texts drawn up by state and local authorities. Liégeois (1980, 17) quotes texts and incidents from many countries in Europe, illustrating centuries of such rejection: exclusion from the right of abode, of moving in groups of more than two or three, and of settlement. The texts he quotes, of French laws of 1504, 1666, 1764, and 1864, follow the spirit of the definition given in the preamble to the law of 1912, which clearly demonstrates society's hatred and fear of these vagabonds:

> *Vagabonds à caractère ethnique, Romanichels, Bohémiens, Tsiganes...roulottiers suspects qui, sous l'apparence d'une profession problématique, traînent leur fainéantise et leurs instincts de maraude le long des routes.*

The 1912 law ensured that every individual carried a *carte anthropométrique,* and the vehicle a registration number, so that they could be identified. Policies such as these are balanced by attemps at integration, by forced settlement, or by indirect methods of obliging the nomad to change life-style. Liégeois also quotes a law of 1972 which permits door-to-door sales but at the same time imposes conditions which make this an impossible business for the nomad: leaving the object with the buyer for several days to allow for a change of mind, presentation of three copies of an invoice etc.

The present situation of gypsies in France, together with the group and subgroup to which they belong and the language name they use, is summarised in Mongin (1980, 6) in the table below.

The Romani groups are those strongly influenced by Romanian, while the Sinto are heavily influenced by German; the Kalo groups have Spanish influence. Some recent arrivals, particularly from Yugoslavia, are said (Calvet in Verbunt 1985, 68) to have brought some of the Balkan dialects of the language with them, although others speak Romani.

These groups and subgroups cohere through two main institutions: marriage and the *kris*. Marriage is used as a form of stabilisation of intergroup relations, with the partners acting as representatives and thus ensuring the continuation of traditions and 'tribal' connections. The *kris* - a form of meeting of chosen representatives who debate the decisions to be taken regarding the division of work, the regulation of differences, and the future of the community - provides leadership, and individuals are therefore not chosen to be leaders in their own right. Since the *tsiganes* do not have leaders as such, they find difficulty in meetng the norms and requirements of French society as a group, and hence are faced with the dilemma of either accepting norms and losing their identity, or of rejecting them by retaining their own (antisocial) culture and finding themselves rejected or forcibly assimilated.

Gypsy groups and languages

Groupe	Sous-groupe	Langue	Dialecte
Rom	Kalderasha	romani	kalderash
	Lovara		lovari
	Tchourara		tchourari
Mânouch	Valashtiké Mânouch	sinto	mânouch
ou Sinté	(Sinté français)		
	Gatshkené Mânouch		sinto d'Alsace
	(Sinté allemands)		
	Piemontesi		sinté piémontais
	(Sinté italiens)		
	Prajshtiké Mânouch		sinté de Prusse
	(Sinté prussiens)		
Kalé	Catalans	kalo	
	Andalous		

Contemporary French attitudes towards gypsies do not seem to have changed much, mainly because the problem is insoluble. Gypsies do not fit easily into concepts appropriate for other ethnic minorities: they are not (noticeably) coloured, they are not recent immigrants, not refugees, and have no country to which they can return; they are not victims of French colonial or imperial attitudes. They reject the process of classification, state help and services, and are above all mobile, living in small groups. They are basically just a nuisance to ordered and settled society, and the local Press is full of the problems of defined parking areas, lack of adequate education for children, and the dangers presented by such antisocial groups.

The current legislation (law of 3.1.69 and circular of application of 8.1.73), by which nomads are controlled, led to compulsory registration of identity, and is intended to lead to progressive sedentarisation and assimilation. Controlled parking, by definition of acceptable parking places and periods of stay, also leads to progressive stability, and the problems placed in the way of nomads are well known, not being by any means unique to France. Nonetheless gypsies, at 0.4 per cent of the population (200,000), still represent a sizeable community of social outcasts.

8.2.2 Language

The chart given above demonstrates the inevitable dialectal fragmentation of the Romany language and its contamination by surrounding languages. Intercomprehension is not helped by rivalries, and the gypsy way of life prevents them retaining a codified language with standard forms: the various dialects are spoken, and all gypsies are at least bilingual. Some of the dialects are distinguished from the surrounding language only by vocabulary: the grammar of Kalo for example is that of Spanish while the vocabulary is Kalo. The Romany spoken in England is similar. On the other hand, one or two words from Romany have entered French: *le gadjé* (group, people), *arnac* or *arnaque* (theft, trickery) made famous recently by the anti-Chirac street chant of *Chirac, arnaque!*; *cacique* (chief), *chouraver* (steal), *kadjo* (non-gypsy, dupe, victim).

There are nonetheless occasions on which the gypsy community assembles, for example at the annual festival in Les Saintes Maries de la Mer in southern France, on marriages and at *kris*, which enable the language to retain its wider unity, although the majority of intergroup communication takes place in French, partly because of rivalries and partly through comprehension difficulties. Likewise the isolation of individual groups from the French community assists in the process of language preservation, although compulsory education and changing socio-economic needs are likely to make dramatic changes in numbers and habits of gypsies in the future, and assimilation seems the most likely outcome.

It is only recently that education, and particularly knowledge of writing, has come to younger generations, and although some correspondence takes place on a national and international basis, the writing system involved is inappropriate for the language. Much intergroup communication therefore takes place by telephone or cassette, and these technological developments may have a role to play in retaining use of the language.

In sociolinguistic terms French gypsies find themselves, as do all gypsies, in a permanent situation of diglossia. They are obliged to be bilingual, and to use French for all official purposes, all writing, and all communication with the society which surrounds them; at the same time their way of life, remaining in small tightly knit groups cut off from close daily contact with neighbours, means that their group language is preserved from excessive corruption, and that the process of inferiorisation is held at bay. Despite the linguistic pressures of life in the twentieth century, with bureaucratic administration, educational requirements for the young, television and radio in particular, it is not expected by the *Centre de Recherches Tsiganes* that the language will disappear or that the way of life will change in the immediate future.

8.3 Armenians

8.3.1 History and present situation

The present diaspora of some two to three million Armenians across the world has come about principally since 1923. In ancient and medieval times Greater Armenia, independent since 189 BC and converted to Christianity in the third century, came under Roman, Parthian, Turkish and Mongol domination; while Lesser Armenia supported the Crusades until it was subjugated. Reunited as part of the Ottoman Empire, the eastern part was captured by Russia in the early nineteenth century. In 1915 the Turkish government carried out a programme of what is considered by Armenians to be attempted genocide, when 1,500,000 were killed, and although the Allies agreed to the creation of a Greater Armenia in 1920, Turkey and the USSR occupied the area. The original Armenia now lies across Iran, Turkey and the USSR, with the Socialist Republic of Armenia as one of the fifteen Republics forming the USSR.

France's Armenian community, the second largest after the United States, numbers some 300,000, and the recent nature of their emigration, and the continuing contacts with the USSR, Turkey and other States of origin, means that political issues relevant to countries outside France are matters of controversy, and that Armenians remember in particular the massacres of 1915. The political situation is hence unstable, and Armenian terrorists intent on assassination have caused problems within France, notably in 1981, when hostages were taken and a policeman killed at the Turkish consulate in Paris, and in 1983, when a suitcase bomb at Orly airport killed four. These events were claimed by the *Armée Secrète Arménienne pour la Libération de l'Arménie (ASALA)*, and the *Mouvement National Arménien* organised demonstrations and other support at the 1984 trial of the four, so although the four actually came to France from Beirut, there is no doubt that some at least of the French Armenian community support the active and terrorist wing of the *ASALA*. Nonetheless, since Armenian militants had been arrested by French police, *ASALA* had attacked French interests in Teheran, and a faction within the *ASALA* aimed further attacks at civilian targets in France and at French interests elsewhere. These concerns however have been countered, within the mainstream Armenian community, which points to the public recognition of Turkish genocide by Mitterrand, and to the welcome offered to Armenians by French society, as indications that neither the Armenian community nor the Armenian language are undervalued within France.

Armenian communities are located in Alfortville, Vienne, Valence and in the Paris region, with their own *Maisons de la culture*, radio stations and several daily Press and monthly newspapers and journals in Armenian or bilingual. The community finances homes and centres, and several well-known Frenchmen originate from the Armenian immigration, among them Henri Verneuil and Charles Aznavour.

8.3.2 Language

Armenian groups retain their own language, religion and customs, with strong community ties. Although second- and third-generation immigrants, educated in France, are bilingual, and the language is used only at home or in such community meetings, there is a strong feeling of loyalty and the groups are likely to retain language use for some time to come. The danger of assimilation - the loss of values and diversity - is alleged by some to be the cause of terrorist or revolutionary acts, and Balian (in Verbunt 1985, 29) considers that the lack of state educational support in Armenian makes it a *langue minorisée* within France.

Armenian is an Indo-European language. Armenians recognise a classical language (Krapar), codified in the fifth and sixth centuries, with its own script and used for religious and literary purposes, alongside modern Armenian, itself divided into an eastern and a western form with a considerable degree of mutual comprehensibility.

The Armenian community retains use of its language, although younger generations are assimilating to French. In the Armenian schools and colleges in Paris and Marseille in particular, the language is taught for use, and it is available at *baccalauréat* level and in ordinary schools and universities. The recent creation of radio stations broadcasting in Armenian, and of newspapers published either entirely or partly in the language, may assist in the continuing use of the language for normal purposes of everyday communication.

8.4 Other immigrants

8.4.1 History and present situation

Immigrants have come to France for a variety of reasons over the centuries, although political repression elsewhere, and economic advantages within France, have been the main factors.

The systematic search for an immigrant labour force started in France in the decade 1880-90, when industrialists in Lorraine sought contract labour in northern Italy. The largest systematic movement for economic reasons however was that of Polish workers, who were invited from 1906, but whose main arrivals took place between the wars. In 1926 these Poles numbered 309,000, and in 1931 the number had grown to 508,000 (Cordeiro 1982, 38). Whole villages or parts of villages were transported to the mining regions of northern, western and central France, and came with their social and religious organisation, with priests, families, teachers, and artisans. Not surprisingly, the Polish communities were inward-looking, and 15-20 per cent were able to return to Poland after World War Two on the invitation of the then Polish government, while those who remained have retained a degree of Polish culture and tradition which has withstood three generations of slow assimilation. This assimilation is nevertheless real: the daily Polish-language newspaper *Narodowiecz* has ceased publication and new arrivals from Poland are few, numbering about 8,000 in total since 1985.

Recent immigration into France has been characterised by waves from different countries and regions. In 1954, 84% of those of foreign nationality in France were of European origin, while in 1975 this had fallen to 62%, and those of African origin had risen from 13.5% to 35%. In the 1982 census, 48.5% were of European origin, 43.5% African, and 8% Asian (Mermet 1987, 171). The 1982 census figures identified 3,627,600 foreigners, some 6.8% of the total population - a very similar proportion to that of 1931, although it should be remembered that second or third generation immigrants born in France have French nationality and therefore drop out of the statistics, many are naturalised, and there are at least a million illegal or unregistered persons of foreign nationality in France: the Interior Ministry figure for the total in 1984 was 4,470,000.

The distribution of countries of origin among the population of foreigners in 1985 is as follows (Mermet, 1987, 239):

Algerians	530,540
Tunisians	127,690
Moroccans	331,911
Sub-Saharan Africa	96,699
Italians	248,141
Other EEC	130,118
Spaniards	235,033
Portuguese	632,804
Polish	59,559
Yugoslavs	59,844
Turks	76,518
Others	342,862
Total aged over 15	2,871,719

Although EEC immigrants as a group (including Spaniards and Portuguese) are numerous, it is particularly the immigrants from the Maghreb countries, from Sub-Saharan Africa (Black Africa - *Afrique Noire* in French), and increasingly from Asia who present problems which are not solely sociolinguistic. It is important in this respect to distinguish between problems of assimilation, which eventually lead to the abandonment of the immigrant's own culture, and problems of 'insertion' into economic and social life, which allow immigrants to benefit from their new life without requiring them to abandon their own culture completely.

Nouschi (in Morsy 1984, 49) points to the main characteristics of the inflow of Maghreb immigrants:

- the number of Maghreb immigrants increased noticeably from 1946-7 and really expanded in 1962, after the independence of the three countries;
- immigrants move always to the same areas of France: the Midi around Marseille, the Lyon region, the Paris region, the North and East;
- immigrants in the 1970s and 80s are just as unqualified as their predecessors, they have no qualifications other than their physical strength;
- they are welcomed by managers but rejected by fellow-workers, who see them mainly as competitors;

- they have great problems of insertion into French society, and these cover all aspects of life, at work, in education, in administrative contacts and in social contact.

Immigrants in general work as labourers or unqualified workers: 69.4% of the immigrant population, as against 32.6% of the total working population, fell into this socio-economic category in 1982. Unemployment rates are higher for immigrants of every age and every category, reaching in the same year 14% as against an overall rate of 8.75%. Immigrants in particular find themselves in illegal, non-declared work (800,000 to 1,500,000 'clandestine' workers according to Mermet 1987, 212), at the mercy of both the official system which does not recognise their existence for social security benefits and of employers able to insist on illegal employment terms and contracts. In general, too, immigrants live in working-class suburbs of large towns; adult first-generation immigrants are illiterate and poorly educated, women in particular suffer from isolation and from communication problems. In general, likewise, immigrant families are larger than those of native French: 23.5% of immigrant families have three or more children compared with the national average of 8%, and on average immigrant women have 3.15 babies as opposed to the 1.8 of French women, with a high of 5.23 for Moroccans, 5.2 for Tunisians and 4.29 for Algerians, and a low of 1.74 for Italians and 1.77 for Spaniards (Mermet 1987, 93).

Immigrants are no longer mainly male workers. Since the war, there has been a decrease in the proportion of workers: from 60% among those entering in 1946 to 42.3% in 1982; an increase in the proportion of young people; and an increase in the proportion of women - from 38% in 1962 to 43% in 1982. It is to be expected, too, that features such as the high birth-rate and clandestine working will gradually disappear, as has happened with previous waves of immigrants and in other countries.

The presence of immigrants, legal or otherwise, in France, has of course become a matter of political debate, with Le Pen and the *Front National* concerned to keep France for the French. France has traditionally been a *terre d'asile,* and most Frenchmen retain a tolerant attitude towards immigrants whether political or economic, but recent election results have shown a proportion varying between 5 and 15 per cent of the electorate supporting proposals ranging from reduction in social security to removal of work and residence permits, forced return to the country of origin and removal of civil rights from immigrants. Racist and antiracist attitudes were strengthened both by fiery speeches in the 1988 presidential campaign and in the subsequent legislative elections and also by the continuance of violence, particularly in Marseille, although the poor showing of the *Front National* in the legislative elections may indicate its demise as a national political force.

8.4.2 Language(s)

The language problems facing first generation immigrants are great, and can be exemplified by considering the case of a middle-aged woman arriving in France, working at home as a housewife, seeing no-one except family and neighbours of the same ethnic origin, living in a working-class suburban flat having come from a rural environment; monolingual in a non-Romance language and illiterate (see de Hérédia 1983, 115). The linguistic environment of such a first-generation immigrant would be a mixture of mother tongue, other languages known, foreigner talk in French (for example from shopkeepers), and the popular French of the suburb. From the point of view of eventual integration into French society, such a linguistic environment is not helpful, and much research has in fact concentrated on the problems of immigrants in terms of their problems in acquiring adequate command of French (see Perdue 1986).

The situation of particular immigrants will differ if the individual expects to be able to return 'home' after making his fortune, rather than wishing to stay and become an integrated member of his new country. In general, most recent immigration into France is of this temporary economic nature, and this is particularly true of other European nationalities such as the Portuguese: Portugal (and Senegal) were the first countries to sign agreements with the French government in 1984 about procedures to support immigrants wishing to return home with financial support from the French government, firms and collectivities. According to de Hérédia (1983, 99), this factor means that little improvement in French-language skills is to be expected from first-generation immigrants, who acquire sufficient to enable them to survive and have little or no wish to acquire a deeper linguistic understanding.

Second generations, having gone through a French-language education, will normally be bilingual. It is probably these children, however, who have most difficulties in the sociolinguistic sense: they have problems of identity, not knowing their original homeland and with parents who are not sure whether they will be staying in France or not; they have linguistic problems in acquiring adequate French, and may have problems of adjustment, in multiracial and multicultural environments, to monocultural

French education; they may have literacy problems in being the first generation of their family to have acquired writing skills. Above all, they will have problems of acceptance of their background and language within a society which takes pride in its own culture and language (see Dabène et al 1983 and Charlot et al 1982).

Malewska-Peyre (in Morsy 1984, 109-19) reports for example on a number of surveys of Maghreb adolescents showing how far they are cut off from their family traditions, particularly in relation to the central role of women and of family honour, and how they are moving towards acceptance of French adolescent behaviour and values; yet the experience of racism still separates them, whether by interiorising attitudes (*Je suis marocaine et pourtant je suis gentille et bien élevée*), valuing the difference ('black is beautiful'), imitating Frenchness (more French than the French), or agressivity (fighting back). Malewska-Peyre notes the growth of a solidarity among youth of all races and the development of a common urban youth culture, cutting across all races, including the indigenous French. This solidarity is well represented also by recent antiracist movements and demonstrations, in particular the campaigns led by Harlem Désir in 1986 and 1987, which were noticeable for their support among the young.

The sociolinguistic problem for all immigrants is the retention or the abandonment of their original language, or, more realistically, the degree of modification which has to be brought to the original language. Different ethnic groups resolve the problem in different ways; none retains its original language as sole means of communication, and the unifying power of the French educational system is evident. In all cases, the French language is accepted by French society as the superior form of communication, so any immigrant language, even Arabic or Portuguese, whose history, cultural traditions and efficiency as communication media are the equal of French, is regarded as inferior. The most striking example of this is the belief, common among educators and social workers alike, that immigrants' problems are associated with their lack of understanding of French, and that the best method of helping them is to improve their French:

> *Les instituteurs considèrent souvent encore avec réserve l'entreprise qui consiste à enseigner une autre langue que la langue de l'école à des élèves jeunes qui abordent le français écrit* (Delrieu in Dabène et al 1983, 26).

The belief may be strengthened by the fact that official educational policy, decided in 1975, is that 'national' languages may be taught in order to assist the integration of children to the French educational system; they may be taught as *activités d'éveil* for no more than three hours per week (thus replacing other school activities); they may be taught at the request of the country from which the immigrants come, by teachers provided and paid for by those countries. Such a background does not assist in attaching a high value to the language, for children, parents or other teachers within the school.

There may be other reasons for the denigration of ethnic languages: Platiel (1989, 44) points out that it is the norm in African multilingual societies for wives, and children, to adopt the dominant language of the husband or his group, so transferring this approach to the new situation in France is not necessarily a rejection of previous cultural habits.

8.5 Social outcasts

8.5.1 Present situation

One can only define a social outcast from the point of view of those who are not themselves outcasts, and although we have said that we shall here examine the language and situation of the 'criminal classes', we shall in fact not confine ourselves solely to the language of arrested criminals or prison populations, but consider the 'underworld', with particular reference to Paris. By comparison with the total population, the criminal fraternity in France is apparently comparatively small: Mermet (1987, 177) shows the growth of crimes of all types in French society: from 1,763,372 *délits* in 1973 to 3,681,453 in 1984. Nonetheless, the number of murders has not increased since 1825, and the major increase is in comparatively petty crime, in drug-related crime, in vandalism and in financial crime. Only some 43,000 criminals were in prison in 1986, 30% of them for sentences of five years or more, and 33% of them for theft.

Criminals are not necessarily always caught, however, nor necessarily always cut off from the rest of society. The groups of social outcasts whose language is usually studied are those located in large cities such as Paris, Lyon or Marseille, based on working-class areas and sectors where criminals are known to congregate: there is, at least for linguists and sociolinguists, a clear connection between the social outcast and the working-class, in terms of language use and attitudes. It is for this reason that the boundaries between the language use of the working class and that of criminals, and between criminals and the police, social workers, lawyers and others who live and work among them, are both unclear and constantly changing. A word such as *dégueulasse*, for example, defined in Sandry & Carrère as *Argot du Milieu* or criminal slang in 1953, is widely used today in the ordinary colloquial language, and the special languages of the courts, the police and the criminal are equally widely understood, as gangster films such as *Les Ripoux* demonstrate.

8.5.2 Language

The **slang** of the Parisian underworld has been studied in a number of works, although most of them concentrate on the history of the phenomenon, or on identifying the origin of words such as *le cambrioleur,* which have passed from Picard dialect (*la cambriole,* small room) to the Parisian underworld and on to the general language. Many terms have indeed entered the general language in this way, including for example *le boniment, le truc, la pègre* (from the Provençal *pego,* pitch, a reference to the pitch on the hands of thieves in the port of Marseille).

The term **'argot'** was first applied to the language of beggars and wrongdoers, who are said to have created a **secret language** of their own in order to avoid being understood by honest people, and the special forms or uses of words - as for example *mouche* or *mouchard* for a police spy or informer - are attested from the thirteenth century. The purpose of a secret language is firstly to prevent easy communication with non-initiates, while secondly providing a vocabulary and expressive possibilities which are needed by the particular activity involved, this second requirement forming a sort of technical vocabulary of crime and punishment. The terms used relate to criminal activities, to food and drink, and to other basic drives such as sex and greed: .

Criminal slang is a spoken language, although it is well recorded in films and on television, and many authors have made effective use of it, among them major literary figures - who have also created as well as used existing terms and expressions. But the main characteristics of criminal slang, rather than its literary representation, are a concentration on the vocabulary of relevant activities, the heavy use of imagery, word-play and creativity; and word-deformation or change. Both Guiraud (1980, 54-77) and Muller (1985, 213-22) give numerous examples of these, and the following brief summary is an outline of their findings.

The contemporary 'technical' vocabulary of crime thus includes, in the area of types of crime, terms such as *le vannage* (picking pockets), *la gouale* (blackmail), *la carambouille* (resale of merchandise not paid for); *le serrage* (mugging, threats), *le piquage* (mugging with a knife), *le braquage* (mugging with firearms, armed robbery). Dictionaries of *argot* are also rich in terms associated with prostitution: *le mac* (abbreviation of *maquereau*, ponce), *la marmite, la boulangère, le biftek* (ponce's first woman), *le doublard* and *le triplard* (second and third prostitutes).

The use of imagery is particularly noticeable in the great variety of terms which euphemistically refer to parts of the body or to the sexual act: Muller (1985, 218) quotes a list of terms describing the posterior such as *disque, faubourg, oignon, rond*. Similarly *neige* for cocaine, *villa* for prison, *purée* for poverty. But expressive language is mostly noticeable in the variety of swearwords and ritual insults, indicating the scorn in which the adversary is held, and which is well recorded and exemplified in literary works such as *Zazie dans le métro* (Queneau) and the novels of San Antonio (Frédéric Dard).

Some words are **neologisms**, but both Guiraud and Muller point out how few of these there are, with many of them being created by literary authors: the majority recall ancient forms or dialect forms attested in the texts of earlier centuries or in dictionaries of *argot*. Nonetheless **redoubling** is a favourite form of creativity: *kif-kif* (same), *nana* (girl), *rififi* (riot, fight), and some **onomatopoeic forms** also occur: *zin-zin* (noise), *fric-frac* (break-in).

One word is often replaced by another. Guiraud (1980, 18) gives the examples of *beau* replaced by *bath, chouette, girond;* of *le bavard* for a lawyer, *le battant* for heart; of a whole series of vegetable metaphors for head, ranging from *la poire* to *la tomate*.

A further way in which words are changed is through their adaptation. **Le verlan**, the process of inverting words *(l'envers = le verlan)*, is a widespread form of such adaptation, and functions as an identity symbol for different groups at different times ('*marque toujours son locuteur comme "marginal"*' - Méla 1988, 70), although the procedure is well understood, used by adolescents and indeed in general slang: it is spreading particularly into publicity, with examples like *la mode chebran* (ie *branché,* up-to-date). Further examples include *haschich = chicha; perdreau* (policeman) = *dreauper; peau de balle (=rien)=balpeau;* the widely understood *ripoux* (*pourri*) and *keuf (flic)*, both used in recent film titles. More complicated syllabic interchanges occur in **largonji, loucherbem,** and **javanais**. The first consists of placing the initial consonant of a word at its end and replacing the first consonant by 'l' (*le jargon* = *largonji, le sac (=1 000 centimes)* = *le lacsé)*; the second does the same and adds the syllable *-em (le boucher* = *le loucherbem, bon* = *lombem, pisser* = *lissépem)*, and the third introduces the syllable *av* or *ag* in the middle of an existing word (*jardin* = *javardin, non* = *navon).*

There are many other ways in which words are adapted to disguise them or simply to ring the changes: the addition of suffixes is much used, for example *-abre (seulabre, jeunabre)*; *-aga (poulaga* (ie policeman, from *poule), pernaga* (ie *pernod)*; *-if (rasif* (ie *rasoir)*; *-ingue (valdingue* (ie *valise)*, and many others. Likewise, words are often shortened: *d'autor (d'autorité,* ie speedily), *estome (estomac)*, and forms such as *impecc (impeccable)* and *sympa (sympathique)* which have long entered the general language.

The purpose of a secret language is not merely protection from the rest of society: it also acts as a signal of in-group membership, of solidarity among the criminal fraternity - which is one reason why its use by policemen makes them part of the same separateness, the same conspiracy. In sociolinguistic terms, the process of creation of a separate language is at once a form of compensation for the difficulties of the life criminals lead, its hardships and squalor, and also an indication of the rejection of society and its values by users: this form of language is both a constructive support to personal identity and a badge of antisocial non-conformism.

Further reading

Betbeder, M-C. 1985. Jeunes portugais: les vertus d'une double culture. *Le Monde de l'Education.* janvier 1985: 10-13

Charlot, M., Dias, M., Dupont, R., Metro, R., and Perotti, R. 1982. Vers une société interculturelle? *Pour*, 86 .

Dabène, L., Flasaquier, J., and Lyons, J. 1983. *Status of Migrants' Mother Tongues.*

François, F. 1983. *J'cause français, non?*

Giordan, H. 1982. *Démocratie culturelle et droit à la différence.*

Girard, P. 1983. *Les Juifs de France.*

Guiraud, P. 1980. *L'Argot.*

Liégeois, J-P. 1980. Le discours de l'ordre: pouvoirs publics et minorités culturelles. *Esprit*, 41: 17-50

Méla, V. 1988. Parler verlan: règles et usages. *Langage et Société*, 45: 47-72

Mongin, O. 1980. Vers un droit des minorités: l'exemple tsigane. *Esprit*, 41: 3-12

Morsy, M. 1984. *Les Nord-Africains en France.*

Perdue, C. (ed) 1986. L'acquisition du français par des adultes immigrés. *Langages* 84

Platiel, S. 1989. Les langues d'Afrique Noire en France: des langues de culture face à une langue de communication. *Migrants-Formation*, 76: 31-45.

Verbunt, G. (ed) 1985. *Par les langues de France.*

Vermes, G. (ed) 1988. *Vingt-cinq communautés linguistiques de la France.* (2 vols)

9   Social variation: occupations

THIS chapter is concerned with the use of French in working lives. The nature of employment or activity affects language use, the words and expressions selected or preferred, just as much as does geographical location or social category, and the variation involved is as systematic. For reasons of space three types of employment only will be considered, in the fields of science and technology, the law, and commerce, although most trades and types of employment have their own recognisable linguistic characteristics.

9.1 Professional discourse

9.1.1 Tasks and groups

We have mentioned above a distinction which is commonly made between primary, or face-to-face, human groups, and secondary groups whose members are linked indirectly (see Sprott, 1958). Primary groups come together in a number of different ways and for different purposes: family members meet around the breakfast table, neighbours might drop in for a chat over coffee, small groups converse in the pub, and most such casual meetings concern themselves with 'making contact', social interaction in which the conversation covers a range of subject areas, and in which social links are established and broken. Chapter 10 below will be concerned with interaction of this type, and with alternative sociolinguistic models, such as networks, for understanding it.

Primary groups may also be formed from people carrying out some defined task. These groups - a board meeting, a plumber and his mate repairing a leaking boiler - occur at all levels of occupational hierarchies and in all types of occupations. **Task groups** may be constituted from those with similar disciplinary and professional backgrounds (lawyers in court, research scientists, garage mechanics) or from representatives of a range of such backgrounds (a multidisciplinary research group, social services case meetings). The language use in task-oriented groups may hence be technical in nature ('jargon'), particularly in groups made up of specialists from the same disciplinary area, while the extremes of this specialist language may be modified and 'translated' for the benefit of the non-specialist in multidisciplinary groups. In all such groups personal interaction is involved, and hence language use will be directed both towards ensuring that 'correct', technically acceptable messages are sent, and also that they are successful: that they achieve their intended effect.

Secondary groups are made up of people belonging to the same profession or activity, or connected by interest, religion or sentiment. In cases of this type - the 'invisible college' of scientific colleagues dispersed throughout the academic world, all lawyers, all doctors - the links between members of the group are generally accepted symbols or modes of symbol manipulation rather than face-to-face spoken exchanges. The links are formed by a similar training or educational background, and maintained by professional discourse, religious or professional symbols such as the Hippocratic oath, or other unifying myths, taboos and practices which together bring about a feeling of identification, a **professional culture**, based on the knowledge (*savoir*) a particular occupation requires and on the way in which this knowledge is put to use (know-how or *savoir faire*), described or mediated through a particular variety of language. The group identity, and indeed the group discourse, may also be found at the micro level in particular organisations: *Electricité de France* (*EDF*), and Bouygues, the civil-engineering concern, have worked hard to ensure a business culture and group identity for their organisations.

Two further distinctions should be made at this stage. Language use at work is of interest to a number of disciplines apart from sociolinguistics: to the sociology of work, to philosophers, to computer scientists interested in expert systems, to psychologists and ergonomists, and to management specialists. Each is interested in different aspects of the nature of work. A convenient illustration of the range of interests and disciplines involved can be derived from the workshops of a 1989 conference convened in Paris by the *Ministère de la Recherche* to study *Travail et pratiques langagières:*

- *Les Savoirs au travail,* with papers on topics such as *Savoir pratique et situation* or *De l'analyse des situations de travail au système expert*;
- *Langage en acte dans les organisations,* with papers on *La Parole et le travail en usine* or *L'Adresse au bureau*;

- *Approches interactionnelles dans les situations de travail*, with papers on *Interaction verbale et organisation institutionnelle* or *Voix et interaction de travail*;
- *Le Langage de l'organisation*, with papers on *La Littérature managériale* or *Formes de communication et division du travail dans une administration publique*;
- *Interprétation et interaction*, with papers on *Echanges entre une psychiâtre et une patiente* or *La Production langagière des sites HLM*;
- *Production des langages techniques*, with papers on terminology.

Secondly, language use at work is not necessarily the same as the language used to describe work. The distinction is clearest in a case such as that of a machine operative who may use very little language while operating his machine but when asked in an interview to describe or explain his actions may display a wide technical vocabulary and a very specific professional discourse. Similarly, a considerable amount of shorthand and slang will be used within the work group, but if the group needs to make a presentation to other groups the language will become more formal and more open, since fewer assumptions can be taken for granted. The distinction becomes more blurred in professions dependent on the use of words: lawyers, politicians and marketing experts may well confuse language at work with language about work.

9.1.2 Analysis of professional discourse: linguistic functions
The language use of people at work may be analysed according to the function or intended purpose of what is said or written. Indeed, the school of **functional linguistics** is based on this concept, and there is a long history of linguistic analysis devoted to correlating language items and their purpose (see discussion of this point in Halliday 1978, 48).

Fundamental to the idea of a functional analysis of language is the model of a communication situation, outlined on page 166, which diagrammatically represents what happens when language is used: the message **sender** S (ie the speaker or writer) encodes the **message** (ie forms words and sentences) within a particular **context** or situation for transmission along a **channel** (ie in the form of speech or writing) towards a **receiver** R (ie the hearer or reader), who is himself also located within a specific situation, which may not be the same as that of the sender.

When we come to analyse the message, its characteristics (choice of lexis, pronunciation, syntax, overall structure) can be related to these elements, but also to the intended purpose of the sender, and to his perception of the receiver. Situated action of this type is hence open to analysis and description in a number of ways according to the purpose of the analysis. Six possible functions of the message have thus been identified, for example by Jakobson (in Sebeok 1960, 350-377), illustrated in the table on page 167.

CONTEXT

S -------> (encodes)   message   (decodes) ----> R   is sent along a channel

CONTEXT

The language use of individual professions may be located and described in relation to such functions: scientific language is thus mainly denotative, some types of commercial language mainly vocative (marketing, selling), while legal language is often concerned with matters of definition (denotation and metalinguistic).

9.1.3 The study of language at work: other approaches

A different approach is that of 'Languages for Specific Purposes' (see Swales, 1980). This is a branch of applied linguistics, aiming to provide accurate descriptions of specialist language use, such as that of science, which may be used to teach non-specialists and foreigners how to communicate in these fields. The movement has developed its understanding of what constitutes specialist language and how it is differentiated from the ordinary language, starting with defined vocabularies and frequency lists, giving the terms most used in a particular specialism, and producing lists such as the *Vocabulaire général d'orientation scientifique* (Phal 1971). A next stage in the development of this approach led to the study of the organisational and presentational terms used in scientific or other writing, and those concerned now consider that the most effective description of a specialist language variety is obtained through examining the discourse structure, or overall organisation, of whole texts. Most work in this area has been carried out on English, and by far the most widespread application of the work has been to teaching language to non-native speakers.

Most research by sociologists in the field has used the techniques of **ethnomethodology** (Winkin 1987), a technique for analysing interaction, based on the work of Erving Goffman, or **transactional analysis**, a technique whose aims are to identify the nature of exchanges between partners. In the work environment, of course, power relationships are also of importance, and analyses have been made for example to identify who has the right to speak to whom, and how, in hierarchical situations.

Communication situation and language functions

Element	Function	Description/exemplification
Sender	emotive/expressive	The message relates to the sender (I), who expresses his own feelings.
Receiver	conative/vocative	The message relates to the receiver (you), for example attempts to persuade and influence.
Context	denotative/cognitive/ referential	The message relates to the outside world (it). Such a message could be a description of the context itself, or communication of factual information about something within it. ·
Channel	phatic	The message consists of attempts to maintain communication and contact (for example sounds made by the listener during a telephone conversation).
Message	poetic/discoursal	Structure markers: for example expressions indicating the structure of what one is saying ('as I just said...; however, on the other hand').
Code	metalinguistic	Messages concern the code, explaining how one has used a particular term or expression.

Language use in the *Groupes d'expression directe* or worker groups, usually led by an immediate supervisor, whose minutes, recommendations and suggestions must be forwarded to the management of the enterprise under the Auroux laws of 1981, and which are similar to Quality Circles, Sunrise (or Sunset) meetings and other discussion groups whose main purpose is to motivate or orient the workforce, have thus been studied, as has the nature of communication within the enterprise through such means as house magazines or team-building exercises.

Linguists have generally concentrated on text-based techniques such as **discourse analysis** in order to identify language use related to the working environment, although **terminology**, as a development from lexicology, is of considerable importance particularly in relation to new and developing technologies.

The interest of these approaches for sociolinguistics lies in the fact that they enable us to identify different varieties of a language, correlating the variety characteristics with features of the context and relating discourse processes to social processes. Many of the studies are more concerned with language use peripheral to work - in discussion groups, talk about work, or reports on work relationships - than with language use at work and in relation to 'productive' processes. In addition, however, there are other, more specifically sociolinguistic problems which will be dealt with below:

- the effect of borrowings from other languages, particularly
  Anglo-American, on expression in French science;
- the problem of change, particularly within technology, and the
  effect this has on language use;
- the relationship between professionals, and between the
  professional and the general public as mediated through language;
- the nature of commercial and transactional interaction.

9.2 Legal language

9.2.1 Sources

Legal training is a lengthy process, lasting several years after the acquisition of an initial degree; law degrees in the French system provide a wide introduction to the field and are taken by those who intend to become economists and businessmen as well as lawyers. Entry to the legal profession itself follows at least two years postgraduate training, after a *Maîtrise en droit* , in specialised institutes such as the *Centre National des*

Etudes Judiciaires. Entry to the *Magistrature* (ie judges and public prosecutors or investigating judges) is open at a young age, as a career and as part of the civil service, through the *Conseil Supérieur de la Magistrature*, and after training at the *Ecole Nationale de la Magistrature*, which graduates about 250 each year (240 in 1987, 320 in 1985). Recruitment in 1986 was 316 *magistrats*, and the total number of them was 6,006 in 1989. Entry to the liberal professions, as *avocat* (18,500 are registered) or as *avoué* (of whom 330 are registered), roughly equivalent to the barrister and Queen's Counsel or senior barrister, lies through the profession itself, which is organised in 180 *barreaux*, one for each court or area. Other legal employment is available, for example as one of the 7,300 *notaires*, whose role is approximately that of the solicitor, or as one of the 2,935 *huissiers*, whose duties include the execution of legal decisions such as the seizure of goods (all figures from *Quid*, 1990).

During their long training process lawyers acquire the terminology and modes of expression of their specialist variety from three sources of written legal language: *les Codes et Lois, la Doctrine,* and *la Jurisprudence* or cases. The style of the Codes and Laws is found also in administrative decisions which have legal force, such as Ministerial Orders, in *Arrêtés* and *Décrêts* but also in a whole range of formal documents such as contracts. Doctrine comes from academic and professional writing commenting on law and the legal process. Jurisprudence is the language of judges' decisions on individual cases. Courtroom language, the cut and thrust of spoken interaction, together with the expressions and terms in which the business of the courts is conducted, is not considered here. From these sources there has developed a technical language which has been characterised as specialist, conservative, formal, static and dense (eg Mimin 1970).

9.2.2 Characteristics

Its specialism is derived from the use of technical terms and expressions, often of direct Latin origin (*nemo dat qui habet, in limine litis, nemo consentur ignorare legem*), and from the use of fixed phrases (*recours pour excès de pouvoir, flagrant délit, ci-après, susnommé, susdit, exposé des motifs, vice de forme*), as the underlined examples in the following extract from a contract illustrate:

> *Le locataire ne pourra sous aucun prétexte introduire dans les locaux*
> *<u>présentement</u> loués aucun animal (chien, chat etc.) sans autorisation*
> *préalable du propriétaire et de son mandataire. <u>Pour l'exécution</u>*
> *<u>des présentes, les parties soussignées font élection de domicile</u> dans*

> *les bureaux de l'Agence Nicolas et conviennent qu'en cas de contestations, <u>le tribunal compétent</u> sera celui des lieux de la circonscription judiciaire où se trouvent les locaux loués.*

Specialist technical terms express concepts and definitions which are fundamental to Roman Law and are hence more important in the French system of codified law which is based on it than in the Anglo-Saxon customary law. These terms must remain invariable, and can have only one meaning, and consequently the central importance of the text itself, the words and forms of the Code, the law, the order or the directive, in the whole French legal process is not to be underestimated.

Legal language is generally conservative, using words and expressions which have long disappeared from normal usage, such as *le sieur* or *ledit*. A further example of this is the retention of suffixes which are themselves unproductive in modern French, such as *-ure* or *-ance*: *clôture, parjure; usance, vacance, redevance.* Particularly in view of the necessity to establish incontrovertible authority, texts are also formal in style, and completely lacking in personality or individualism. Hence, for example, a much greater use of passives and negatives than in 'normal' French, as in *la bonne foi est toujours présumée, la présente loi sera exécutée, il est établi un procès-verbal, il sera rendu compte, nul ne peut être adopté par plusieurs personnes si ce n'est par deux époux.* Norms appropriate to a strict **text typology** are followed, and hence laws are presented within a strict format, with subdivision into *livres, chapitres, articles* and *alinéas*, and legal judgements similarly follow set patterns, contributing also to the impression of formality.

The static appearance of legal language is as dependent on the unchanging nature of these forms as on the actual terms used. Legal language is also dense, in that 'content' or 'full' words seem more frequent than the organisational or grammatical words, by comparison with everyday French. This impression is caused by stylistic uses such as the frequent recourse to participles (*la saisie, le fondé de pouvoir, l'inculpé, le trop-perçu*), and verbal nouns (*l'habitant, les comparants, l'occupant, les tenants et aboutissants*), and to a heavily substantival style, as the extracts from the *Code de l'expropriation* given below demonstrate.

The following extracts show the styles of Laws, Doctrine, and Jurisprudence:

Codes and Laws:

Lorsqu'un délai d'un an s'est écoulé à compter de la publication d'un acte portant déclaration d'utilité publique d'une opération, les propriétaires des terrains à acquérir compris dans cette opération peuvent mettre en demeure la collectivité ou le service public au bénéfice duquel la déclaration d'utilité publique est intervenue de procéder à l'acquisition de leur terrain dans un délai de deux ans à compter du jour de la demande. Ce délai peut être prorogé une fois pour une durée d'un an sauf dans les cas où une décision de sursis à statuer a été opposée antérieurement à l'intéressé en application des dispositions du code de l'urbanisme. (Code de l'expropriation (Décret du 28.3.77) Article L. 11-7).

Doctrine:

Pour la doctrine classique, l'action administrative était caractérisée par l'inégalité entre l'administration et les administrés, par l'existence au profit de celle-là de pouvoirs n'appartenant pas à ceux-ci. Ces propositions doivent aujourd'hui être nuancées. On sait maintenant que les moyens exorbitants du droit commun peuvent consister, non seulement en des prérogatives, mais aussi en des sujétions; d'autre part, l'action administrative, quel que soit l'organe dont elle émane, n'utilise pas toujours - elle utilise même de moins en moins - des moyens exorbitants du droit commun et abandonne souvent la 'gestion publique' au profit de la 'gestion privée'. (P Weil 1964, 44).

Jurisprudence:

Sur le moyen tiré de la force majeure: - Considérant que, si le requérant soutient que le tassement de la terre qui a provoqué l'acident est survenu brusquement et d'une manière imprévisible, l'exactitude de ces allégations ne résulte pas de l'instruction.

Legal language is normally written language, and the discourse structure involved varies considerably from one text type to another. Thus the style and presentation of administrative decisions, which have force of law, is based on the style of parliamentary laws and the underlying Codes, but the structure, for example of an *arrêté* or a decree, is very precisely determined, with the whole being organised in the form essentially of one sentence starting with the main subject (the office of the authority decreeing or deciding), giving next the *considérants* (mentions of relevant texts, decisions or opinions), introduced by a participle or participial phrase such as *considérant que* or *vu*; continuing with the verb *arrête, décrète* or *décide*, according to the nature of the document; following with the decisions themselves, arranged in numbered *articles* which have internal paragraphs or other subsections, often themselves numbered, and concluding with the closing signature formula:

> *Le ministre des armées,*
> *Vu l'article 4 de l'arrêté interministériel en date du 12 mai 1969 autorisant l'ouverture de concours pour le recrutement de techniciens d'études et de fabrications des travaux du bâtiment du service du génie,*
> *Arrête:*
> *Art. 1er. - Les épreuves des concours portant recrutement de techniciens d'études et de fabrications de travaux de bâtiment du service du génie ouverts par l'arrêté interministériel susvisé se dérouleront les 2, 3 et 4 juillet 1969 dans les centres de Paris, Lille, Rennes, Bordeaux, Lyon, Metz et Marseille.*
> *Art 2. - La date de clôture des inscriptions est fixée au 1er juin 1969.*
> *Fait à Paris, le 22 mai 1969.*
> *Pour le ministre et par délégation:*
> *Pour le directeur des personnels civils empêché:*
> *Le sous-directeur des personnels civils extérieurs,*
> *Arnaud.*

Although each text within the legal variety shares many of the characteristics outlined above, there are nonetheless identifiable differences, in discourse arrangement, which the above extracts are not long enough to illustrate, but also in the nature of the vocabulary used and in the general tone. Thus Codes are often limpid, dealing with concepts and permitting actions (with the use of the present tense and modals such as *pouvoir*), while the Doctrine, in presenting detailed concepts and in arguing a point of view, analysing a case or examining the basis for a law or judgement, is more developed and artistic in intent, while retaining a level of formality well in excess of most academic writing. Judgements themselves tend, even today, to be stilted and formal, to make much use of double negatives, passives and dependent clauses, and generally present a style of considerable subtlety but also requiring linguistic dexterity in the reader.

The context of each text type, and its purpose or function, clearly condition some of these differences in style. Codes and Laws state simply, in the present tense, what is (or by implication should be) and do not use terms such as 'ought' or 'must'. These are majestic texts, authoritarian and impersonal. The Doctrine has to persuade, and is hence constructed in order to please and interest as well as to inform; the personality of the author is intended to come through. In judgements, the written form requires a formal style, in complete contrast to the spoken style of the courtroom. The main task is to keep track of the events and arguments used in the courtroom, to attack or support them on a basis of logic, and to arrive at defensible conclusions: the texts are therefore well structured, with numerous indications of the process of the message (*Sur le premier point, Sur le moyen unique pris en sa seconde branche*), with each argument introduced by *attendu que* (whereas) and concluding with set phrases: *Par ces motifs, reçoit X en son appel, le dit fondé...confirme le jugement...condamne Y à payer, déboute Z*. It is worthy of note that law students are required to write commentaries on judgements within their course, so this style is quite deliberately taught as a part of the education of every lawyer.

9.2.3 Attitudes

Lawyers themselves are occasionally concerned to ensure that legal writing and speech does not become too remote from everyday usage. Thus a Circular of 15.9.1977 from the Minister of Justice to Court Presidents (*Journal Officiel, Brochure* 1468, 289-97), conveyed the results of work carried out by a committee for the modernisation of legal language. The report proposed the replacement of some Latin expressions by French equivalents (*res nullius - chose sans propriétaire, de cujus - défunt*), together with the modernisation of other forms (*le sieur - monsieur, es privé nom - en son nom personnel*). Particular attention was drawn to terms and expressions which had become impolite, such as the habit of writing Dupont René instead of M. René Dupont; to the use of empty and pompous language, such as '*Dit que le jugement sortira son plein et entier effet pour être exécuté selon ses formes et teneur*', which could be replaced by '*Ordonne l'exécution du jugement*'. Similarly, expressions which were unclear: *louer* in its two senses of *donner* or *prendre à bail*, or *intérêts de droit* in the sense of *intérêts au taux légal*. In general however few recommendations were made for changes, and the committee actually commented on this by saying that it found little to criticise. The general public was not surveyed in this instance.

Administrative forms and questionnaires are further examples of a quasi-legal text type which shares many of the characteristics of legal language. Attention has recently been focused in France on the problems which inadequately designed forms can pose and revisions to the main income tax form among others have considerably changed its previously forbidding appearance, although such revisions seem to be more concerned with typographical changes or layout, for example in the use of colour, than with the style of language used. A case study of the design of forms concerned with building permits (Gallouédec-Genuys 1981, 199-236), involving an assessment of the form together with interviews both with those who complete them and with those who deal with them at local level, demonstrated the problems involved for over a million such requests each year, and provided an assessment of specialist and public opinion on administrative communication practices.

There was general satisfaction with the overall design: a four-page form printed on one sheet of paper; with the layout, use of colour and type-styles. Problems arose with the language of the form and with the nature of the details requested, and in the latter case in particular were often solved by the local agents entering into 'a sort of alliance' where the lower-level inspectors used the form as a shield to protect the local office from the central administration, by filtering the contents, ignoring uncompleted, poorly or inaccurately completed parts whose relevance to their own task was unclear. Many such local inspectors completed their own summary cards with the main information, extracted from the form, and used the form itself merely as a file cover. They understood the desire of individuals not to reveal information, such as the value of the plot of land, which could be used by other civil servants (eg in the tax departments), and were happy to help in filling in the form, interacting directly with requesters by phone and speech: an example quoted was the replacement of the term '*garage*' (taxable) by 'lean-to' (*auvent*) (non-taxable) in one case. Interestingly, they saw the written form as providing extra information to clarify the drawings and plans which were their main concern, whereas those completing the form saw the written form as the main item, with the drawings providing extra detail: expectations for each group were thus quite different.

The opposite reaction to this friendly interchange was also reported, with requesters not being provided with adequate copies of the form in the first place and having to make their own photocopies, or being provided with a local version which demanded extra (and sometimes illegal) information; being passed from one office to another; being asked for yet more supplementary details and generally being treated by the administration as a nuisance.

The language of the form itself was criticised, particularly for its vagueness in asking general questions ('Describe the external appearance...Provide details on tall trees' (what is 'tall'?)); for its over-technical language, and for its inbuilt assumption that those who complete the form intended to cheat or to lie - although in the interviews this indeed appeared to be the intention of many, who did not want to reveal their own tax position or who wished to ensure that their application did not fall foul of the established guidelines and hence manipulated the details to fit. Examples of excessive linguistic complexity and technicity included such expressions as *sous-sol non aménageable, surfaces hors oeuvre brutes/nettes, stationnement des véhicules dans la construction,* all of which had to be interpreted by the requester. An example of the implied mistrust concerned the calculations required, where technical terms and the accepted norms of architects and surveyors were sometimes used and sometimes not, an example being the calculation of the *plancher,* which in normal terminology is floor area but here includes roof space.

The general impression was that the form appeared complicated whereas it was not: the formality of the language, combined with the nature of some details requested, whose relevance to the matter in hand was not understood by either party, led to a sort of 'blockage' and a degree of mistrust which was in practice often overcome by spoken-language intervention. Sociolinguistically the relationship between administrators and administered, formal in the written medium, was modified by both the use of the spoken medium, particularly in 'translating' technical terminology for the non-initiated, and by the complicity of both at local level in what was seen as conflict with an impersonal and overinquisitive State.

9.3 Science and technology

9.3.1 Sources
The task of natural, medical, social and human sciences is to describe and explain the world, and the scientific method - the obtaining and classification of data, the establishment of hypotheses, the search for proof and refutation, the elaboration and reformulation of theories - results in the

creation of specialised language varieties to do so. Two aspects of the specialised languages of science are of prime importance within sociolinguistics: terminology and text typology, and one of the main sociolinguistic problems for French is the prestige value of English-language science and the associated import of English terms and manners of thinking.

Scientists are trained in the universities and the *Grandes Ecoles*. Of the 253,593 holders of the *baccalauréat* in 1985, 11.8% entered scientific higher education, 6.4% medecine and 9.7% the preparatory classes for the *Grandes Ecoles*. 1986 graduates, at all levels from the two-year *DEUG* or *DEUST* to the *Doctorat d'Etat* representing a lifetime's work, numbered 40,360 in science, 21,297 in the medical sciences, with under 4,000 engineering diplomas awarded in the *Grandes Ecoles* (*Note d'Information* 87-23 and 88-45). Research scientists (all disciplines) employed through the *Conseil National de la Recherche Scientifique* (*CNRS*), industry and the universities were estimated at approximately 300,000 in 1984 (*Quid*, 1990). In total therefore, and despite a two per cent decrease between 1975 and 1985 in entry numbers to scientific higher education, a high proportion of the French population has come into contact with scientific thinking at an advanced level, and high prestige continues to be attached to scientific methods and approaches, expressed in relevant language forms.

9.3.2 Characteristics

All sciences classify and organise the information they require in a terminological system, which enables the relative importance of concepts to be expressed in a hierarchical structure within which all terms interrelate. The basic terms may be mathematical, first-order units or elements of observation naming prime elements; these are usually then arranged in a taxonomy in which more general terms are modified by the addition of prefixes or suffixes or by the addition of other modifiers to represent subdivisions. A simple example is the naming process for plants, which creates a taxonomy of families, genera, species - *famille, genre, espèce: rosacée, rosa, rosa canina*. Professional terminologists can assist in identifying the terms involved, usually by examples, contexts and the use of associated terms (antonyms, synonyms) and correlate French usage with international usage. The terminology of a particular science is recorded in dictionaries, nowadays often by computer, and these term banks are then used by scientists, lexicologists, translators and information scientists to re-group existing terms and develop new ones.

Terms are often based on translations from English, or on the direct adoption of English terms (*pipeline, feedback, pattern*), both of which when used in French limit the meaning, and the connotations, of the original English word: so 'pipeline' if translated as *oléoduc* can refer only to an oil pipeline, while translating 'pattern' as *modèle* gives only one sense of the many underlying 'pattern'. French is thus cut off from some of the links and connotations which English-speaking scientists would draw upon, and particularly from the creativity which an understanding of such basic terms can give.

Examples of some computing terms, together with their definitions and connection with English, as defined in French government decrees include:

> <u>*Accès direct*</u> nm.   *Mode d'écriture ou de lecture de données se faisant au moyen d'adreses qui repèrent leur emplacement*
> *Anglais*: Direct access, random access
>
> <u>*Logiciel*</u> nm.   *Ensemble des programmes, procédés et règles, et éventuellement de la documentation, relatifs au fonctionnement d'un ensemble de traitement de données*
> *Anglais*: software
>
> <u>*Progiciel*</u> nm   *Ensemble complet et documenté de programmes conçu pour être fourni à plusieurs utilisateurs, en vue d'une même aplication ou d'une même fonction*
> *Anglais*: package

The same *arrêté* (*Journal Officiel, Brochure* 1468, 1985, 153) lists 54 terms, of which 47 are nouns, 2 are verbs (*visualiser* and *lister*), 3 are adjectives (*autonome, interactif, numérique*) and 2 are adjectival phrases (*en ligne, de secours*). Of the 54 terms, 20 are not given as translations of English words, although most of them are based on roots similar to those found in the English equivalents, such as *microprocesseur* and *interface*.

A recent survey of French scientific usage is Kocourek 1982, which defines the main characteristics as being textual coherence, syntactic condensation, impersonality, nominalisation, precision of lexical units and wealth of graphic resources.

In French, as indeed in English, scientific language distinguishes itself from everyday usage principally by its preferential use of nouns and noun groups, and by the nature of these. Thus *pressage* will be preferred to *presser*, and *la disponibilité des données* to *les données sont disponibles*. Noun groups are often much longer than in standard French, but also contrast with the comparative simplicity of noun-group construction characteristic of English or German. A phrase such as *système radioélectrique d'appel sélectif unilatéral*, for the English 'radio-paging', requires the addition of link-words such as *de*, and leads to the construction of a type of recursive noun-phrase which is practically never-ending: *l'importance de la publication de la traduction du résumé de l'examen de la réfutation de l'analyse de la comparaison de la distribution des prises de bonites*, or *palan électrique à engrenages à chaîne à maillons à commande par boîte pendante à boutons-poussoirs* (Kocourek 1982, 67 & 54). Nominalisations of this type, whether derived from verbs or verb phrases (*un faible pouvoir oxydant du soufre*) or from adjectives (*la souplesse des fibres*) are frequent. Similarly, noun groups are formed from verbal participles used as adjectives, replacing more active forms of the verb: *l'étape de collage sur le mandrin est souvent remplacée par la projection de métal fondu directement sur la nappe de fibres*, or from other verbal forms: *le témoin détecteur, la remorque autochargeuse*, and indeed from the simple juxtaposition of nouns, although this last process is becoming more evident also in the everyday language: *équipements tous terrains, microscope monture forte*.

Verbs and verb groups are often simple, concerned with the manipulation of these nominal elements, and could be regarded as 'operators' in the mathematical sense, working on the 'objects' or nominal groups which carry the prime sense. Thus the range of verbs found in scientific texts is very restricted, with the majority being synonyms of *être* or simple presentational devices. Tense usage is likewise reduced, limited mainly to the present or simple past. The passive is much used, particularly in the description of experiments carried out or actions undertaken: *Quelques échantillons ont été inclus*.

One of the main features of scientific texts is their impersonality, caused partly by the wide use of impersonal constructions themselves: *il est erroné de supposer que..., il est raisonnable d'admettre..., il a été établi que*; but also by deliberate suppression of the personality of the author, maintaining a sober impersonal tone throughout. Pronouns, for example, are limited to the third person, and authors refers to themselves as *nous* rather than *je*.

Sentences are long and syntactically complex, with frequent embedding of clauses, references or additions: *les espèces pour lesquelles la population a fortement diminuée depuis 35 ans (c'est le cas des canards) ne pourront sans doute jamais retrouver leurs effectifs d'antan*.

Much scientific writing is illustrated by figures, tables and other 'non-language' material. Indeed, research reports are often extremely short, with the main information being contained in equations or diagrams, and the minimum of words setting in context the problem, its solution and discussion of the results.

9.3.3 Text types

Scientific text types fall into three main divisions: training materials, such as textbooks; texts for specialist communication, including research articles, conference and seminar papers, working papers and notes; and texts for popular consumption, including mainly newspaper features, popular science books and documentaries for television.

Texts used in presenting scientific research information are frequently brief and utilise note form, diagrams and illustrations, formulae and technical shorthand. The structure of such texts typically follows a set pattern: identification of the problem, review of relevant research (these first two may be reversed); presentation of a hypothesis, presentation of data, experimental results or the reasoning leading to support, rejection or modification of the hypothesis, conclusion together with (often) contributions to wider theory. Scientists follow such a set pattern because they publish in accepted outlets which 'normalise' - indeed, sometimes rewrite - articles received, and also because changes to the discourse structure would impede comprehension and render the text too personal.

Training and educational material is above all clear, systematically organised in a logical sequence. The text is subdivided into chapters, sections, paragraphs, often with clear numbering systems to enable reference, understanding of the identity of most and least important items in a group, and with much authorial guidance through the text. The text is supported with a range of presentational devices used to facilitate understanding: diagrams, graphs, illustrations, and, in some cases, particularly with more elementary texts, different types of underlining, marginal annotation, arrows in the margin pointing to important elements and many others.

Text types involved in wider scientific communication, such as presentations to the general public (scientific journalism), education and abstracts or résumés have also been analysed, and the range of types involved means that it is often difficult to define a specifically 'scientific' journalism different from serious journalism in other fields, although occasionally the scientist's inbuilt optimism and excitement in his work is reflected in the journalist's evangelical tone.

9.3.4 French and English in scientific language
Particularly in the scientific world, but also in management and commerce, French, along with other languages, is now faced with the major importance of Anglo-American as a means of communication. This fact is important both for analysing language use itself and also for assessing the language attitudes of specialists. A survey (Loquin 1982) noted that, of a total of 47,250 scientific articles examined at the end of 1980, 30,729 were published in English and 4,651 (9.8%) in French, the second most popular language. Gablot, in Chambrun and Reinhardt (1981, 29), basing her conclusions on a smaller survey carried out in 1976, notes that, taken across all the sciences, only 20% of French researchers published in English, although this figure varied greatly by discipline, from 80% in biochemistry to 0% in geology and low figures in technology. Students however were using mainly English-language textbooks (90% of material used was in English), and electronic data-bases of scientific information, of importance to researchers, all used English as their 'housekeeping' language. Three reasons were advanced for the growing dominance of English: most developed countries had English as a native language; for reasons of professional and personal advancement scientific publication must be speedy and widespread, and this was only possible through large-circulation English-language journals or abstracting services; the most reputable outlets were English-language services.

The dangers of this 'over-use' of English are not felt to be solely linguistic, however: 'Even scientific facts, expressed differently, allow differing interpretations, create different hypotheses and reflect different experiences' (Dausset in Preface to Loquin 1982), a sentiment which is echoed in Lévy-Leblond 1990: 'Words are not neutral clothes for ideas; new ideas often emerge from their free and unexpected use. Using a foreign language can only restrict the associations and slips through which creativity comes'. Similar feelings have been expressed in a number of fields, for example by computer specialists, particularly in debate over the nature of *informatique française,* implying intellectual creation in and through French, as against *informatique en français,* merely recoding from English to French the language of a neutral, international *informatique* (*La Lettre de l'AILF*, particularly issues 5 and 6, Dec 1983 and March 1984). De Broglie (1986, 40) sums up the fear:

> As the language of knowledge and thus of applications of that knowledge, English tends to become that of control and thus of

power. The danger is not just economic, but also intellectual and social.

His solutions are twofold: a separation of research, which has to be communicated rapidly and which might as well be spread in English, from scholarship and particularly from teaching, which ought to be carried out in French; and secondly, international support, from all the Francophone countries, for the use of French in conferences by French speakers, together with adequate provision of translating and interpreting facilities.

Of the 8 indicators used by Loquin to measure the world importance of languages in the scientific community, English came first on 5 (languages known by the scientist, understanding, scientific weight (measured by the number of pages occupied by each country in The World of Learning for 1978-79), cultural effort, and publication spread), French on 2 (languages understood by the scientist and potential for more widespread use) and Russian on 1 (competitiveness).

There were hence some reasons for optimism: the conclusion of this survey pointed out that although French was on average a second language in scientific fields, 'three quarters of the world's scientists understand French...the proportion of English language use is decreasing as other languages come onto the scene' and is already less than 50 per cent in certain areas. The two factors in which French came first were thought to put French in a position of great potential for the future, provided defeatists did not assume all was lost.

Most French scientists now publish directly in English, and public expressions wishing otherwise are now infrequent: statements by eminent scientists and commentators are more likely to note that 'There is no longer a role on the international scene for a French language scientific journal. One may regret this but it is nonetheless a fact which cannot be ignored' (Reggi 1984). The French Scientific Academy accepts English- language articles, accompanied by a French translation or abstract, and scientific congresses and conferences normally use English as the main or only conference language. The *Institut Pasteur* caused a certain amount of concern in 1989 when it decided to rebaptise its prestigious *Annales* as Research in Microbiology, a decision which caused a degree of embarassment to the French representatives at the 1989 Francophone summit in Dakar. Despite this, the 1987 edition of the official list of Francophone associations notes 32 associations concerned with all branches of science, 24 of which include among their objects aims such as the maintenance or the expansion of the use of French in science, and conferences (eg Chambrun and Reinhardt 1981) on the topic continue the pressure. A number of these associations have been set up with overt or covert aid from government, and official linguistic policy in relation to this topic will be reviewed below (Chapter 11).

9.3.5 Control of scientific language

Terms, particularly new ones, are approved or created by ministerial or interministerial committees, working together with the *Commissariat de la Langue Française* and professional term-bank organisations such as *AFTERM* (*Association Française de Terminologie*) which established *FRANTERM* under the overall control of *AFNOR* (*Association Française de Normalisation*), the equivalent of the British Standards Institution or the German *DIN*. *AFTERM* has so far approved about 11,000 French standards and more than 4,000 international ones, each of which requires its standardised vocabulary and international comparisons. Each industry and scientific area also has a *Commission de Terminologie*, under the overall direction of the *Commissariat de la Langue Française* and with interministerial representation, lexicologists and experts from the area: the decisions and recommendations of these comittees are eventually incorporated in linguistic legislation. Brochure 1468 of the *Journal Officiel de la République Française* contains the resulting decrees, ministerial decisions (*arrêtés*) and Circulars which have force of law in government documents and elsewhere.

9.4 Commerce and management

9.4.1 Sources

Over the last twenty years a major shift in employment has taken place in France, as elsewhere. Whereas in 1968 11.5% of the working population was involved in agriculture, this has dropped to 7% or less; there has been an increase from 5% to 9% in the proportion employed as managers; the 21% employed in offices has risen to 26%. The reason for this shift is explained by Mermet (1987, 251) as follows:

> Initially concentrated on mass production, industry today has changed, concentrating on designing new products, managing resources, selling, distributing, exporting, planning for the future in a climate of increasing competition and increasingly sophisticated markets.

In consequence, the proportion of service activities in the economy has increased, and the role of management has gained in importance. At the same time, the number of small shopkeepers has decreased, although there is evidence that improved services, such as later opening hours, have slowed this development. Over the same period the previous fall in numbers and proportions of *'artisans'* (small businesses) has also been arrested. Generally speaking therefore there is now employment for better qualified and trained people in the service sector, while employment in both the primary (agriculture) and secondary (manufacturing) sectors has declined. The sociolinguistic consequences of this shift can be easily foreseen, in enhanced communication requirements, and in the greater use of persuasive language in the vocative function, in domains such as marketing and selling, management control and management-staff negotiations.

For certain types of employment in commerce there exist structured training courses of different durations and in a variety of different establishments, starting within the school system, and leading to a range of vocational and semi-vocational qualifications. Theoretically, such courses within the school system now start at the entry point to the *'2e'* (*deuxième classe,* entered normally at the age of fifteen; the French system starts at age eleven with the *'sixième'*), and take place within the *Lycées professionnels*: they hence are available only to those who have not dropped out of education before this point, and to those who do not continue with the traditional *enseignement long* or long course leading to universities and Higher Education and to the traditional *Baccalauréat* taken at the age of 18. The qualifications include the *Certificat d'Aptitude Professionnelle,* usually taken only by those intending to become factory or agricultural workers; the *Brevet de technicien* or *Brevet d'études professionnelles,* awarded after two year courses in the schools for those who enter after the *3e*; the *baccalauréat* (technical, or, for commerce more usually the G options), likewise awarded after two years, but available to those who enter after the *2e.* At university level, the *Diplôme d'études universitaires générales* (*DEUG*) can be taken after two years, with specialisation for example in 'Economic and Social Administration'; or in the *Instituts Universitaires de Technologie (IUT)* the two-year diploma can be taken with specialisation in management. Degrees (*Licences*) are awarded after one further University year, and the *Maîtrise* requires two years after the *DEUG*; each can have professional specialisation in the commercial field.

Outside the 'normal' school and university system, training courses are organised by both public and private establishments, leading mainly to national awards, which can be obtained by a unit-credit system. The Adult Training Association (*AFPA*), groups of universities and schools, the Continuing Education centres of universities, and the *Conservatoire National des Arts et Métiers (CNAM)* which has fifty-five centres outside Paris, are the main providers. The requirement that 0.1 per cent of the wage bill for every undertaking must be devoted to training courses, coupled with the right of workers to take a specified number of days training each year (*congé-formation*), means that there is a high level of provision and take-up of training.

For managers, however, most large firms, and an increasing number of smaller ones, now look for recruits with a diploma from a leading business school, while certificates and diplomas are also often now required for a range of technical executive posts in specialisms such as marketing or finance. There is in France a strong tradition of training through the *Grandes Ecoles*. Those which were set up to provide the officer corps for military units, or for the leaders in the service of the State in technical areas such as mining or civil engineering also included aspects of management within their courses, and their products have traditionally moved freely between the higher echelons of the civil service, state agencies, and public and private industry.

Entry to the four top business schools (*Hautes Etudes Commerciales - HEC*, *Ecole Supérieure de Commerce de Paris - ESCP*, *Ecole Supérieure de Sciences Economiques et Commerciales - ESSEC*, *Ecole Supérieure de Commerce de Lyon - ESCLyon*) is by a common competitive entrance examination and interview, prepared by two years of special classes after the *baccalauréat*, or possibly by entry from the university after at least the *DEUG*. The eighteen other *Grandes Ecoles* (*Ecoles Supérieures de commerce et d'administration des entreprises: ESCAE; 'sup d'éco'*) have a similar three-year course, a common entrance examination and the requirement for preparatory classes. There are in addition many public and private '*écoles de commerce et de gestion*' offering four or five-year courses directly after the *baccalauréat*, others offering three-year courses, and some giving two-year courses. The names of the institutions do not necessarily reveal their situation on this 'pecking order', and names such as '*Institut Supérieur d'Etudes Appliquées*' (two-year course) or '*Ecole Européennee des Affaires*' (three-year course) have to be 'interpreted' in order to assess the relative value of their diplomates. Generally speaking, if the Ministry of Education approves the award, the quality and the reputation of the school will be enhanced.

In addition to the business schools providing initial education, organisations such as *INSEAD* (*Institut Européen d'Administration des Affaires*) or the *Institut Supérieur des Affaires* (*ISA*), the latter located on the *HEC* campus, offer courses at MBA or doctorate level, as indeed do the universities themselves; these are attended, usually on a secondment basis, by practising mid-career managers. The *Ecole Nationale d'Administration* (*ENA*) is the most prestigious of a number of schools originally providing initial or continuing education for civil servants, but now often offering entry to others on a very competitive basis. Continuing education, in the form of short courses, is a feature of many of the business training establishments.

It is nonetheless true that entry to managing posts within family firms is still limited by nepotism, that flair and enterprise - or inherited capital - still enable progress to be made without training, and that training and certification are not essential prerequisites for the use of commercial language. In this, as in other ways, there is a strong contrast with the legal and scientific domains.

Language-based training has always played a large part in the traditional establishments, in exercises such as drawing up reports, *notes de synthèse,* memoranda, letters and other internal documents. More recently established *Grandes Ecoles* concerned solely or mainly with training managers for commerce and industry have been heavily influenced by American teaching methods and materials, many adopting the case-study approach in most areas of study. Such training processes are based on spoken and written small-group interaction, and it is said as a consequence that management style itself is changing in France from the authoritarian and paternalistic to the consensual and problem-solving. Much training material, as in the scientific field, is written in English, and some courses, seminars and workshops may well be conducted in English; in any case, students will be expected to follow courses in English and to demonstrate a high level of fluency in this and indeed usually in one other foreign language as well.

The case-study approach uses a real-life problem, described in comparatively straightforward terms, and supported by a number of appendices giving any further information required by a student, such as the results of market surveys or descriptions of the technical characteristics of a product. 'Banks' of these case-studies are retained by the business school, or are available in published collections, and serve to start discussion on the possible solutions, techniques needed, range of possible outcomes to the situation described. As there are no 'correct' solutions to the problems involved, discussion could become heated and lengthy in the training sessions, with considerable interaction which itself mirrors real-life problem-solving. Interestingly, Beedham (1981), examining case-studies discussed in the English tradition, found that

> The discussion is fast, spontaneous, and ranges widely...is linguistically extremely demanding...opinions are expressed with varying degrees of certainty, irony, politeness and aggressive argumentation

whereas analysis of video-ed discussions within a comparable French business school found fewer examples of disagreement, interruptions, and the expression of opinion by students, and a more directive, pedagogic style by the lecturer. It is likely therefore, and this is again supported by direct classroom observation within French business schools, that French business training methods, even at a high level, remain more directive and hierarchical than in the English or US tradition.

9.4.2 Characteristics
9.4.2.1 Correspondence

Commercial correspondence is characterised by the heavy use of set phrases and stereotyped expressions, by a tone of impersonality and general politeness, and by the limitation of information to that specifically required for the relevant purpose. An example of classic commercial letter style, laid out in the 'French method' (ie with the destination address to the right, and paragraphs aligned on the comma of the introductory '*Messieurs*') is given on page 187 (Ponthier 1987, 13). The example lacks, here, the headed notepaper, logo, paper quality and other elements of house style which would normally be important features of such a communication.

Recently developed forms of commercial communication are changing this style. Both telex and electronic transmission (fax) are having direct linguistic consequences: for example, as in telegraphic style, salutations and closing formulae are being shortened, abbreviations are more widely used, prepositions such as *à* or *de* are being omitted where at all possible, and messages are being reduced to the absolutely essential nouns and numbers. An example of a telegram (Ponthier 1987, 153) is:

> Expédiez avion urgent contre remboursement joint culasse Maserati Modèle X sortie usine mai 1970.

This type of stylistic reduction is used also in forms such as the telex, an example of which is reproduced on page 188 below. It is evident that in the telex, direct communication is established between the salesman and his client, so a number of shorthand forms are used (*Mls slts* for *Meilleures salutations,* for example), and the communication, although recognisable, is reduced to essentials.

Commercial letter

Etablissements Dupont SA,
23, avenue Général Galliéni,
33100 BORDEAUX

Boulogne, le 23 septembre 1986

Réf. JS/MB
Objet: Notre commande no. 721

A l'attention de M Bernard Martin

Messieurs,

Comme suite à la visite de Monsieur MARTIN, nous vous avons commandé cinquante caisses de Bordeaux 1975 qui devaient nous être livrées le 1er de ce mois, règlement à 90 jours fin de mois.

A ce jour nous n'en avons reçu que 25 (vingt-cinq) et, à la dégustation, nous avons constaté que ce vin n'était pas conforme à l'échantillon.

Nous vous prions, en conséquence, d'annuler provisoirement l'expédition des 25 caisses restant à nous livrer et nous attendons de votre part une proposition concrète pour régler ce différend.

Etant donné les relations de confiance que nous avons toujours entretenues avec votre maison, nous ne doutons pas de parvenir à un accord et, dans l'attente de votre réponse, nous vous prions d'agréer, Messieurs, nos salutations distinguées.

Jean SIMON
Président-Directeur Général

Telex

ATTN.: MR J VILLE
1. SELON VT DEMANDE, DEMAIN NOUS ALLONS LIVRER 2
BOUTEILLES A GAZ INERTE A NT TRANSPORTEUR TRANS
ALPINE EXPRESS.   DETAILLES D'ARRIVEE A SUIVRE.
FRAIS DE TRANSPORT A VT CHARGE.

2. A CAUSE DE LA PANNE SUR L'UNITE POLYCOLD, VOUS
CONSEILLONS D'EVITER SON UTILISATION POUR LE
TRAITEMENT MULTICOTE SUR VERRE (MINERAL).

3. VOILA NT MEILLEUR OFFRE NO 87027 DU 11-03-87

PC.1 A700454-M SUPPORT COMPLET.   SFR 1'064,70
PC.1 B700470-R SECTEUR SPHERIQUE POUR VERRES DIA 80
SFR 798,60

PCS.12 ANNEAUX PORTE-VERRES - SFR 55,- CHACUN

DELAI DE LIVRAISON: DANS 6 SEMAINES DE VT
CONFIRMATION
PAIEMENT   : COMME D'HABITUDE
EXPEDITION   : SELON VOS INSTRUCTIONS
CES PRIX NE COMPRENNENT PAS FRAIS DE TRANSPORT,
DOUANE, ASSURANCE, ETC

DANS L'ATTENTE DE VT COMMANDE,
MLS SLTS
EXPORT DEPT

At this level, commercial French is fairly easily recognisable, simply taught to French and foreigner alike, and presents little to discuss in the context of sociolinguistics, apart from noting both its easily identifiable nature and therefore familiarity to a large number of the population, and the fact that Anglo-American influence, principally in simplifying the complexities of traditional French commercial language, but also in removing recognised politeness formulae, and in certain technical terms, is growing. Indeed, English may have entered business French to the extent of replacing terms like *Rayon Exportation* by Export Department, and thus forming part of the internal language within the firm. Similarly, in the telex and other forms of on-screen communication, misspellings, abbreviations and other shorthand forms of communication are evident.

Commercial and business French is not however limited to correspondence, and executives, secretaries, clerks and other 'front-line' personnel would need to be familiar with the terminology and format of text types such as the reports, documents and forms, illustrated in Holveck et al 1985, which form part of commercial training courses.

9.4.2.2 *Publicity*

Advertising, or the publicity given to a product or service, is one manifestation of the marketing of an item, and it is normal to present its aims as correlating to three of the functions mentioned in the table on page 167: cognitive, in disseminating information about the product to those who are unaware of its existence; affective, in an attempt to move the potential buyer from awareness to liking and preference; and conative, in persuading the buyer to purchase (see Lavidge & Steiner 1961, reprinted in Enis & Cox 1985, 408-12; illustrations and examples quoted in Mermet 1987, 127). The first aim corresponds to advertisements of a type consisting of announcements, descriptive copy, slogans and statements. These aim at making the public aware of the existence of the product or service; an example would be the simple picture of a bottle of port with the announcement of its name. In the second, affective, type and stage of the selling process, advertising copy is argumentative, competitive, based on the image and status of the product, and intended to move the public from awareness to liking and then to preference for this particular form of service or product. An example from Mermet 1987 (127) is the 'dream' a picture of a fantasy couple, half dressed, behind a picture and the name of a cup of coffee; or the 'sublimated reality' of a picture of a pot of Danone yoghurt sitting on a dish of caviar with the slogan *Ça change du caviar!*

Only in the third stage is the potential purchaser encouraged to move, from preference to conviction and towards direct purchase, by price appeals, testimonials, deals, point of purchase advertising and the concept of the 'last chance'; at this stage the seller attempts to move towards 'closure' and the act of purchasing.   An example is the direct call to the reader: '*Dévorez! C'est léger! Cuisine légère de Findus*'.

Advertising, the sharp end of publicity, can thus be of various types, and the selection both of relevant language and of appropriate accompanying images for display in the Press, on television or film, or on public hoardings, is a matter of skilled appreciation of both linguistic and contextual problems. Examples of these different types of advertising can be readily identified, although the majority of Press and magazine advertisements will necessarily lie in the first and second stages.

The following text is an example of the second type of advertising. Accompanied by a luscious picture of ripe cheese, its effect on French people can be readily imagined:

> *Nous savons préserver nos traditions !*
> *Au coeur de nos plus petites provinces, vivent de grands fromages, héritiers d'une longue tradition. De grands fromages au goût tendre ou viril, envoûtant ou subtil, aussi généreux que ceux qui les fabriquent, aussi vrais que le pays qui les abrite. De grands fromages aux noms aussi variés que ceux de nos provinces: le Neufchâtel, le Cantal, le Salers, le Beaufort, le Pont-l'Evêque, le Bleu des Causses, le Munster, le Crottin de Chavignol, le Brie de Meaux, le Pouligny-Saint-Pierre, le Laguiole, le Maroilles, le Bleu d'Auvergne, le Roquefort, le Selles-sur-Cher, le Saint-Nectaire, le Livarot, le Chaource, le Bleu de Cex ou du Haut-Jura, l'Ossau-Iraty Brebis Pyrénées, le Brie de Melun, le Reblochon, la Fourme d'Ambert et de Monbrison, le Comté, le Vacherin du Haut-Doubs ou du Mont d'Or. De grands fromages d'appellation d'origine, reflet d'une tradition fromagère que l'on retrouve, au coeur de nos provinces, derrière tous nos bons fromages.*

The pure poetry of the litany of names, associated with the deliberate references to tradition, provinces, greatness, history, artistry, the skill of the hand craftsman, phrased against the background of evocative adjectives such as *subtile, virile, généreux,* is designed to catch all the characteristics of the peasant lying at the heart of every Frenchman and all the attitudes towards food identified by observers as important:

The French inability to tolerate foreign cooking...the French master cook's first principle is to show off the fresh, succulent ingredients he uses...it is the variety of the produce they use that explains their success...this constant imaginative quest that explains the growth in popularity of regional dishes (Zeldin 1983, 289-300).

Likewise Mermet (1987, 380):

a good meal shared with friends is one of the most sought-after ways of celebrating...cooking and eating are unlike any other activity: the fundamental being is expressed through the basic human need to eat; nothing can be gratuitous in the rites which surround the celebration of eating.

The design of publicity for specific markets - the young, women, one social class rather than another - extends to packaging, symbolism and image, so that the mountain air of Evian replaces the prosaic reality of a plastic bottle in a cardboard case, and the sporty fast car rolling through the open countryside replaces the mundane steel box with its dented panels, stuck in the permanent traffic jams of the *boulevard périphérique*. Again, the design of appropriate messages is dependent on careful assessment of French character, attitudes and preferences,and hence the study of successful messages is one method of understanding the nature of French personality and through it, French society. It is no accident that *Francoscopie* (Mermet), an evaluation of the French in 1985, 1987, and 1989, is profusely illustrated with the most striking of such images, which encapsulate the 'Styles of Living' exemplified in more concrete and quantifiable ways throughout the book; and indeed Mermet makes the point openly (1987, 127), when he observes that publicity acts as a direct reflection of society.

9.4.2.3 Management communication

Commercial communication includes also communication within an organisation, and small-group interaction, whether within working groups or in management-worker confrontation, is a fundamental aspect of this. Negociation, as an example of small-group interaction, has been analysed with the intention of improving performance by management, and from such analyses one can identify the structure and phases of the process (see Guittet 1983,97) :

- establishment of procedures and agenda; creation of relationships and respective roles (domination, conciliation);
- search for problem areas and points of difference;
- list of possible points for negotiation;
- analysis of gains and losses for each side, identification of negotiable and non-negotiable areas;
- identification of possible solutions;
- agreement and resolution.

Within each of these stages, communication is based on exchanges within a pairs structure, which again can be identified (see Goffman 1981 and the French translation and adaptation: Winkin 1987). The frequency of occurrence of one type of pair as against another, together with the terms used and their phrasing, can characterise the type of interaction involved, and thus distinguish negotiation from conversation, the recruitment interview from the appraisal interview. The pairs identified by Guittet are:

- question/response
- challenge/rejection
- statement/reformulation
- attack/defence
- offer/acceptance or refusal

At the same time negotiation is conducted within traditional argumentation types: deduction, induction, analogy, pragmatism, dialectics, examination of restrictions and rejection of proposed solutions, paradox, alternatives, appeals to general values, appeals to authority.

Analyses of union and employer discourse have been undertaken on a basis of quantification over a number of years by the research group on political lexicology, based at the *ENS* St-Cloud, and forming part of the *CNRS*-supported *Institut de la Langue Française* (Lefèvre & Tournier 1987). In particular, published work by Gardin bears on the identification of union discourse and on corpus-based analysis of management-worker negotiation exchanges. A special issue of *Langages* (no. 93, March 1989) was also devoted to the question of *Parole(s) ouvrière(s)*.

Further reading

Bourcier, D. 1979. Le discours juridique: analyses et méthodes. *Langages* , 53, mars 1979: 5-32

Boursin, J.-L. (ed). 1981. *Le Livre scientifique et technique de langue française.*

Chambrun, N. de and Reinhardt, A. S.-M. 1981. *Le Français chassé des sciences.*

Broglie, G. de, 1986. *Le Français, pour qu'il vive.*

Enis, B. M. and Cox, K. K. 1985. *Marketing Classics.*

Gallouédec-Genuys, F. 1981. *Le Dialogue écrit administration-administrés.*

Gardes-Madray, F. and Gardin, B. (eds). 1989. Parole(s) ouvrière(s). *Langages,* 93.

Goffman, E. 1981. *Forms of Talk.*

Guittet, A. 1983. *L'Entretien.*

Holveck, A., Mull, C., Neusch, A., and Reinbold, P. 1985. *Connaissance de l'entreprise: documents commerciaux.*

Kocourek, R. 1982. *La Langue française de la technique et de la science.*

Lefèvre, J. and Tournier, M. (eds). 1987. Le Discours Syndical Ouvrier, *Mots,*14, mars 1987.

Locquin, M. V. 1982. *Enquête sur la situation du français par rapport à l'anglais, l'allemand et le russe dans l'ensemble des sciences.*

Maingueneau, D. 1987. *Nouvelles tendances en analyse du dscours.*

Mimin, P. 1970. *Le style des jugements.*

Phal, A. 1971. *Vocabulaire général d'orientation scientifique.*

Ponthier, F. 1987. *Le Grand Livre de la corespondance commerciale et d'affaires.*

Sabourin, P. 1981. *Place et avenir de la langue française dans les sciences juridique, politique et économique.*

Sprott, W. J. H. 1958. *Human Groups.*

Swales, J. (ed). 1980, *Episodes in ESP.*

Winkin, Y 1987. *Les Moments et leurs hommes: textes d'Erving Goffman.*

1985. *Langue Française,* Journal Officiel de la République Française Brochure 1468.

10   Interaction

10.1 Approaches and methods

SMALL-GROUP interaction, or the language use of primary groups in face-to-face situations, is a topic of much interest to philosophers, psychologists and sociologists as well as linguists. It is not surprising therefore that there exists a plethora of approaches and methodologies for analysing it, and for extracting from an example such as a conversation a range of different interpretations according to the purpose of the analysis. Since our concern is with the different ways in which French can be used, and the different forms the language can take, we shall attempt to avoid too much discussion of particular schools of thought and concentrate on the data, taking insights from different approaches as and where they seem appropriate to illuminate the variations in French language use which mainly concern us.

Three such insights or approaches are particularly helpful in this: the idea of the social network, which helps to relate language use to context, and two methods for analysing text itself: discourse analysis and conversation analysis.

The communication situation outlined in the previous chapter represents a setting for communication between a sender and a receiver, both located within a particular situation and each bringing to the exchange his or her own personality, experiences and social 'persona' (sex, age, class, race, geographical origin, etc.). Life is made up of communicative events taking place within such settings, and by following the events in which any one individual participates, identifying those with whom he speaks and the frequency and nature of the links he has with them, it is possible to discover his **social** or communicative **network** (Milroy 1980). The relationship of one or a group of such networks to others, or to aspects of the wider social environment, enables understanding of its communicative specificities, and helps us to characterise and differentiate between one network and another. This approach has considerable advantages in understanding the relationship between concepts such as 'working-class speech', ie the language variety of a particular social category, and the actual use of language by individuals in specific situations: it avoids, for example, the necessity to consider a speaker as limited or restricted to a specific variety of language, in that the range of networks in which he is involved may require him to master a repertoire of different language varieties for use with each.

Conversation analysis has been developed in recent years in attempts to understand social relationships (Schiffrin 1988). The structure of conversations is identified, and the tasks undertaken by each speaker in constructing joint meaning, in managing the interaction, are related to the linguistic or non-linguistic devices used to carry out those tasks. But conversation is not seen as solely a matter of language or para-language: 'conversational patterns can have very broad symbolic meanings for participants: they can become an index to the larger social worlds (of self, other, and situation) in which talk occurs' (Schiffrin 1988, 265).

Discourse analysis (Blakemore 1988, Stubbs 1983), of interest to historians and political scientists as well as to linguists, is essentially a type of linguistics concerned with language in use, and aimed at identifying 'the way that hearers recover messages from utterances' (Blakemore 1988, 231). 'Utterances', or 'texts', can be spoken or written, and are relevant to their context in the sense that a hearer/reader (or an analyst) can identify the intended meaning: ie can follow the implications, and can understand the speech acts that the speaker produces. Speakers produce utterances that are both thematically coherent, in that a theme or subject is followed through the subdivisions of the utterance, and grammatically cohesive, in that the constituent parts - phrases and sentences - are linked by cohesive devices, such as the use of anaphora or pronouns. Discourse analysis is therefore essentially concerned with language 'above the sentence', and with understanding how stretches of language can be interpreted.

10.2 The communication situation

OUR understanding of the communication situation described in the preceding chapter can be refined in various ways, particularly to make clear that the context referred to by the referential or denotative linguistic function can be viewed as made up both of an **immediate situation** within which people talk, and also of a **wider situation** which is in effect the geographical, political, social and cultural framework of society, its traditions and history, and its way of life. Both the immediate and this wider setting have an effect on the nature of interaction, and both should be taken into account in any full description of a particular interchange.

To give a full description of the wider setting of any particular conversation in any degree of completeness would however be an immense task, equivalent to explicitly defining French culture. **'Culture'** is defined by anthropologists and sociologists as 'a complex entity which comprises a set of symbolic systems, including knowledge, norms, values, beliefs, language, art and customs, as well as habits and skills learned by individuals' (Hamers and Blanc 1989, 115). This mental background, the configuration of learned behaviour and the symbolic meanings attached to it, is shared, perhaps unevenly, by every French citizen, and forms his or her cultural identity. Language has a special role within this definition of culture: it is a component part, on the same level as values or beliefs; it is a product of culture, transmitted as part of the socialisation of the new generation; it forms culture, in that our beliefs and norms are formulated in language; and it is the transmitter of culture, enabling individuals to internalise their understanding of their society. French culture, in this sense, is hence a necessary part of linguistic interaction, whether between French people who will have it in common and can therefore make allusions and use 'shorthand' within the conversation, or between a French person and a foreigner for whom certain aspects have to be explained or with whom conversation can never take place on a completely equal basis. Lack of understanding of cultural differences, as we know, produces culture shock, problems for immigrants, and unsuccessful international business negotiations.

The immediate situation of a conversation or other form of interchange is more easily described. Hymes (1972) established the elements which have to be taken into consideration in the **'ethnography of speaking'** approach for the description of communicative events, and more recent approaches to variety differentiation (Downes (1984), Gumperz (1982), Crystal (1987), and Duranti (1988)), do not materially invalidate it.

This Hymes framework is appropriate for describing and analysing situations which have taken place. Against this framework the analyst can then identify the particular means which have been used to construct the communicative event itself. Such means include not merely language, but also non-verbal (*heu, hein, bof*) and non-vocal items (body language, gestures, facial expression), for each of which there is a range of possibilities.

Ethnography of speaking

Mnemonic (SPEAKING)	Explanation
S	setting (physical location) and scene (type of social occasion, such as 'committee meeting')
P	participants and their communication roles
E	ends: conventional outcomes (eg 'a diagnosis') and personal goals
A	act sequences: message form (eg a conversation) and content (topic of conversation)
K	key: tone, manner or spirit of the interaction
I	instrumentalities: channel (spoken/written) and forms (dialect or language variety)
N	norms: of interpretation (ie expectancies for this speech event) and of interaction (eg turn-taking conventions)
G	genres: such as poem, lecture

The content of an interaction, the **'information'** exchanged, itself is not solely cognitive: Argyle (1972) describes three types, which can be related to the table of functions on page 167:

- cognitive information, relating to the outside world and hence conveying factual content;
- indexical information, corresponding to the expressive and conative functions. This type of information enables the recipient of the message to 'place' the speaker against his social, geographical or occupational background, and to situate the exchange against the wider context;
- interaction management: this type of information, dealt with in the present chapter, enables the participants to 'construct' the interchange, managing their interaction in terms of their communicative roles as well as in terms of the sequencing of the different phases of the interaction. Information of this type corresponds to the phatic (contact-making and maintaining) function, the poetic/discoursal function and the metalinguistic function, commenting on the code itself, and ensures the success or otherwise of the exchange.

10.3 Monologue and group interaction

10.3.1 Monologue

Observers note that French education stresses the judgement of the individual. Although from many points of view the purpose of education is to socialise children and thus create conformity, and the French educational system does this effectively in terms of imposing a common language and common textual forms, pupils are nonetheless expected to demonstrate individual judgement in expressing their own point of view within these frameworks. Thus the standard form of the *dissertation française* (Desalmond & Tort 1977), still the main means by which examinations are answered and therefore a fundamental part of the French way of life, has a tripartite structure: arguments for a proposition, arguments against the proposition, and a personal conclusion evaluating these and moving the discussion forward (caricatured as 'yes, no, perhaps' or less politely as '*oui, non, merde!*'). Likewise many French examinations are oral, and the candidate is expected to analyse a problem and expound his own point of view within the set structure of the '*exposé*'.

The consequence of this intellectual training in self-oriented discourse forms is that an extended expository monologue is not regarded in conversation as inappropriate, as it would be in English, and the didactic expository tone of many individuals in conversation which would be offensive in English is quite normal in French. The characteristic of monologue, as opposed to dialogue, is that there is little audience feedback, although even formal monologues, written to be spoken, such as political speeches, business presentations or lectures, normally react to, and expect, some audience feedback on delivery. Informal monologues in French are likely to continue much longer than in English, and anyone in a position of authority or expertise will be expected to possess the ability to keep talking.

Monologues, particularly spoken monologues, are successful if they are clearly understood; and comprehension depends not merely on content but also on **coherence** of thought and **cohesion** of presentation. Lexical cohesion can be achieved in a number of ways: by simple or equivalent repetition of the lexical item, (for example the repetition of *avion* or when *avion* is replaced by *moyen de transport*); by replacement of the item by another item, such as a pronoun; or, at a higher level (close to coherence of thought), by reference to the overall meaning of the message, using synonyms or words for the same set of terms. Cohesive devices are best understood as linking devices in French, as in Corbeil (1968), which uses the concept of the '*charnière*', or 'hinge', categorising devices as

- *liaison:* conjunction: *et, d'ailleurs, or*;
- *de traitement:* cataphoric: *c'est-à-dire, d'abord*;
- *de rappel:* anaphoric: *ainsi, je vous rappelle que*;
- *de terminaison:* terminal: *donc, enfin*.

Whitcombe (1980) analysed cohesion in radio French, identifying both the ties used and their distribution as between different types of broadcast material. She found that short, staccato messages such as headlines and information '*flash*' used practically none, since there was little repetition; newscasts used practically equal amounts of lexical cohesion and reference; while reporter's comments were heavy users of lexical devices; and formal speeches had very high frequencies of all types of tie. Both these types of discourse, particularly the reporters' comments, approximate to the characteristics of monologue in everyday speech. Whitcombe found that, in lexical cohesion, a high amount of simple repetition was involved, with equivalent repetition being the next most frequent type. Among the cohesive devices, formal speeches were greatly dependent on simple additive connectors, in particular the ubiquitous *et*, while reporters' comments used slightly fewer of these but more *ou* and *mais*, more *en fait* and other adversatives such as *toutefois* or *cependant*, more (and more formal) causals such as *car* or *puisque*. *Charnières de traitement*, such as *alors, il s'agit de* or *c'est-à-dire*, were frequently used, as were recall devices, in particular *ainsi, comme vous le savez, voilà*, and *cela dit*. Terminators, such as *enfin, au bout du compte*, were comparatively rare in these monologues however.

Other types of monologue have also been studied, in particular the academic lecture and political speeches (eg Lucci 1983, Encrevé 1983). The differences in the frequency of occurrence of items, in the use and selection of words and expressions, again indicate that French speakers seem to be consciously aware of the structure of what they say, to plan and organise with care their use of discourse markers indicating the stages of their thought, and generally aim to reduce the chaos of speech or writing to systematic order. This is particularly characteristic of the discourse of intellectuals, mainly academics and (more recently) media personalities, and the high importance of the role of the intellectual in French society is described by Zeldin (1983, 412) as equivalent to that of 'the Church of England and Her Majesty's Opposition': 'France has in a way been created as much by intellectuals as by kings and armies conquering territory'.

Zeldin (1983, 398-401) feels that the role of the intellectual in setting the tone for, and establishing a model for monologue in French is undeniable and rooted in history, and that, since for intellectuals 'how he says things is as important as what he says', 'it is their language that has coloured the debate as to what France is about'.

One major contributor to the characteristic style, in speech and writing, of the intellectual is the expectation the speaker/writer has of the audience that they will share the same knowledge, experiences and assumptions; this permits ellipsis, 'shorthand' reference to known events and people, and a general allusiveness in tone. If the speaker/writer can be sure of his audience, the incidence of such allusiveness will grow, and the monologue contain proportionately more discourse (coherence and cohesion) markers, as the analysis of an editorial in the weekly opinion magazines such as *L'Express* or *Le Point* will illustrate (see Ager, 1972).

Monologue, in spoken language, is likely to be didactic or pedagogic, explaining and clarifying something. The monologue speaker is explaining or expounding facts he or she knows, or a point of view; the role the speaker plays implies superiority, and the tone of the discourse may hence, particularly in French, be reminiscent of the more structured and careful forms of writing rather than the many mistakes, false starts and other performance errors of spoken interaction. It is likely, too, that monologue will be more formal than informal in tone, and that formality indicators such as speed of delivery, increased liaison and careful enunciation will be more noticeable in spoken monologue than in interaction.

10.3.2 Group interaction

At the other extreme from the monologue is the situation in which a number of people speak at once. In practical life such a situation rarely arises except at times when, in a group interaction such as a committee or problem-solving group, or even in an informal family context, people are uncertain whose turn it is to speak next. The situation rarely permits members of the group to keep speaking at the same time as each other, and one speaker will eventually 'win' the right to speak. In this setting, the contrast between 'Anglo-Saxon' and French norms have been noticed (Wylie 1981, 324):

> When a general conversation takes place among Americans, the whole group listens to the speaker...we are embarrassed when, in a group, a Frenchman standing next to us talks to his neighbour at the same time...the French are capable of passing from a general

conversation to a particular one without embarrassment or lack of comprehension.

This French ability to maintain group and two-person (dyadic) conversations at the same time and hence to continue to speak at the same time as others is a measurable fact, and coincides with observed differences with other cultures in non-verbal aspects of interaction such as the definition of personal space, body language and eye-gaze direction.

André-Larochebouvy (1984, 42) is quite sure that groups rarely exceed three active participants and that larger groups soon break into smaller ones. Nonetheless, the presence of others above this number, who become passive onlookers, has a regulatory role, modifying extremes of language use such as slang or technicality, so the presence of larger numbers is not irrelevant to the nature of the interaction. Even within groups of three, however, André-Larochebouvy notes that interaction leads to 'dialogue plus an intruder', with the role of 'intruder' being passed from one to another. In the conversation she exemplifies (husband, wife, and friend of the couple who is also a colleague of the husband), the husband and friend speak of a mutual acquaintance with the wife silent; then five minutes of generalities with all three speaking; then wife and friend speak of bridge, with the husband silent; the last part lies again between husband and friend, with the wife making an unsuccessful attempt to change the conversation but otherwise remaining silent. Such coalitions imply that 'natural' conversation in French is based on dyadic interchange.

10.4 The structure of dyadic interaction

10.4.1 Purposeful interaction

Guittet (1983) reviews the practice of 'functional interchange' or interactions in which the participants are obliged to converse in order to achieve some end or purpose. The participants are defined by their professional relationships, roles, and by this purpose, whether the precise setting is a market-research survey or a clinical, psychiatric interview: these two settings forming the extremes of a range in which the 'interviewer' is involved with his interlocutor to a greater or lesser degree.

The professional roles of speakers in purposeful interchanges are important in defining the legitimacy or otherwise of what is said. A judge is able to use certain types and styles of language when talking to the defendant in court which the defendant is unable to use in reply, and similarly a manager can use the forms of apparently friendly communication to a greater degree than the person managed: the 'manager' of the interaction sets the tone and remains in command, precisely because the role relationship permits this to happen and both participants regard it as the norm:

> *l'efficacité symbolique des mots ne s'exerce jamais que dans la mesure où celui qui la subit reconnaît celui qui l'exerce comme fondé à l'exercer* (Bourdieu 1982, 119).

Guittet analyses the characteristics of the following types of interchange:

- information: obtaining information, as in the market-research survey, or providing information, by explanation, transmission, influencing or instruction;
- diagnostic, evaluating, as in appraisal interviews;
- recruitment or selection;
- negotiation, including a range of more or less amicable settings;
- counselling or assisting.

Purposeful interchange is dependent for its success on both linguistic and non-linguistic aspects, and Guittet devotes considerable space to such factors as the physical setting (on whose territory will the interview take place?), the posture and gestures, the joint body language (do they indicate cooperation or conflict?), facial expression, direction of eye gaze, degree of control and indicators of stress, in addition to para-linguistic factors affecting speech such as voice quality (*timbre*), pitch, dynamism or effort, rhythm and intonation, all of which have some effect on the participants, although some individuals have greater or lesser awareness of them than others.

Corraze (1983) and Morris et al (1981) also review some aspects of these non-vocal or non-verbal communication systems, although neither is specifically oriented towards French. Indeed most of the research in this area is based on work with the upper primates, with psychotherapists and their clients, or with non-Europeans, although Morris et al (1981, 274-91) provide an extensive bibliography of works covering European countries.

Wylie (in Reynaud et Grafmeyer 1981) points out some particularly French characteristics of non-vocal behaviour. He notes particularly contrasts in the French muscular tension, whether in standing or sitting, by contrast to American relaxed attitudes and stance; habits such as shaking hands around the group; and greater use of gestures. Franco-American similarities however exist for example in the definition of personal space (intimate up to 1 metre, social from 1 metre to 3).

10.4.2 Conversation

Conversation, in contrast to these purposeful and managed or controlled interactions, is defined as any dyadic interaction without immediate or definable purpose, although the boundaries between a purposeful and a non-purposeful interaction are necessarily fluid. Because of the immense variety of conversational situations in which people find themselves, much research in this area describes actual conversations and attempts to find structures, whether linguistic or social, which can impose order and classification, in terms acceptable both to linguistics and to the study of behaviour. The close relationship between the two means that analysts often seek to identify motivations and social purposes even within conversations which, in general terms, have been defined as 'purposeless'.

A recent 'semio-linguistic' analysis of conversation in French is André-Larochebouvy (1984), which reviews the 'rules' of conversation against an overall concept which assumes that participants 'mobilise all their capacities to present themselves to their best advantage' ('*faire bonne figure*'). This idea is basic to the Goffmann ethnomethodological approach, in which participants protect their 'face', and assumes that participants use linguistic and non-linguistic items in pursuance of an underlying interactional strategy. The following résumé combines the main outlines of the André-Larochebouvy analysis with other work on interaction.

Three types of analysis, represented diagrammatically below, can be applied to conversations: the linguistic, strategic or sequential. The underlying concept for each is the couplet, or cue and response pair: speaker A provides a stimulus to which speaker B responds.

In a linguistic analysis the main constituent of the cue-response couplet, also called an exchange, is the speech act, although in some analyses a speech event is defined, which itself is made up of speech acts. The speech act also usually includes non-verbal and indeed non-vocal material (Roulet quoted in Guespin, 1984, 50).

Within a strategic analysis, a sequence of speech acts forms a 'turn', and a sequence of turns on the same theme or subject forms an 'episode' within the conversation. The turn of one speaker may be assisted by a cooperation signal from the listener, indicating the fact that the listener is paying attention, or perhaps indicating approval or disapproval, but in any case contributing to the construction of the dialogue. As with the linguistic analysis, non-verbal and non-vocal elements will be identified on the same level as the speech act.

The sequential analysis divides a conversation into openers, body and closers.

Hierarchy of elements in conversation analyses

sequential analysis (all elements at the same level)	strategic analysis	linguistic analysis
- opening	- episode (ie theme or subject)	- exchange or couplet (eg greeting and reply)
- body of conversation	- turn	- cue (or reply) - speech event
	- speech act - cooperation signal	- speech act (eg opener, closer)
- closure	- verbal, non-verbal or non-vocal element	- verbal, non-verbal or non-vocal element

The types of analysis are interlinked, in that the identification of linguistic material enables the clarification of strategies within the overall sequence of the interaction. Thus within 'openings' one can identify, in French, the following strategies and examples of language items used to achieve them:

- greetings: these are exchanged, so the exchange is a 'confirmatory' one in which reciprocity is required in order to maintain relationships: *bonjour - bonjour*;
- introductions: these vary according to the formality level: *Connaissez-vous M. X...*; *Permettez-moi de vous présenter M.X*;
- vocative/contact request: *dis maman; Paul, tu es toujours là?*;
- contact-making strategies; these vary according to relative status (ie whether the speaker is 'authorised' to make the contact proposed or not - anyone can address a shop assistant but not a well-dressed lady in a public place), and also vary according to permitted topics - weather, time, directions.

Telephone interaction is somewhat different from face-to-face conversation, and necessarily the selection of 'openers' is different. Three types of opener can be distinguished: unmarked, marked for business, and marked for intimacy, as follows, noting the French concept that the telephone caller is disturbing the called, and therefore needs to excuse himself, by contrast with Anglo-Saxon usage, which expects the called person to be available:

> *Unmarked*
> C: calls number
> A: *Allô?*
> C: *C'est bien le 798 01 23?*
> A: *Oui*
> C: *Bonjour, c'est Monsieur Valentin à l'appareil. Excusez-moi de vous déranger; est-ce que je pourrais parler à Madame votre mère?*
>
> *Business*
> C: calls number
> A: *Allô, Maison Valentin*
> C: *Je voudrais parler à Monsieur Valentin lui-même, s'il vous plaît*
> A: *Oui, ne quittez pas, je vous le passe; c'est de la part de qui, s'il vous plaît?*
>
> *Intimacy*
> C: calls number
> A: *Allô?*
> C: *C'est bien le 798 01 23?*   or   *C'est toi, Georges?*
> A: *Oui*
> C: *Bonjour Georges, c'est moi Jean-Paul* or *C'est Jean-Paul*
> A: *Bonjour Jean-Paul; c'est Georges*

Opening items in face-to-face conversation are considerably more varied than closing items, which tend to be limited to set phrases, such as *salut, bon week-end, au revoir,* and are often preceded by a 'pre-terminator' such as a short silence, or the use of a proverb or saying such as *la nuit porte conseil.* Within the body of an interaction turn-taking strategies (where speaker A takes the speech turn from B, keeps it, or passes it on to B) are classified by André-Larochebouvy as follows:

Taking the turn
vocative
    by name: *Paul tu te souviens...*
    by an excuse: *Pardon excuse-moi mais là je ne*
                suis pas d'accord...
run-on: *et pourtant ça dépend, moi je pense...*
completion: *Ce n'est pas toujours avec tous qu'on peut se sentir*
        si...(B pauses, A completes with...)
          .. si détendu hein...
simultaneous speech: B: *C'est pas pareil qu'avant hein faut dire*
          A: *Ah non plus pareil moi je*
          suis d'accord

Keeping the turn
repetition: *je me rappele, moi, j'avais qu- j'avais quoi- j'avais*
        pas- j'avais quinze ans..
voiced pause: *et heu c'est assez heu donc heu et Louise heu...*

Passing the turn
A pauses
A fails to complete the utterance
A names the interlocutor
A poses a question

(Note: the vertical line | indicates speech taking place at the same time)

André-Larochebouvy then reviews other linguistic 'signals' which indicate a range of discourse functions. Examples include a desire to change the subject (*à propos*), to maintain distance and separation (*hé mais dis donc*), to establish or maintain collaboration (*oui d'accord, c'est bien mon avis*), to punctuate the exchange (*bon disons que, quoi*). Many linguistic signals have, as elsewhere in speech, a range of possible interpretations: the examples quoted are the laugh (*le petit rire*) and repetition, which can both mean many different things in different settings.

Exchanges can be classified into a number of standard types of 'expectancy pairs', the first part expecting the second:

question/response
greeting/greeting
appeal/response

offer/acceptance or refusal
thanks/acceptance of thanks
complaint/sympathetic or negative response
challenge/acceptance or refusal
compliment/acceptance or refusal

If the expected response is not forthcoming the exchange will be unsuccessful; as Goffmann (1957, quoted in Laver and Hutchinson 1972, 348) points out:

> In our society a system of etiquette obtains that enjoins the individual to handle these expressive events fittingly, projecting through them a proper image of himself, an appropriate respect for the others present, and a suitable regard for the setting.

The extreme of expectancy pairs are the ritualised exchanges which communicate little more than respect for the setting and the other participants. Such ritualised exchanges are again exemplified by André-Larochebouvy (1984, 191), who quotes a particularly notable example of a conversation almost entirely composed of them:

A: *Ben dites donc, i fait chaud hein!*
B: *Ah ne m'en parlez pas, c'qu'i fait lourd!*
C: *Ah ben oui oui ça...oui ça faut dire*
A: *C'est pas un temps de saison quand même!*
B: *Ben non, en général en mai*
C: *En mai en général l'fond de l'air est frais*
B: *Tandis qu'là hein*
C: *Ah non j'vous jure, moi-moi j-j'en peux plus*
A: *Sûr qu'c'est fatigant, cette chaleur, sûr*
C: *Et pis et-et pis i fait chaud partout dedans dehors Ya rien à faire quoi!*
B: *Ah ça oui c'est lourd!*

10.5 Formality levels

10.5.1 Stereotypes

When language is said to be formal we understand by the term that the variety is stereotyped, of good quality and therefore having high prestige, and used in open, public, rather than in private intimate settings. The difference between public and private language has been mentioned several times. Cutting across this distinction however are two others: that between the written and thé spoken code, and that which correlates language selection with the level of formality present in the interaction. Usually setting and language are more formal if the participants are not acquainted with each other or are playing social roles which require them to behave as though they were not acquainted.

Language is often stereotyped because the situation is itself to a certain extent 'ritualised': the interaction that takes place contains a minimum of content and cognitive information exchange, and a maximum of phatic communication, and information dedicated to establishing or maintaining human contact and the norms of the personal interaction itself. The most obvious way in which such ritual exchanges are noticed is in the use of clichés about the weather, as we have noted, but other 'fillers' such as 'clichés, bromides, proverbs, greetings, leave-takings and other politeness formulas' (Fillmore 1979, 94) are much used to the same ends. The special case of telephone conversations requires much more evident 'fillers', and callers will check that their interlocutor is still there, still listening, by direct questioning, if the supply of '*oui, bien, c'est ça, non*', and other pause-fillers dries up. In these cases it may well be that the language variety used is not notably 'formal' in the sense of being of high quality, carefully chosen and delivered, but merely that it is impersonal.

A range of other formality indicators exists in both spoken and written French: the most important for the spoken form is probably that 'optional' liaisons such as *je vais essayer* or *ses plans ont réussi* are more frequent in formal situations. For Encrevé (1983), analysing the spoken language of a range of major political figures, there is no doubt that '*le taux des liaisons facultatives réalisées croît avec la hauteur du style*', although even in the most formal situations only some 49 per cent of the total theoretically possible were actually realised; more importantly, in situations of formality such as speeches, the rate of liaisons without *enchaînement* (ie pronouncing the liaison consonant, not at the beginning of the following syllable, but at the end of the preceding one, thus 'detaching' the first word) increased, even to the extent that some liaison consonants were pronounced before following consonants: *quand je* or *quand vous* (62). The conclusion must be that liaison is clearly felt as a marker of formality.

10.5.2 T/V oppositions and forms of address

French has, like many other languages, a clear marker of social distance in the second-person *tu/vous* opposition, with *vous* being the normal, unmarked and polite form, as well as the plural. The reciprocal use of *tu* hence is apparently limited to members of the same (extended) family: the family boundary starts where one starts using *vous* to individuals. The T/V opposition however spreads outside the family unit: reciprocal *tu* can express intimate relationships within any primary group, for example at work or in close-knit organisations such as military or student units, while giving non-recoprocal *tu* can express superiority: adults use it in talking to children and by extension so do policemen talking to suspects. Reciprocal *vous* is hence widely used as an 'unmarked' pronoun, while giving non-reciprocal *vous* indicates social distance or respect.

Brown and Gilman (1960) characterise the reciprocal use of the T/V oppositions as indicators of 'power' and 'solidarity': he who gives *tu* and receives *vous* is normally the more powerful, while reciprocal *tu* is used among friends, comrades and those who wish to indicate their common purpose or solidarity. Reciprocal *vous* is unmarked.

The apparently simple opposition is open to subtle play and variation:

- In a Paris-based advertising agency everybody uses *tu* except to the owner and the cleaning woman.
- *Tu* used to be used only to intimate acquaintances and people considered (extremely) subordinate. The impersonal *vous* was used to authority figures: the scholmaster, the father, the colonel, the local priest.
- There is nothing intimate or friendly in the *tu* used by the policeman who is checking the papers of a young person or an immigrant worker.
- Upper class leaders of society still use *vous* widely to intimates: Raymond Barre in talking to his wife, Giscard d'Estaing to everybody in his household, including his wife, children and dogs. (*L'Express* 20.10.79, 85-6).

Although apparently simple, the T/V opposition is subtle: moving from a *vous* relationship to one based on *tu* is usually an irrevocable step, marked by the 'superior' person: the older, the female, or the hierarchical superior. One of the consequences of the événements of 1968 was a wider use of *tu*, and its use is much less restricted today than formerly. Many non-standard French speakers, for example those from Africa, use *tu* more widely and thus come into conflict with social norms in France, since an unsolicited *tu* is perceived as an insult.

The pronoun *il* or *elle* is sometimes used to give extraordinary respect: *Monsieur veut-il prendre son petit déjeuner?* or *Madame prendra du café?* would thus be used in formal receptions and even some cafés. The pronoun *on* is also sometimes used to neutralise the power/solidarity oppositions: *On va sortir?*, rather than *Tu vas/vous allez sortir?*

Social distance is also indicated by the use of titles and names. In the following list of address forms used at work M = title (Monsieur or Madame etc), N= surname, P=(*prénom*) first name, V= *vous* and T= *tu*. The subtleties of interactions indicated by exchanges of these forms are many; a secretary for example would receive PV but give MNV, and be very surprised to receive any other form (see Guigo, 1989):

> MV *style distant*
> MNV *style respectueux,* used between the sexes and where age or hierarchy requires with the same sex
> NV *style militaire,* used between two males of the same 'level'
> V *style poli*
> PV *style américain,* used in three types of situation: boss to secretary; between the sexes when the *'tu'* would be too familiar; between women of the same age and 'level'
> NT *style potache,* used between two males recalling schooldays
> T *style camarade,* often used in work groups
> PT *style amical,* used between women; between men, relationships outside work would be required for this level.

10.6 Written and spoken differences

THERE are such considerable differences between the forms of spoken and written French today that it has been claimed that they are in effect two different languages. Commentators instance a different verb system: the written language has different forms for the six persons, while the spoken language normally uses only three. There exist innumerable homophones (*cent, sans, sang, (je) sens; temps, tant, tend, taon; quand, Caen, quant, camp*) and comparatively few homographs, syntax is often fundamentally different (*il pleut?* is the universal spoken question form as opposed to the other possibilities for the written: *pleut-il?* or *est-ce qu'il pleut?*). Likewise verbal forms such as the past historic or imperfect subjunctive survive only in the written code; and there are considerable complexities in the expression of number and gender (some liaisons, elision, agreements of past participles) which require precision in writing and which are completely ignored in the spoken version of the language. The largest differences lie probably in matters of style and sentence organisation, in which the spoken language proceeds by chunks and parts of sentences, rarely completing the syntactic sequence which is necessary in the written form to produce a 'complete' idea, and uses repetitions, emphasising devices such as the sequence *c'est lui qui* or *moi je*, and direct vocatives much more frequently than the written.

Differences between spoken and written French have been extensively treated in the research literature, in many grammars and textbooks, and in dictionaries. A useful presentation of the main differences is that given in Muller 1985 (78-113) summarised in the next two sections.

10.6.1 Differences of code

Since the written language cannot represent the individual pronunciation and performance norms of the speaker, it is necessarily less subjective and less able to provide information other than cognitive information. The relationship between the phonemes of the spoken language and the graphemes of written language is irregular: no single phoneme is transcribed by one grapheme, and no single grapheme represents a single phoneme. Thus there are 23 possibilities for writing the nasal [ɛ̃], 30 for the open [ɛ] as in *père*, and 8 for /s/, while many letters are either silent or have a variety of possible interpretations, as for example the grapheme 'e' as in *sept, pied, peloton, femme* or *enivré*. There remain, particularly for new words, variations in spelling. Muller notes finally the influence of written forms on pronunciation, where people now try to pronounce the word as it is written, for example in words with double consonants (*effet, attendre*), or in words with originally silent consonants (*donc, sculpteur*).

Generally utterances are longer in the written form; that is a sentence will require more graphemes than phonemes, and as much speech is composed of incomplete sentences, false starts and disconnected expressions, a written transcription of speech will lengthen to 'correct' these and incorporate the missing parts. Hence an utterance will be clearer in the written form than the spoken: in the latter much of the 'missing' information is provided by the situation. This is true even at the level of the redundancy of the written language, in which for example indication of the plural is given by pronouns and verb forms where none is heard in the spoken language: *elle parle au pauvre* and *elles parlent aux pauvres* are indistinguishable in the spoken form.

10.6.2 Other differences

The written form generally prefers a term from the prescriptive norm: *chose* rather than *truc*, *livre* rather than *bouquin*, *cinéma* rather than *ciné*. Likewise the affective intensifiers (*effectivement, formidable, drôlement*) much used in spoken forms are replaced by terms such as *bien* or *très*. Technical terms, imported words or slang words are replaced by standard forms.

In syntax, spoken French prefers shorter and more simple constructions, and we have already noted the high proportion of 'mistakes', false starts and fragmentary utterances. Parataxis is frequent, replacing the more complex conjunctions: *Il pleut. Je ne sors pas,* as opposed to the written *Parce qu'il pleut je ne sors pas.* The normal question form in written French is inversion, whereas the spoken form is the statement with appropriate intonation. Dislocation, both to the right and to the left, is normal in spoken French: *Les hommes sont lâches* becomes, in the spoken form, *Les hommes, ils sont lâches* or *Ils sont lâches, les hommes*, or even, *Lâches, ils le sont, les hommes.*

Morphological differences are most obvious, in particular the different verb conjugation and tense systems. The present tense of *parler*, for example, has six different forms in the written code: *je/il parle, tu parles, nous parlons, vous parlez, ils parlent* ; while the spoken forms are three: *je/tu/il/ils* [parl], *nous* [parlɔ̃], *vous* [parle]. Similarly in the tense systems the past historic, imperfect and pluperfect subjunctive are not used in spoken French. In the spoken code the article has much greater importance than in the written: it is for example the sole indicator of number and sometimes gender, as in the group *les nouvelles maisons,* which has three plural markers in the written form but a single marker on the article in the spoken form.

Blanche-Benveniste et al (1986) neatly summarise the range of attitudes linguists and society have towards spoken French as three *mythes séparateurs*: confusion between spoken French and popular (and hence inferior) French; the view that spoken French as in some sense 'incorrect' French; and the converse view that spoken French is 'advanced' French. The first is illustrated in three variables: absence or presence of *ne* in negation, absence or presence of final [l] in *il* or *ils*, and simplification of consonant groups such as *chambre* or *ouvre*. All of these are characteristic of spoken French in a range of settings including formal settings yet are frequently quoted as characteristic of popular and hence socially denigrated French; as a consequence, spoken French itself will be considered as inferior to the written form. The second point is illustrated in the condemnation of dislocation structures such as *Le petit cheval il a mangé l'herbe*, or in attempts to teach written language at school from a completely false analysis of a spoken French which only exists in structured formal monologues. In this tradition spoken French will be regarded as imprecise, disordered or inaccurate, and hence equally inferior to the written form. The third view, that spoken French represents the French of tomorrow, is illustrated by studies such as Harris 1978, which trace a development in word order from the 'standard' Subject-Verb-Object of *j'aime Marie* to a 'new' Verb-Subject-Object order based on dislocation as in *je l'aime, moi, Marie,* and deduce from this the changes to come. Spoken French will here be regarded as more 'acceptable', and indeed as the only 'real' French, with the written form a derivative.

It is clear that spoken French is different from written, that the differences can be identified, and that spoken French is itself not uniform. The differences are the greater in less formal and elevated settings, with the written language reflecting the norms of formal spoken monologue rather than those of informal unstructured interaction. It is clear also that the varieties of spoken French correlate with a range of situational variables, of which social class is only one: others include particularly the social function of language and the nature of the interactional setting.

10.7 Registers

UP to this point in our discussion a number of different social, functional and interactive factors affecting language choice have been identified, and corresponding linguistic variation noticed; we have organised our discussion, very approximately, around the Hymes approach to the ethnography of communication. The British tradition in applied linguistics has however defined language varieties 'according to use', by opposition to 'dialects' seen as varieties 'according to user', as 'registers'. Language elements here correlate to situational dimensions such as field (purpose and subject-matter), tenor (relations between participants) and mode (ie channel). The register concept is a fairly blunt instrument which combines many if not all of the factors we have been at some pains to distinguish in the present work, although as a concept which strikes an immediate understanding in the analyst it is of considerable use in education (see Ager 1972), in the language industries such as translation, and in lexicography.

It is however clear that the linguistic variables open to choice may well produce similar results no matter which dimension is at play: it is often difficult to say precisely that a particular variant (eg lack of final liquids in *quat'*) correlates to one particular factor (social class, spoken use, informality, topic) rather than another. Different factors such as age, social category, spoken/written differences, regional and interactive characteristics often lead to a very similar overall selection of items, and it is the number and interplay of these, rather than them as individual items, which contribute to establishing the indexical information conveyed by the text.

Batchelor and Offord (1982, 6) provide a description and examples of a three-part register system based mainly on formality, in which R1 is close to extreme informality and R3 is closer to the limit of extreme formality. In this interpretation, the term 'register' is hence used as a convenient shorthand for 'language variety determined by social, regional and/or situational factors':

R1	R2	R3
very informal, casual, colloquial, familiar, careless, admitting new terms almost indiscriminately, certain terms short-lived, at times truncated, elliptical, incorrect grammatically, prone to redundant expressions, includes slang expressions and vulgarisms, likely to include regional variations.	standard, polite, equivalent of 'BBC English', compromise between the two extremes.	formal, literary, official, with archaic ring, language of scholars and purists, meticulously correct, reluctant to admit new terms.

Examples of the different choices which could be made in vocabulary selection (others are given in pronunciation etc.) include:

R1	R2	R3
donner un coup de main	*aider*	*assister/seconder*
crevant/marrant/rigolo	*amusant/drôle*	*cocasse*
tordant		
d'acc/OK	*d'accord*	*entendu*

The descriptions of register are subject, as is almost any statement in sociolinguistics, to the use of value-loaded terminology, and it is not difficult to find texts in high-class journalism (*Le Monde, Nouvel Observateur, L'Express*) which are full of 'ellipsis and redundant expressions'.

For practical purposes the three-part differentiation presented by Batchelor and Offord is sufficient. However, Joos (1962), in a seminal article concerned with such **levels** of use, distinguished five for English: frozen, formal, consultative, informal and slang. Stourdze and Collet-Hassan (1969) identified six for French (*classique, littéraire, soignée, courante, familière and populaire*), which could be rephrased and illustrated, even from literary sources, as below: *savant (technique, scientifique, juridique), cultivé (littéraire, poétique, didactique), courant, familier,* and *populaire* or *argotique (criminel, estudiantin, militaire)*.

Vulgaire
En tout cas, moi qui vous cause, je lui ai dit un jour à mon mari: 'Tu veux que...Pollop, que je lui ai répondu.   Va te faire voir par les crouilles si ça te chante et m'emmerde plus avec tes vicelardises'
R. Queneau: *Zazie dans le métro*, Gallimard, 1959

Familier
Oui, après Uzés, j'ai vachement flippé.   Je suis parti.   Pour sortir d'Avignon, je me suis changé de fringues, tout ça, je me suis fait couper les cheveux, j'avais les cheveux vachement plus longs que ça avant, j'ai pris l'air minet.
Jean Bilski, *Libération*,19.5.76

Courant
'Tout ce qu'il raconte est absurde ou immonde. Sa vogue est un défi au bon sens et au bon goût'. Cette opinion, qui n'est pas rare, Brassens sait bien qu'elle est juste. Il se contenterait d'ajouter qu'il défie encore d'autres puissances que la raison et la politesse.
A. Bonnafé, *Brassens*, 1963

Cultivé/littéraire
Le recteur n'était pas homme à épier ses ouailles: ce fut sans le vouloir que de sa fenêtre il aperçut Miserere. Il craignit un malheur et sortit. L'îlien avait disparu.
R. Queffélec, *Un homme d'Ouessant*, 1953

Savant/juridique
Tous droits de mutation et tous frais de délivrance des legs ci-dessus mentionnés seront supportés par ma succession, de manière que les légataires susnommés perçoivent le montant de leur legs francs et quittes de toutes charges.
Le Parfait Secrétaire, Larousse 1954

Registers or levels of language do not present examples of automatic and predetermined correlation between the register description and language item choice. The linguistic choices represent the speaker's awareness of social and situational requirements, together with those geographical and social conditioning factors which might impose certain choices on him. The effectiveness of communication is dependent on such awareness and on skill in the selection of appropriate language, together with other personal factors such as the adequacy of performance in pronunciation or in sentence construction which a particular speaker might possess.

Furthermore, for Muller (1985, 225-94) and other commentators, the boundaries between registers or levels of language are constantly in flux, and tend to disappear in today's less formal, less hierarchical and less static society. Muller instances the different categorisations of terms such as *pépin* (=problem) as *courant, familier* or*populaire* in different contemporary dictionaries, showing thus that not even lexicographers are absolutely certain of the finer value of a term. He notes also the way in which individual language items have passed from R1 to R2 or even R3 in the course of time, and vice versa.

Further reading

André-Larochebouvy, D. 1984. *La Conversation quotidienne.*

Argyle, M. 1972. *The Psychology of Interpersonal Behaviour.*

Blakemore, D. 1988. The organization of discourse. F. Newmeyer (ed). *Linguistics: The Cambridge Survey.*

Brown, R. and Gilman, A. 1960. The pronouns of power and solidarity. T. Sebeok (ed). *Style in Language.*

Corbeil, J.-C. 1968. *Les Sructures syntaxiques en français moderne: les éléments fonctionnels dans la phrase*

Corraze, J. 1983 (2nd. ed). *Les Communications non-verbales.*

Crystal, D. 1987. *The Cambridge Encyclopedia of Language.*

Desalmond, P. and Tort, P. 1977. *Du Plan à la dissertation.*

Encrevé, P. 1983. La liaison sans enchaînement. *Actes de la recherche en sciences sociales,* 46, mars 1983: 39-66

Guespin, L. (ed). 1984. Dialogue et interaction verbale. *Langages,* 74, juin 1984.

Guigo, D. 1989. L'adresse au bureau. *Travail et pratiques langagières - communications.*

Guittet, A. 1983. *L'Entretien.*

Gumperz, J. 1982. *Discourse Strategies.*

Gumperz, J. and Hymes, D. (eds). 1972. *Directions in Sociolinguistics: The Ethnography of Communication.*

Harris, M. 1978. *The Evolution of French Syntax: A Comparative Approach.*

Joos, M. 1962. The Five Clocks. *International Journal of American Linguistics,* 28: 5.

Laver, J. and Hutchinson, S. 1972. *Communication in Face-to-Face Interaction.*

Lucci, D. 1983. *Etude phonétique du français contemporain à travers la variation situationnelle.*

Maldidier, D. (ed). 1986. Analyse de discours nouveaux parcours. *Langages ,* 81, mars 1986.

Mermet, G. 1989. *Francoscopie 1989.*

Milroy, L. 1980. *Language and Social Networks.*

Morris, D., Collet, P., Marsh, P., O'Shaughnessy, M. 1981. *Gestures.*

Muller, B. 1985, *Le français d'aujourd'hui,* Klincksieck

Newmeyer, F. J. (ed). 1988. *Linguistics: The Cambridge Survey,* Vol 4: *Language: The Sociocultural Context.*

Reynaud, J. D. and Grafmeyer, Y. 1981. *Français, qui êtes-vous?*

Roulet, E. 1981. Echanges, interventions et actes de langage dans la structure de la conversation. *Etudes de Linguistique Appliquée,* 44.

Savile-Troike, M. 1982. *The Ethnography of Communication.*

Stourdze, C. and Collet-Hassan, M. 1969. Les niveaux de langue. *Le Français dans le monde,* 65, 18-21.

Stubbs, M. 1983. *Discourse Analysis.*

11 Language policy

11.1 Historical overview

THE thirteen volumes of Brunot (1966) provide much information on the history of the formation of contemporary French, while Wolf 1983a, Genouvrier (1986, 114-38), Grillo 1989, Rickard 1989, among others, summarise the process of language control and codification, and the relevant groups and persons involved, to the present day.

The Frankish kings who invaded France in the fifth and sixth centuries, and their successors through to the period of the French Revolution in 1789, attempted to expand their control of territory from northern France and particularly the Paris basin towards 'natural' frontiers of the sea, rivers and mountains. This military process was accompanied by the spread of their dialect of the French language, which had developed from the Latin spoken by Roman administrators and the soldiers, traders and settlers who followed them and established themselves across Europe. The first 'French' text, recognisably distinct from Latin, is generally regarded as the Life of Ste Eulalie (842) and the slow linguistic development which was to follow over the Middle Ages led to the modern language, recognisable as such from about 1600 and codified in the seventeenth and eighteenth centuries. The development reflects in part the history of the triumph of the Ile de France dialect over other *langue d'oïl* dialects and then over the regional languages, and in part, and closely associated, that of the triumph of centralising, élitist, military, diplomatic and ecclesiastical power over feudal fragmentation and over the lower orders of society.

The first official French text directly concerned with language planning as such is article 111 of the Edict of Villers-Cotterets (1539), which required that legal and administrative texts use French and only French, and that the courts use French in their affairs. Within ten years it is reported that the civil, military and ecclesiastical administrations owing loyalty to the French king were using French without exception for these purposes, and that the language also held sway in areas (Béarn, Savoy) where French control was not yet exercised. The ruling classes, and all those administrators, lawyers and traders needing to use a written language, hence used French and became 'translators' both of language and, through their knowledge and use of language, of power, while the mass of the population continued to use local languages and dialects in an essentially oral tradition, becoming divorced from power and influence.

During the seventeenth and eighteenth centuries the French kings reinforced their hold over the aristocracy through the creation of courtly life and the concentration of subordinate nobles in Paris and Versailles, their hold over the growing bourgeoisie through financial control, and their power over potentially dangerous movements such as Protestantism through religious persecution, in such acts as the Revocation of the Edict of Nantes in 1685. At the same time the French language was codified, systematised and controlled by grammarians with progressively stronger links to the Court: while Malherbe (1555-1628) asserted that the stevedores of the hay port were the best arbiters of usage, Vaugelas (1585-1650) found guides in the 'sanest part of the Court'. Such organisations as the Jansenists of Port-Royal based their approach to language use on logic and reason, but significantly the *Académie Royale*, founded originally in 1634 as a private meeting of minds and almost immediately taken over for the purposes of the State by the King's Minister Richelieu, was created for the purpose of discussion and debate over the 'best' forms of language to use. Although no legislation as such was enacted, the controlling hand of the royal will was evident, and the *Académie* was given the task of devising a grammar and a dictionary, together with a *Rhétorique* and a *Poétique*, in order to codify the language for administrative and scientific as well as literary and cultural purposes: the relevant article of its statutes requires it to work 'with due diligence and care to give rules of certitude to our language and to make it pure, eloquent and capable of treating the arts and sciences'. The first edition of the dictionary appeared in 1694.

Immediately before the Revolution the (cultured, written) French language was used widely throughout Europe as the normal language of international diplomacy and culture, and the spoken language of the Paris Court was recognised as the élite version to be imitated and taught in schools for the nobility from England to Russia. The Revolution was prepared in French, and for the men of 1789 French was the language of liberty. For them the opponents of the Revolution spoke German or English, or one of the many regional languages which the Church used 'in order to keep the peasantry in ignorance'. Hence the 1790 survey by the

Abbé Grégoire, leading to a report presented in 1794 'On the necessity and means of suppressing the patois and universalising the use of French'. This survey showed that out of the 25 million population of France, 6 million (mainly in the South) had no knowledge of French at all, 6 million more barely understood it and were incapable of maintaining a conversation. Only 3 million (12% of the total population) were fully conversant with the language, and only a small proportion of these were capable of reading and writing. As a result of this survey and the speech by Barère at the *Comité du Salut Public* (quoted in Genouvrier, 1986, 131) the revolutionary government passed a number of decrees, the most famous of which (20 July 1794: 2 Thermidor an 2) required that 'no public act be written in any part of the French Republic except in French'. The consequential 'linguistic terror' in Alsace in particular caused considerable problems as zealots attempted to put the decree literally into practice in an area where French as such was barely spoken.

The Revolution's educational decrees also instituted schools to teach French, but were not to be implemented until 1832, with the establishment of primary education, nor to be effective until 1882 when the schools were made free and obligatory. Napoleon's institutional reforms and centralising administrative structures formed the basis for effective linguistic control through the 'mandarin' system of open written examinations for all posts as employees of the State, and the use of the educational system to normalise the language throughout France continued until the early years of the twentieth century. There were other indirect influences in this process, among them the movement of populations caused by transport improvements such as the railway system from 1830 on, or by the introduction of conscription from the Revolution onwards, by the wars of the Revolution, by those of Napoleon, of 1870, 1914 and 1939, and by the administrative system of moving public employees throughout the country. The growth of the Press, the new electoral systems with universal male suffrage from 1848, and the slow introduction through the nineteenth century of commercial systems based on written exchange also forced greater acceptance of the prestige version of the language; but it was still the public schools which were the greatest single instrument in fostering the spread of the norm of French, both in the direct teaching of an officially approved version of the French language and also in the use of texts approved directly by the Minister in all subjects.

The language was normalised officially both through insisting on the use only of approved dictionaries and grammars and also through ministerial decisions identifying and officially approving grammatical and spelling norms, and deviations from them, as for example in the *Tolérances* of 1901. The single greatest influence was the training of teachers through the 'normal' schools, and the imposition, by teachers, of measures countering the use of regional languages and dialects in the school premises, such as obliging defaulting children to wear a sign around their neck and suffer other punishments if caught using the local forms. The prestige of the rural schoolmaster, particularly in the nineteenth century, was considerable.

Through the twentieth century the belief in a *'bon usage'* has been maintained and strengthened through the publication of comment in the Press by distinguished and regular contributors, by the publication of grammars countering regionalisms - Grévisse, the standard work, was originally conceived to counter Belgian deviations from standard French - and through the continued strength of the competitive system of recruitment to administrative posts and for entry to prestigious educational establishments. The language-based educational system, requiring expertise in language manipulation skills and conformity to norms of presentation such as those of the *dissertation* also contributed, although this latter is now under some attack from the comparatively recent preference for mathematically based education in the popular and prestigious mathematics C stream of the *baccalauréat.*

Historically speaking therefore French language planning has derived from a set of policies and practices having their origins in government and in political life, in economics and in employment, and in certain social and cultural, usually élitist, environments and attitudes. The resulting linguistic practice is not always incorporated or prescribed in specific 'language laws', but the educational and social consequences of these formal and informal planning procedures have brought about the practical acceptance of the norm just as effectively. French language planning is hence on occasions formal, official and legal, incorporated in laws, ministerial orders and regulations; on other occasions it derives from economic pressure, both pressure to preserve economic advantage for France, and also, according to some analyses (see Bourdieu 1982), to preserve economic advantage for the social group in power. At other times it reflects cultural prestige and the preferences of the educated. In the last two cases planning is informal and realised through the prestige value accorded within society to a particular norm.

11.2 French opinions and attitudes

11.2.1 Awareness of language questions

We have reviewed the language attitudes of the French at several points above. Attitudes, in the sociological literature, are the outward manifestation of a society's, or an individual's, beliefs, which are themselves based on underlying values. In summary, therefore, perceived language attitudes can be said to be based on the belief that French achieved perfection in the eighteenth century, and that this perfection renders it a universal human possession worth defending, by centralised control, against change, against internal fragmentation or 'creolisation', and against external attack, by unified, fierce, defensive and offensive moves. The general public is thus said to be proud of the language, proud of owning it, and proud of its symbolic value.

The general public is also said to be greatly interested in language questions. Many commentators have noted that as many language books are published in France as books on cookery for example. The French should hence value language matters highly; should attach great prestige to correctness and accuracy, and in practical terms should:

- defend French against borrowings, particularly from English; - oppose the degradation of the language, particularly by the use of words, terms or pronunciations which are socially undervalued;
- reinforce the socially prestigious norm; eliminate the use of regional languages;
- aid the spread of the French language abroad;
- render the 1975 law, on the use of French within France, effective.

The evidence for the existence of these beliefs and values among the general public is however somewhat sparse. Ball (1988) is of the opinion that their origin is language insecurity, due to the flimsy nature of the arguments for the international importance of French and the rapidity of linguistic development, leading to the idea of crisis, although again no quantitative evidence is provided apart from the flurry of book publication since 1970. His final conclusion (p 104) is that 'Despite the eloquence with which it is expressed and the publicity it attracts, linguistic *angoisse* in modern France seems to be a luxury reserved mainly for *belles-lettristes*'. St-Robert (1983, 70-80), the former *Commissaire de la Langue Française*, seems at various points in his report on the first two years of his work to suggest that educated people in France, particularly journalists but also some politicians and many businessmen, are either permissives who do not care about language anyway or are excessively libertarian, feeling that any attempt to control and direct is an infringement on their personal liberty. His account of the misrepresentation of an attempt through the courts to prevent the use of the English word 'showroom' complains that accusations levelled at his *Commissariat* went as far as to accuse it of fascism and a police mentality.

One piece of evidence to the contrary however is precisely the report by St-Robert (1983, 30) that the general public wrote regularly to the *Commissaire de la Langue Française* to express their worries and views about language. Again the popularity of a television programme such as the Bernard Pivot spelling programme, or the television game '*Chiffres et Lettres*', could indicate that these values and beliefs are widespread. Readers of *Le Monde*, and indeed of other papers, write regularly on language matters, and although the attitudes expressed vary somewhat from one newspaper to another most are concerned to condemn rather than to praise.

11.2.2 The general public

Bourhis (1982, 40-1) after pointing out that no quantitative work had been done on French language attitudes, summarised the general feeling among those who have studied the topic as follows:

> One might expect that on a prestige (high-low) continuum of speech styles in France, the Ile de France standard would be rated very favourably by both standard and non-standard speakers. Conversely, one could expect regional accents and dialects to be rated below the Ile de France style, while urban nonstandard and ethnic speech styles would be rated even lower on this prestige and evaluative continuum. Finally the Parisian argot and the foreign-accented French of migrant workers from North Africa and Eastern Europe would most probably receive the lowest ratings on this continuum. On the other hand, one might also expect each of the above nonstandard varieties to be rated favourably in their respective milieus for usage in informal settings...To many a Frenchman, attachment to standard French has grown deep as a symbol of the unity, prestige and vitality of French culture in the world.

The survey on the *Francophonie* concept conducted for the 1986 summit meeting of heads of Francophone states, reported in Section 6.3 above, did not demonstrate any great measure of language awareness among the French community generally, with many of those questioned maintaining that they felt closer to the concept of Europe than to that of *Francophonie*.

An opinion poll conducted by the *SOFRES* in April 1988 among 1,000 respondents and thus representing the 'average Frenchman', welcomed as the 'first poll we have on the image which the French have of their language', came to a number of conclusions, presented in Pécheur 1988a and here reformulated from that summary, in terms of percentages of answers received in response to particular questions, below:

What is important for French influence abroad?

exports of French products	65
French culture	42
use of French language	28
diplomatic action	26
military power	21

Which elements of the French inheritance are the most important?

Literature	56
Language	51
Customs	not given
Popular traditions	not given
Cinema	20
Music	19
Painting	18
Theatre	13
Dance	7

What is the value of good French?

To help in professional life	49
Means to make oneself understood	45
Access to culture	29
Advantage in social progress	28
Pleasure in itself	25

When you hear a mistake in French, what is your reaction?

It would concern me (*me gêne*) but I would take no action	47

I would correct it	23
Of no importance	23

Has the use of French improved or worsened in the last 30 years ?

Worsened	62
Improved	22

(Agriculturalists, liberal professions, intellectuals and executives with educational levels of secondary and above, more than other professions; and women, more than men; feel that language use has worsened)

Which factors have affected how the French language is spoken and written?

School	66
Television	62
Family context	37
Press	27
Literature	27
Radio	21
Advertising	21
Songs	15
Cinema	8
Political speeches	6

Is the use of English and American words in French good or bad ?

Bad	50

(because French would lose its own character)

Good	45

(because a language must assimilate foreign words to enrich itself and develop)

(The latter view supported particularly among 18-24 year olds, employees and executives)

Is 1992 and the Single European Market good or bad for French?

Good	44

(because it will increase French influence in Europe)

Bad   18
(because it will diminish French influence)
No difference   26

Pécheur summarises the main conclusions as showing that the French have a mainly utilitarian view of their language: are attentive towards its practical value, pessimistic about the way in which it is used, but optimistic about its influence. They feel that its history is more important than its future.

11.2.3 Politicians

Philippe de St-Robert, *Commissaire de la Langue Française* from 1984 to 1987 and a man with known right-wing Gaullist sympathies when he was chosen for the post by the left-wing President Mitterrand, was well placed to observe language attitudes in the contemporary French scene, since it was his task both to advise government and the administration, and to receive the views of the general public on matters such as the implementation of the 1975 law on language use. His rather acid book on his early experiences (St-Robert 1986) shows how far some language attitudes are connected to a set of political attitudes and beliefs. We could derive from him the simple statement that purist views are politically right-wing, while left-wing views are either permissive (*laxiste*) or directive (*dirigiste*).

He starts by observing (p 84) how low in the list of governmental priorities language matters were in the 1984-86 period:

> One can imagine how happy I have been for the last two years, swimming between a hostile press and a government so indifferent that it was able to let me know that I was not there to do something, that the time was not now, particularly not on the eve of elections

and most of the book is concerned with the problems of working with civil servants and Ministries jealous of their own privileges. St-Robert points out (p 12), that 'conservatism (including language conservatism) tends to conserve special interests at the expense of the common good', and those who wish to preserve French from any change have forced the language to borrow in order to cope with neologism, the creation of the necessary new terms to describe new realities. The implication is that purists associate linguistic purism with nationalism and with a set of right-wing attitudes opposed to attacks on the status quo. These '*Cassandres à cocarde*', excessively patriotic mouthpieces of impending doom, are to be found on the political Left as well as the political Right, but are united by their opposition particularly (in this century) to American influence (see Hagège 1987, 105-13).

The Left, however, divides into those who wish to take no action, the *laxistes*, on the one hand, and on the other the *dirigistes* who wish to control and channel future developments, while accepting that development is inevitable. St-Robert reserves vituperation particularly for the former, whose number included journalists and indeed professional linguists, and who attacked attempts at language policy on the grounds that they were an admission of inferiority, a sign of inward-looking approaches and dictatorial, if not fascist and racist.

The value of St-Robert's book is that it enables the distance between public pronouncements on language matters to be measured against effective political action. In the French political scene it is appropriate for politicians of all parties to make the equivalent of speeches in favour of motherhood: condemning excessive American influence and supporting French identity and nationalism, in favour of Francophone links and supporting a greater influence for France in the world and in Europe, and associating these questions with the future of the French language.

As with foreign affairs, French political attitudes in language questions admit of little differentiation between the parties: the problem for those who observe the French situation is to identify how high up the agenda of political action language matters are at any one time. As we have noted, language-planning has been on the agenda of political action in 1982, with the creation of the Giordan report; in 1984, with the reformulation of committees into the *Conseil Supérieur de la Francophonie* and the *Commissariat Général de la Langue Française*, and with various measures concerning regional languages and education. However the question of a reformulation of the 1975 law on the use of French has been shelved a number of times, and action by politicians has been mainly confined to technical matters, and to a campaign through the media to awaken interest in language matters generally. The political scandal 'uncovered' by the incoming Chirac government in 1986 around the grandiose concept of a Communication project in the Défense area of Paris has also had some effect in damping down interest in direct and open language planning.

11.2.4 Intellectuals

It is easy to generalise about language attitudes, and quite difficult to determine how widespread those published in book-length works about language in France actually are. Assuming the *SOFRES* survey reported above, based on a representative sample of 1,000 respondents, can be taken to represent as accurately as possible 'the general public', we still need to identify the opinions of the academics, philosophers, historians and *'belles-lettristes'* who form the cultured *beau monde:* users of language whose passion for the tool of their trade often leads them to an over-protective or excessively purist view of what language is or should be.

The general opinion here appears to be based on the notion of an élite culture, of which the French language is the jewel: de Broglie (1986), former vice-president of the High Committee on French and President of the National Commission on Communication and Liberty, controlling the media, is better qualified than most writers to offer opinions in the field. Starting by declaring that French is in fact threatened, he is sure that it must be 'respected, protected, known, brought to life and animated' (p 10), which he proceeds to do by considering in turn the crisis of French, the genius of the language, the forms of its distribution (book, audio-visual), the choice of objectives, the roles of those concerned, the means available, international policy, and the future of French.

In this last chapter, he places himself firmly in the group of those who believe that deterioration is not inevitable: that 'usage is weakening but the written language retains its strength; that none of the scenarios for the future reduces the role played by people, and that Francophones themselves can control the future of French' (p 268). He also identifies tendencies and possibilities that inspire fear: a cosmopolitan, internationalised, permissive culture, or even counter-culture; liberalism, deregulation and privatisation, with the consequential loss of centralised influence; a loss of national identity and of national self-confidence. His hopes for the future centre on what he sees as a change of policy since 1984: 'a policy has been outlined, although it lacks a voice, echoes in public opinion and the push to completion which can only come with energy' (p 270, adapted). While avoiding the two reefs of, on the one hand, 'elitism, purism, bombast and abstraction', and on the other, the drive towards creolisation and language mixture *(métissage)*, he hopes that French will retain its complexity, subtlety and nuances, and that the debate will centre on the international role and relations of French: an introverted policy would lead to weakness.

Two other examples must suffice: Fernand Braudel, the recently deceased eminent historian and member of the *Académie*, participating in a debate in March 1985 on French identity, quite firmly noted that 'France is the French language', and felt that the former colonial possessions, the countries of the East, and Latin America, still remained faithful to the language. His main point however was that the identity of France was formed from her centralisation and her unity; in second place he noted her poor performance in economic matters; and thirdly, her success lay in her renown and in the spread of her cultural influence: 'a triumph of culture and a spread of civilisation'. For Braudel, the future of France lay in Europe, although her own identity was not in danger of disappearing, and her greatest asset was not so much her language as the human values of reason, liberty and cultural priority it is recognised as conveying (Kajman, 1985).

Jean Dutourd, in a speech to the *Académie Française* on 19 December 1986, also noted the feeling of smallness, of restriction widespread in a country which had been used to a greater world role: 'Our national passion, at this moment, is humility'. But his conclusions were that the danger for French arose from the disappearance ('towards 1960') of agrarian and artistic society and its replacement by a scientific and technological one. For Dutourd, 'the French language is a national palace...a house for every Frenchman, even the most deprived'; and his analysis of the 'crisis' was that developments in French were now coming from the top rather than from the slow process of popular change: 'intellectuals full of jargon, scientists, technicians, higher civil servants...merchants who want to sell and publicity agents prepared to help them by spreading the midatlantic jargon whose magic effects they have noted'. These had created a situation where contemporary French was being degraded, had become like a 'classical statue covered with graffiti by crowds of illiterates and pedants'; 'a language of men, an instrument for describing and forming the mind, for going into the nuances of the heart and of thought' could not be, and should not be, replaced by, a child's language 'for measuring visible objects or giving recipes for manipulating matter'. The point is made with brutal simplicity as follows, with Dutourd remembering how, as the more intelligent, he was told by his elders to give way in argument with those 'little brutes' less intelligent than himself:

> You are the more subtle, the more powerful, the more exact, the sharpest of human languages, the best adapted to everything, whether it is the soul, literature, politics, war, even science. Give way therefore. Give way to a barbaric patois, which is the language of the modern world and that of the year 2,000. Your millions of books, your thousands of men of genius no longer count for anything

Dutourd's proposals for correcting the problem were to institute financial penalties for those misusing the language, creating a group of inspectors on the lines of the tax inspectorate, and thus to ensure language planning which would be effective (Dutourd, 1986).

An interesting exemplification of the concern of intellectuals for the language was the publication of a statement in favour of French by a group from all political persuasions. This advertisement appeared in *Le Monde* (17.4.1983), before the reorganisation of the *Haut Comité de la Langue Française,* and was signed mainly by writers, together with St-Robert and Farandjis (then Secretary of the *Haut Comité*):

> French is by tradition a language of culture and international exchange. In recent decades this position has been degraded, as the language has become poorer and less clear.
>
> Increasingly obvious loss of richness of vocabulary, of syntactic complexity and finesse in grammar; an uncontrolled extension of specialist vocabularies, necessary in themselves but incomprehensible beyond a certain point outside their specialised domains, leading to a lack of reciprocal understanding; a parallel decline, even more accentuated, of the language widely spoken, towards a basic form of French: all these are indications of this process of degradation and impoverishment threatening the heart of our language.
>
> At a time when it is of pressing importance to defend national inheritance across the world, it is urgent that the French should restore its value to their own language, the first of these inheritances.
>
> Is it not by entering their language and by learning to use its subtleties that the French will be enabled to become the scientists, philosophers, technicians, businessmen, writers our country needs?
>
> Is it not also in this way that, by enriching their personality, they will be able to help the indispensable dialogue of cultures, and be positively open to everything which other languages convey of universal value?
>
> We hence call for action on behalf of the French language, action to maintain its richness and depth and to renew itself according to the laws which are its own.
>
> It is not only a question of fighting to maintain the language, but also to retain its vitality and capacity for invention.
>
> We hope that all modern means of communication will in their different ways assist in this.

We wish the teaching of French - of its vocabulary, its grammar, its literature of the past and present - to be restored to honour within education, from primary and throughout secondary education, and that its fundamental place be granted to it, accepting its absolute necessity.

Scientists and medical specialists have been active recently in the debate, and have been particularly concerned with the effect of the growing use of English. But in practical terms for the majority of practising scientists there is no choice: they publish in English or their career is slowed. Only in the social and human sciences, and in some limited scientific areas, such as certain branches of mathematics, is it still possible to publish on an international level in French. This has led to the widespread belief, spreading beyond the bounds of the scientific community, that English (and indeed Spanish) is a utilitarian language with no inherent value other than that of being able to communicate factual and material information; a modern version of Napoleon's condemnation of the English as a nation of shopkeepers, and a trap into which even President Mitterrand falls on occasion when he condemns a 'grey and uniform' universe, and associates this with the use of Anglo-American. Even professional linguists can be led a certain distance along this path (Hagège 1987, 12, condemning 'the uniformisation of cultures' as a 'danger for all languages').

11.2.5 Linguists

Apart from sociolinguists and others professionally concerned with such matters (see Marcellesi 1986), language specialists as such rarely enter the debate, with recent notable exceptions in Genouvrier (1986), Hagège (1987) and Walter (1988), reviewed below. Traditionally the view of language specialists has been that their task is to describe and explain, sometimes to predict, rarely to prescribe: they see their task as a part of the scientific endeavour, and discussions on language planning as too much the result of opinion rather than fact. As Hagège (1987, 11) puts it

the Francophone linguist...is neither a purist nor the watchdog of a culture. Do not expect speeches from him banishing borrowings from English, nor that he would take sides in the combat to promote French.

But Sauvageot (1978, 21), basing himself particularly on the experience of language planning in Norway, Finland and Hungary, shows how French developed from the usage of the élite in Gaul, was imposed from the top during its formative years of the Middle Ages and to the seventeenth century, by priests, by administrators, by the entourage of the King, by and through the written language and close comparison with Latin. He is sure that French today is the result of a continuous process of planning, and that 'French today needs a new set of rules similar to those of 1694' (the first edition of the Academy's dictionary) (1978, 181). His suggestions (pp 181-4) are that pronunciation distinctions should be clarified (eg the [a] of *patte* and that of *pâte*); that certain forms should be regularised and simplified, such as the plurals in *-aux*; that word usage should be planned, as for example in allowing the feminine forms of any word denoting a woman (eg *une otage, une professeur*), and that generally traditional words and expressions should be preferred to modern creations, so that one should write and say *croyable* rather than *crédible*, *illettré* rather than *analphabète*. Seeking clarity, economy and beauty, he notes that French is not necessarily the best of languages in any of these domains; 'let us nonetheless try to make it an efficient instrument, as beautiful as we can' (p 180).

Genouvrier (1986) reviews the diversity of French in France, examines the written language, and then discusses the problems of 'living in French': traversing the crisis, the vocation of the language, functions and culture, and teaching problems. His main concern is with the crisis of French in the educational field, but his conclusions on the general level are that the pessimists, basing themselves on a 'need for security joined with juvenile mythology', inculcated a belief in a glorious past when knowledge of the classics was joined to perfect command of spelling and grammar, and think that nowadays there is a widespread ignorance of French culture, a language used without care or precision, a language which is no longer universally used and respected throughout the world. He believes by contrast that these 'sour remarks' are quite wrong: education is in fact a great success; the proportion of errors, for example in spelling, is small, given the quantity of published material; illiteracy is rare, given the success of education; publicity and advertising may destroy the language but they merely reflect modern usage; education may be no longer classical and atomistic but it has other aims, in educating for success in domains other than literature and the arts (pp 161-3). Genouvrier sees two vocations for French: to act as the unifying factor within France, and as the link point for Francophone nations across the world; he also sees Europe as another area for French influence. In essence, after reviewing the evidence for the belief that French is being undermined by Anglo-American, he feels that there is no internal crisis of the French language which might form a threat in itself, in its lexis or in its structure. On the other hand the cultural crisis is evident (pp192-3).

Hagège (1987), another linguistics specialist, sees the vigour of French attacked on two fronts: 'the first, internal, is the language itself, attacked in its vocabulary and even its grammar by a flood of Americanisms capable of drowning it. The second, external, opposes English and French in unequal struggle for universal dissemination, previously realised to its own advantage by French which is now forced out by English.' (pp 9-10). Hagège examines, in considering these two aspects of the problem, the reality of the invasion of Americanisms, the causes for it and the ripost, before passing to a consideration of the possibilities for the year 2000: the diagnosis (French dominated, English dominating), French and market forces, ways and means for action, and finally the destiny of French.

Hagège points out (pp 239-52) in this last chapter certain of the realities facing French: language nationalism is not shared by all the French, and material well-being overcomes the symbolic values attached to languages, as the case of the disappearance of French in Louisiana demonstrates. Likewise, even if the symbolic values associated with French are important for the French of France, that is not the case for all Francophone countries, and it would be necessary to use a symbolic country, a *patrie francophone*, to act as the relevant unifying symbol. There could, it is true, be an international role for French as the third possibility between the Russian of the Soviet bloc and the American of the Coca-Cola culture; but one should remember that there are now already more Francophones outside France than within it, and that French is progressing there, despite the fact that French is still often the language of the elite and that local variation is strong. Hagège moves from the assessment of the realities of the situation towards suggestions and requirements: the need to promote French in those parts of the world where it is absent or disappearing (Latin America, non-Francophone Africa); to spend more on *Francophonie*, accepting the fact that most countries are poor; to be more confident of the value of contemporary French culture and creativity ('instead of digging in behind punctilious purism and thunderous defence of a prestigious past, we should be making our language the laboratory of new creations which will ensure it can discover a new prestige' (p 248)). Particular attention should be paid to the language industries.

Hagège notes that now many nations are conducting legal or even military battles to establish their linguistic rights: the Albanians of Kosovo, the Hungarians in Transylvania, the Turks in Bulgaria; the plurilingualism of India, the problems of Sri Lanka. The domination of Anglo-American is by no means a proven fact, and even in the USA the advance of Spanish and the future of the nation demand greater awareness of language diversity. If *Francophonie* is to be a powerful force it must be aware of diversification: 'today the truth is not that French is declining, but that English is advancing faster' (p 250). A privileged location for French would be Europe, where the use of French would underline the autonomy of the Community, as well as providing another basis, in addition to the Arab and the African, for the greater use of French. Hence the defence of French includes that of other languages: in the bicentenary year of the French Revolution, French as the language of liberty can act as a model of survival for the other languages of the world.

Walter (1988) represents a third point of view among professional linguists. She notes that the French regard their language as an 'unchanging institution, corseted in its traditions and practically untouchable' (p 18), instancing two examples in which Frenchmen interviewed or giving lectures use words (*taciturnité* and *cohabitateur*), excusing themselves for these perfectly comprehensible creations by asking whether they 'are French': that is, whether they already exist in the dictionary. The French have not merely 'a sharp sense of observation (identifying differences from traditionally accepted forms)' but also a 'more or less conscious refusal to accept the existence of diversity in the use of French' (p 19). Walter explains this phenomenon by proposing a duality: every Frenchman is aware of an 'ideal, perfect, rounded, pure and complete' French but uses, also, 'every day without fuss or bother, a multiple, changing, version, adapting it to circumstances and and familiar situations' (p 19). The myth of perfect French is maintained in grammars and dictionaries, and every user is aware of the duality.

Walter is optimistic for the future, despite warning that French must adapt or perish. She notes that the language reacts if innovations become too dangerous: *micro* in the sense of *micro-ordinateur* has not yet supplanted *micro* in the sense of *microphone*, and the use of Anglicisms such as *sponsoriser* and *nominer* is justified in the search for a precise nuance of meaning. Generally she does not take up positions in the debate, but is content to exemplify and observe developments.

11.2.6 Pressure groups

The *Commissariat Général de la Langue Française*, together with the *Secrétariat d'Etat auprès du Premier Ministre, chargé de la Francophonie*, produces an annual list of organisations, associations and groups working for the French language and for Francophony. The list contains 246 organisations, of which 15 are 'official'. The remaining 231 vary from large activities such as the *Alliance Française*, running French language schools throughout the world, to pressure groups in sensitive regions such as Belgium or Quebec. Fifteen of the Paris-based associations share the same two postal addresses, and at least ten have as their objects or as part of their objects 'the defence of the French language'; one, created in 1958, is simply called '*Défense de la Langue Française*'.

One such group, established in 1986, is the *Académie Francophone*, which publishes *Le Courrier Francophone*. An extract from the April 1988 issue (no 11), commenting on a European Community report on regional and minority languages, indicates the nature of the magazine and the strength of feeling involved:

> It is scandalous to learn that the 'European Communities' want to ressuscitate the various patois forgotten in Europe and particularly in France. While at the same time these same European Communities are doing everything to sabotage the French language in their institutions. Before the entry of England to the Common Market, French was the only working language, then one of the conditions of England's entry to the Common Market was that French should remain the working language in the European institutions. Alas, all the functionaries have adopted English as the working language. French is relegated to the forgotten corners, despite promises, and today the same people have dreamed up a 'Charter' for minority languages which have long been forgotten. With this new Charter, French will not survive long, because there will be an official language which will be English and different regional dialects. It will be the most abominable and cruel dictatorship: a global Anglo-Saxon. For them promises are scraps of paper: they come, they establish themselves and they impose themselves. Imposing their language, they impose their culture, their way of thinking, their identity and all the vices we don't need. We have quite enough with our own! Do I conclude that the European Communities want the destruction of French culture? It is time to be aware of the facts and to organise ourselves for our own survival   (p 10).

Most pressure groups and individuals such as Etiemble, whose series of books illustrating and attacking *'franglais'* have adopted a similar purist and defensive line, are equally forthright in their statements, summarised for example in Hagège 1987, 114-9. The military or medical vocabulary of 'struggle', 'defence', 'declarations of war', 'eliminate the virus', 'cure the disease', is typical of purist writing in this field, in which opinion and attitude is paramount, usually fierce, and normally associated strongly with firm views on the value of the French identity.

11.2.7 A language crisis?

In summary, French language attitudes represent a continuing theme of crisis and disaster: a language crisis has been identified since 1900 at least, and Gueunier (in Maurais 1985, 3) presents a striking list of the following titles which all repeat this notion:

> *La Crise du français* (G. Lanson 1909), *La Défense de la langue française* (A. Dauzat 1913), *Le Français langue morte* (A. Thérive 1923), *Le Péril de la langue française* (C. Vincent 1925), *Le Massacre de la langue française* (A. Mouflet 1930), *Au Secours de la langue française* (A. Mouflet 1948), *La Clinique du langage* (A. Thérive 1956), *Parlez-vous franglais?* (Etiemble 1964), *Le Jargon des sciences* (Etiemble 1966), *Les Linguicides* (O. Grandjouan 1971), *Hé! La France, ton français fout le camp* (J.Thévenot 1976), *Quand le français perd son latin* (J.Le Cornec 1981), *Les Avatars du français* (Tanguy Kenech'du 1984).

Gueunier examines the evidence for the existence of a crisis in language knowledge and expertise, covering research, evaluations carried out by and for the Ministry of Education, and information provided by and through associations, pamphlets and other publications. In summary she finds 'a general optimism in university research, countered by anxiety from the educational evaluators, and a large range of opinions among the journalists and other observers, from the deepest pessimism to a relaxed view' (Gueunier 1985, 31).

In university research she identifies a number of tendencies of the contemporary language: changes in pronunciation such as the decrease in liaison accompanied by increasing use of an emphatic accent; in spoken language, or in its analysis, the fact that division into sentences is no longer really appropriate, together with other tendencies such as increases in nominalisations, with verbal structures becoming of less importance, while increasing use of acronyms recalls the idea of a 'secret' language for the initiated. She notes that research plays down the number and the effect of Anglicisms, considering them to represent less than 2.5 per cent of the lexical stock, and finds in summary that research does not generally confirm the idea of degradation of the language.

In the school-based evaluations, Gueunier quotes surveys of 1979 and 1982 for the primary level, and finds that generally results are poor: for example if the agreement *vous voyez* is correct in 86%, *il les utilise* is so only for 45%, and only 10% of children at this age spell *les cerises rouges* or *une jolie robe* correctly. At secondary level, '10 pupils out of 24 on average do not achieve the normal level of the middle course and four can be called illiterate'; while the Prost report of 1982 noted that 'the quality of written expression of *lycéens* is below that of their predecessors'.

Qualitative assessments of language knowledge that she reviews are based on the number and type of comments in language columns of the Press, in pamphlets, and in the published remarks of associations and others. In pronunciation, negative comments centre on the non-pronunciation of mute /e/ and on excessive use of liaison and double consonants; in morphology, on the regularisation of irregular verbs (*acquérir, fuir*) and the wide use of *on* to replace other pronouns; in syntax, on dislocation (*une guerre, ça se raconte pas*), on inversion (*je me demande à quoi penses-tu*), on the adverbial uses of adjectives (*voter socialiste*), and on the formation of expressions by juxtaposition (*un coffret métal, une opération sourire*), while in lexis Gueunier notes that comments centre on Anglicisms but also occasionally on excessive latinisation, particularly in the preference for complex rather than simple verbs (*comporter, constituer* for *être, procéder à* for *faire*), and on the use of acronyms.

Gueunier concludes by feeling that 'it would be imprudent to consider the crisis more apparent than real in the sense that it seems to us to be evidence of a lack of confidence, both in respect of the possibilities of the instrument and of any attempt to control it' (Gueunier 1985, 32).

Three components of the cultural and social environment in which the crisis is described seem to recur: firstly the notion that attacks on French come from outside the country, in borrowings in language and culture, in science and technology, and in life-style, bringing with them substantial changes in language itself. Secondly, social changes inside the country, ranging from the widespread 'democratisation' of education to the use of 'vulgar' language, the language of younger generations, and increased immigration have their effect. And finally the language insecurity, associated with cultural insecurity, of a nation which is still shocked at finding its world role no longer taken for granted and which is concerned about the effects on its hard-won territorial and cultural identity of fragmentation both inside and outside the country, has inevitable consequences. This last factor finds expression in opposition to regional languages and dialects as much as in metropolitan dislike of non-standard uses by native speakers from Africa and the Caribbean.

These three components have led to a complex of language attitudes traditionally placing high value on the prestige form, now itself widespread throughout the country and in all social levels; placing high value on the written form and on details of spelling and accuracy; and placing high value on cultural identity. Above all, this traditional attitude was based on stability and on the never-changing perfection of a complete and rounded means of expression.

If one attempts to correlate language attitudes with the social attitudes outlined in Mermet 1987 (398) as characteristic of the French (see Section 7.2 above), it is clear that the majority of the French can be expected still to support this point of view: Mermet's 'materialists' (26.8% of the population in 1987), 'egocentrics' (22.5%), and 'rigorists' (20.1%) clearly outnumber the 'laid-back '(17.3%) and the 'activists' (13.3%).

There are nonetheless changes. The French are becoming more adaptable, as noted already, in their awareness of and readiness to use the prestige form but also more practical everyday forms: the repertoire of forms available to all is widening. And the adoption of aspects of American culture, of 'modernisation', has made France an importer of culture rather than an exporter; has changed the expectation that the role of France in the world is to be a focus of radiation and dissemination (*rayonnement*), with a civilising mission, to a new awareness, even though this is often combined with resentment, that others are now acting as a source of sought-after goods and cultural priorities. The crisis, if crisis there be, is one of attitudes towards cultural identity rather than towards language alone.

11.3 The norm

ANY objective description of French is of necessity an abstraction, divorced from any actual use. *Langue*, the system, and even systematised usage (*langage*), can be identified and exemplified in its main outlines in its written form in textbooks, whether for native speakers or for foreigners, in grammars (Grévisse, latest edition) and in dictionaries (ranging from the larger *Robert* to the annual *Petit Larousse Illustré*), and in its spoken form by a description of the usage of a notional individual resembling a 'French person from Paris or the Centre, cultured, possessing easy and fluent speech' (Genouvrier 1986, 62). Walter (1987, 225-78) similarly describes the 'hard centre' of the language in terms of its pronunciation, words and meanings.

It is an axiom of sociolinguistics however that no language is monolithic, and that language varies according to the circumstances of its use: different norms will exist for different purposes: a norm for scientific language, a norm for Lyon and a different one for Marseille, a range of norms for specific interaction settings, a norm for 1900 and a different one for 1990. If we are to continue with the concept of a single 'objective' norm, this must therefore be defined in socio-cultural terms as the form of the language which is accepted by the majority of the population as applicable to many such settings, or a form which 'does not attract attention and deflect it from the comprehension of what is said' (Martinet and Walter, quoted in Genouvrier 1986, 62). This 'average' form of the language is unexceptionable, and often called the descriptive norm, to distinguish it from the quite different notion of the prescriptive norm, the socio-culturally prestigious form, which can be erected into a national possession and hence defended against external aggression with as much passion as any other piece of property.

Genouvrier (pp 49-71), reporting surveys of language attitudes in different regions, shows that language insecurity, measured by the feeling that one has an 'accent' and deploring the fact, is higher in regions such as Lille, Limoges and Réunion than in Tours. Similarly, 'doctors, bosses, lawyers, teachers, and radio announcers' are felt, particularly by those in 'lower' social classes, to speak better. The feeling that good French is an 'inheritance' (*patrimoine*), is widespread, and 'maximal standard spoken French' as used in semi-formal situations such as radio news broadcasts can be said to represent this possession, and will be defended by 'recourse to the Academy and to morals' if any questions are posed on it or attacks made on it.

Since the concept of norm depends on subjective evaluation, according to how and for what purpose the norm is being identified, there has to be a prescriptive norm for education, although there may well be a descriptive one for translation and the language industries, where some degree of variation is permitted. An explicit norm exists in dictionaries and an implicit one can be derived from the actual usage of individuals; a prestige norm is identified as the defensible possession of the nation, a (range of) social norm(s) can be defined according to the social group involved and an individual norm, or expected manner of speaking of any one individual, can also be described.

Similar discussion and definitions of the concept of the norm are extensively reviewed in Bédard and Maurais (1983), in which chapters concerned with French deal with the process of normalisation, with the language of the State, with dictionaries and the norm, with the norm as seen by Press columnists, differences between the norm and overseas variants, and with the attitudes of the French (as reported in Genouvrier 1986 above). It is generally accepted that French language attitudes support the prescriptive norm, 'the strong position held by the notion of "bon usage" in French linguistic consciousness, a position which has never seriously been in question' (Wolf 1983a, 133), and that the prescriptive norm is necessarily socially defined - the language of the socially prestigious group - and defined in time - the language of the past.

A rather different point of view is expressed in Marcellesi, 1986, where the concept that users of French identify the norm 'under the dictat of an ideology which they do not control' (p 27), leads to the idea that it is the task of sociolinguists to ensure that language users are enabled to conduct their own language planning (*autogestion langagière*), in the same way and to the same extent that they should be encouraged to conduct economic planning (*autogestion économique*), for example in defining communication patterns within certain work environments such as science or medecine (Marcellesi 1986, 28). Two further examples are given later in the volume (p 127) - Brussels and the situation in Occitan, where bilingualism would form a 'less frustrating' solution than the Belgian language laws or the contrast between social militants arguing for a revival of Occitan and the general feeling arising from empirical surveys that the language has disappeared. '*Glottopolitique*' is hence defined, in opposition to language planning or centrally directed language policies, as a liberating social process.

11.4 Contemporary language legislation

11.4.1 General language laws

It is officially stated that French linguistic legislation consists of three laws or groups of laws: the Edict of Villers-Cotterets of 1539, preceded by an Edict of Louis XII in 1510 and confirmed in January 1563; the legislation of the Revolution; and the law of 1975 as modified in 1977 and 1982, and completed by a range of decrees and arrêtés on matters of detail (Fichet in *L'Avenir de la langue française*, 1985).

The most recent legislation affects three areas: the use of French in commerce; the establishment of terms in science and technology; and the use of French in education. Law 75-1349 of 31 december 1975 forms the basic text for controlling the use of French in commerce:

> Article 1
>
> In the naming, offer for sale, presentation, written or spoken advertising, instructions for use, extent and conditions of a guarantee of goods and services, as well as in invoices, bills and receipts, the use of the French language is obligatory. Recourse to any foreign term or any foreign expression is prohibited when there exists an expression or term approved under the conditions of the decree...concerning the enrichment of the French language. The French text may be completed by one or more translations in a foreign language.

The same rules apply to all information or programme presentations on radio and television, except when these are specifically intended for a foreign public.

> Article 4
>
> ...the employment contract in its written form, and which is valid in French territory must be drawn up in French. It may not contain any term or expression in a foreign language...
>
> Article 6
>
> Any inscription placed by persons using, on whatever basis, a property belonging to a public authority...must be drawn up in French. The French text may be accompanied by one or more translations...
>
> Article 8
>
> Whatever its object and form, contracts made between a public authority or establishment and any person must be drawn up in

French...Contracts made between a French authority and a foreign public or private contracting body may be accompanied by a foreign language text which shall have the same legal authority as the French text.

The parliamentary debate leading up to the passing of this law was both poorly attended and notable for anti-American and nationalist attitudes. The law itself was much modified in the debates and in committee, and took nearly three years from the deposit of the original proposal in 1973 to its final acceptance. The law itself was modified in 1977 by a prime ministerial circular which placed responsibility for production of the French version of text accompanying imports on the importer, rather than on the manufacturer; the EEC Commission obliged the Prime Minister in 1982 to modify the interpretation of the law again in view of European legislation on competition; in 1983, and in subsequent court cases in 1984, the situation was clarified (!) and responsibility, for example for translations, placed on the final stage of commercialisation of goods from other EEC members, except in the case of fruit and vegetables, which are freed of restrictions other than safety labels. Nonetheless the Customs service brought 266 'language' cases in 1982, with 47 found guilty; 251 in 1983, with 174 guilty; and 187 cases in 1984 , although the fines imposed were generally derisory (Herbin in *L'Avenir de la langue française*, 1985, 135-43).

There was much discussion in 1982 and sporadically since about the possibility of reformulating and strengthening this law, and a proposal to this effect was eventually made in the name of the Socialist Député Georges Sarre (*Proposition de Loi* no. 2451, 15.11.1984). Press opposition was widespread and the proposal was not pursued at the time.

11.4.2 *Terminology* arrêtés

In addition to the 1975 law, various decisions on terminology have been passed since 1966, when the *Haut Comité de la Langue Française* (replaced in 1983 by the *Commissariat Général de la Langue Française*) was set up by de Gaulle and itself coordinated the work of terminology commissions in each Ministry. The decrees have the force of law, and are published in the Official Journal: the terms they prescribe must be used in all official documents and in all documents produced by those contracting with the state.

An example is the *arrêté* of 24.1.1984 on 'audio-visual' vocabulary, which provides French terms for English or other words in two appendices, one giving definitions and the other merely listing terms to use and those which are proscribed. A selection from the second appendix follows:

Term to avoid	Term recommended
advanced lay-out	*maquette*
artwork	*document*
big close up	*très gros plan (TGP)*
booster	*suramplificateur*
brain-storming	*remue-méninges*
cameraman	*cadreur*
compact disc	*disque audionumérique, mini-disque*
design	*stylique*
flash-back	*retour en arrière*
mailing	*publipostage*
nominé	*sélectionné*
package	*achat groupé*
rough	*esquisse*
script	*scripte*
sponsor	*commanditaire*
sponsor (to)	*parrainer*
videoclip	*bande vidéo, bande promotionelle*
walkman	*baladeur*

Hagège (1987, 127-9) notes that some at least of these recommended terms have now been generally accepted, for example *cadreur* and *baladeur*. Others such as *remue-méninges* have not so far been successful. Walter (1988, 284) is even more dismissive: 'users continue to talk of *tuner, clips* and *disques compacts*'.

11.4.3 Ministerial control in education
In education, the Ministry exercises indirect linguistic control by approving texts and manuals used in schools, by publishing *Programmes* of detailed syllabus guidelines which teachers must follow, together with guidance on methodology which is often detailed, and by evaluating the work of individual teachers through the inspectorate. In addition the Ministry published, in 1901 and 1976, *Tolérances* which identify linguistic items to be marked correct or incorrect in public examinations.

The 1976 *Tolérances* covered thirty-three points which were not to be counted as errors (*fautes*) in public examinations, and some of them, for example the expletive *ne*, had already been covered in 1901. The first group concerned matters of agreement, permitting the use of the verb either in the singular or in the plural after expressions such as *une bande de moineaux* or *un de ces hommes,* or with the presentative *c'est/ce sont* - ie *c'est de beaux résultats* was accepted along with *ce sont de beaux résultats.* The 'modern' usage of the present subjunctive after a past tense in the main clause was accepted - *j'avais souhaité qu'il vienne;* and the agreement of the past participle was relaxed - *les musiciens que j'ai entendu/s jouer.* With nouns, the second group, points included the use of singular or plural with expressions like *ils ont ôté leur/s chapeau/x;* and the use of masculine or feminine pronouns after expressions like *madame le professeur...il/elle va nous quitter.* Similar points of detail were relaxed: *elle a l'air doux/douce; l'un et l'autre document m'a/m'ont paru intéressant/s;* the expletive *ne* was regarded as unnecessary (*je crains qu'il (ne) pleuve*); and fine points of spelling were also relaxed, permitting *arc-en-ciel* or *arc en ciel, dit-on* or *dit on.* The concluding paragraph of the *arrêté* enjoined correctors not to penalise 'subtle grammatical particularities'.

Indirect official control, for example in examinations and professional certification, is exercised through the widespread use of competitive examinations for entry to the public service. These examinations, whose structure and content is laid down by ministerial decision, also control entry to non public service posts such as teachers of fencing.

11.5 Contemporary official language policy

11.5.1 1981-1986

The main lines of French governmental policy remain those outlined in the debates around the law of 1975, modified by presidential, prime ministerial and ministerial statements since. The three major axes of this policy are the promotion of French across the world, the establishment of a satisfactory relationship between French and other languages within France, and defence of the position of French within Europe, all aspects of these policies being supported by technical work, particularly in the area of new technologies. M. Stélio Farandjis, at the time Secretary General of the *Haut Comité*, presented the detail of the policy in 1983 in eleven points in a document produced by the *Haut Comité* for general distribution.

1. Illustrate the vitality of French
2. Favour the enrichment of French
3. Improve the teaching of French
4. Harmonise the policy for French and that of a general language policy by mastery of new technologies in communication
5. Arouse a new social dynamic of French
6. Improve French linguistic legislation
7. Ensure the quality, modernity, accessibility of administrative and legal language
8. Develop French as a commercial language
9. Relate a policy for French to a general intercultural policy
10. Support a wider dissemination of French abroad
11. Build a living Francophone community.

St Robert, then *Commissaire de la Langue Française*, expressed the policy thus in a speech to the *Académie des Sciences d'Outre-Mer* on 12th April 1985:

1. Respect, in France as elsewhere in the world, for all world languages
2. Defence of French in France
3. Specific research to establish the numbers of speakers of French in the world, its dispersion through the world, identify its ethnic, religious and economic varieties
4. Encouragement of French as an international scientific language in all scientific areas
5. Encouragement of the exchange of cultural goods throughout the French-speaking area: books, films, discs.

11.5.2 The Chirac government

The Chirac government (1986-88) placed some degree of disarray into the situation, by the creation of a Ministry for *Francophonie* which developed additional policy lines. During the period in office of the Chirac government Mme Lucette Michaux-Chevry, elected from Guadeloupe and named Minister for *Francophonie*, eventually obtained control, and the budget, of the *Commissariat Général de la Langue Française*, provoking the resignation of Philippe de St-Robert and his replacement as *Commissaire Général de la Langue Française* by Bernard Billaud, an aide of M. Chirac in the Paris local government (*Le Monde* 7.3.87). *Libération* (5.3.1987) provided some asides on the degree of disagreement between Mme

Michaux-Chevry and M. de St Robert, indicating that the Minister's interference, for example in determining subsidies and priorities, had made the *Commissaire*'s role impossible.

11.5.3 The Rocard government

M Alain Decaux, historian and television personality, was appointed as Minister for *Francophonie* and for International Cultural Relations in the Rocard government of 1988, assisted by M Thierry de Beaucé as *Secrétaire d'Etat*. His priorities were to publicise the notion of *Francophonie*, particularly in France, to build on the success of the practical decisions taken at the Quebec meeting of Heads of State, and to underline the consensual nature of the movement (Pécheur 1988b). He noted that the topic of *Francophonie* was a common problem for several ministries, and that his task, particularly in preparing for the Dakar summit of May 1989, would include coordination. In terms of particular initiatives, Decaux mentioned publicity actions such as the entertainment *Francofolies* held at La Rochelle; and insisting on the use of French at scientific congresses. He saw no contrast between priorities for Europe and for *Francophonie*: for France, 'both options are complementary', the use of French allowing Francophone countries access to Europe. He saw that the future of French 'is linked to the willingness of Europeans to make Europe multilingual and multicultural...and hence the necessity of immediate steps to ensure that schoolchildren learn two foreign languages, and that all European countries follow the same policy...'

The seriousness of the *Francophonie* concept and its relationship to major matters of State and foreign policy were greatly reinforced in August 1989 when Decaux was sent to the Lebanon as the responsible Minister to negotiate possible cease-fires and to present the French position in the conflict there.

11.6 Language control and support mechanisms

THE *Académie Française* was founded in 1635 and celebrated its 350th anniversary in 1985. Made up of thirty 'immortals', its language work continues in comments on the dictionary (the first part of the ninth edition appeared in 1986) and on contemporary usage, but this work is very slow and the *Academie*'s comments on usage are generally met with the respect due to aged notables who are somewhat out of touch with the realities of the world.

The *Haut Comité de la Langue Française* was created by de Gaulle in 1966 at the same time as a *Conseil International de la Langue Française,* which continues today, in order to carry out detailed work on language-related questions and to further the Francophone cause. The *Haut Comité* was replaced in 1983 by three organisations, officially created in 1984: the *Commissariat Général de la Langue Française,* presided by the Prime Minister but whose Commissar was Philippe de St-Robert, replaced by Bernard Billaud in 1987, and renamed the *Délégation Générale de la Langue Française* in 1989; a *Haut Conseil de la Francophonie,* presided over by the President and whose Secretary Général is Stélio Farandjis, with the particular task of preparing the Francophone summits and intermediate meetings; and a *Comité Consultatif de la Langue Française,* whose original Vice-President was Roger Fajardie and which was reorganised by the Chirac government in March 1987, to be renamed the *Haut Conseil de la Langue Française* in 1989. The tasks of the Haut Conseil are advisory. The technical work, particularly in terminology, is carried out by the *Délégation* but more and more by independent organisations like *CIREEL* (see below), particularly after the collapse of the ambitious programme for a communications-based development at Défense.

In addition to these formal governmental organisations there exist a number of groups and pressure groups, noted above, of which one, the *Association Générale des Usagers de la Langue Française (AGULF),* has been involved with legal actions under the 1975 law. The list of Francophone organisations lists 246 organisations in total, and many of them receive subsidies through the *Commissariat Général de la Langue Française* or otherwise have official or semi-official status. Of the total, a small number are concerned more directly with technical matters, including two official organisations dealing with education:

The *Bureau pour l'Enseignement de la Langue et de la Civilisation Françaises à l'Etranger (BELC),* deals with educational research concerning *FLE* (*Français langue étrangère,* French as a foreign language), the preparation of relevant materials and the training of teachers of French

The *Centre de Recherche et d'Etude pour la Diffusion du Français (CREDIF),* attached to the *Ecole Normale Supérieure de Saint*

Cloud, deals with research on the teaching and learning of French, with linguistics and sociolinguistics, and with the training of teachers.

Other organisations are less official, but provide specific services in education and the language industries:

The *Alliance Française* provides teaching in French for adults outside formal educational structures.

The *Association des universités partiellement ou entièrement de langue française (AUPELF)* supports international cooperation in universities, reflecting on the role of research and universities, and supporting the dialogue of cultures.

The *Centre d'information et de recherche pour l'enseignement et l'emploi des langues (CIREEL)* provides an information service on language teaching and use, supports research on the same topics, and organises *Expolangues* annually.

There are more than 150 organisations, groups and associations known to the Commissariat and which deal with different aspects of French and its world role. The general impression created by this plethora of language and culture-related organisations and groups is of disorganised fragmentation, with ministerial subventions from different Ministries provided without an overall plan or policy, despite the rationalisation of 1984, and many organisations dependent on the charisma of an individual, grouping very few active and dedicated members (de Broglie 1986, 225-30). But public realisation of the stakes is growing, and the technical work is proceeding, with potential both for *Francophonie* in general, for the role of French abroad, and for a coherent internal language policy to replace that carried out by and through the *Académie* for 350 years.

Further reading

Ager, D. E. 1987. La politique linguistique de la France contemporaine. *ACTIF 1987*: 31-40

Balibar, R. and Laporte, D. 1976. *Le français national.*

Ball, R. 1988. Language insecurity and state language policy: the case of France. *Quinquereme*, 11, 1: 95-105

Bedard, E. and Maurais, J. 1983. *La Norme linguistique.*

Broglie, G. de. 1986. *Le Français, pour qu'il vive.*

Brunot, F. 1966-1972. *Histoire de la langue française des origines à 1900.* 13 vols (original editions 1905-53)

Calvet, L.-J. 1987. *La Guerre de langues et les politiques linguistiques.*

Certeau, M. de., Julia, D., Revel, J. 1975. *Une Politique de la langue: la Révolution Française et les patois.*

Genouvrier ,E. 1986. *Naître en français.*

Gordon, D. C. 1978. *The French Language and National Identity.*

Grau, R. 1985. *Les Langues et les cultures minoritaires en France.*

Grillo, R. D. 1989. *Dominant Languages*.

Hagège, C. 1987. *Le français et les siècles*.

Marcellesi, J.-B. 1986. Glottopolitique. *Langages* , 83 septembre 1986.

Maurais, J. (ed). 1983. *La Norme Linguistique*.

Maurais, J. (ed). *La Crise des langues*.

Muller, B. 1985. *Le Français d'aujourd'hui*.

Rickard, P. 1989. *A History of the French Language*.

Sauvageot , A. 1978. *Français d'hier ou français de demain?*

St-Robert , P. de. 1986. *Lettre ouverte à ceux qui en perdent leur français*.

Walter, H. 1988. *Le français dans tous les sens*.

1982. *Rencontre internationale sur l'application des législations linguistiques dans les pays francophones*.

1985. Langue française: enrichissement du vocabulaire: textes législatifs et règlementaires. *Journal Officiel de la République Française* Brochure 1468

1985. *L'Avenir de la langue française - 2e rencontre internationale sur l'application des législations linguistiques dans les pays francophones*.

Index

Académie Française, 9, 15, 219, 247
accent, 2, 26
address forms, 209ff
administrative forms, 174-5
advertising, 189-91

affective ties, 6, 7, 27
Albigensian Crusade, 37, 38
Algeria, 89-90, 154-8
allophone, 3
Alsace, 25, 29, 50-9, 220; regional
    French, 25
années creuses, 114
Aosta, 87
Arabic, 11, 89-91
argot, 160-2
Armenians, 152-3
Atlas linguistique, 28
attitudes to language,
    see language attitudes

Basque, 19, 29, 60-3
Belgium, 87-8
Bernstein, 140
bilingualism, 7, 72, 147, 153, 157
birth-rate, 114
Boileau, 15
borderlands, 84
borrowing, 7, 92
boundaries, 7, 27
Bourdieu, 141, 221
Brittany, 19, 25, 29, 64-73; regional
    French, 25

Cambodia, 16
Cameroon, 92
Canada, 97-104

Catalan, 19, 29, 73-5
case-study approach, 185
Celtic, 10, 72
centralisation, 30, 65, 218-21
channel, 166
child language, 114-17
Chomsky, 1
coalescence, 8
code-switching,
    see language-switching
codification, 9, 10, 74
coherence, 198
cohesion, 198
colonialism, 31, 42, 84, 89
commerce, 182-93
communication situation, 4, 165ff, 195-7
communicative events, 196;
    styles, 33, 121, 139ff
community, 5ff
Comores, 94
competence, 1
conceptual systems, 32
conflict, 30ff, 42-3
context, 166
conversation analysis, 195, 203-7;
core-periphery, 31
Corsica, 29, 75-9
creole, 83, 93, 94, 96, 110
criminals, 159
culture, 196

deficit hypothesis, 117, 140
Deixonne Law, 55, 71, 74, 78
denigration, 9, 32, 123; see also *langue
    minorisée*
dialectology, 26-8
dialects, 2, 18-22, 26, 44,
    54, 69, 77, 80;

fragmentation, 27, 39, 41, 44, 47, 151
difference hypothesis, 140
diglossia, 8, 45, 46, 72, 75, 78, 87, 94, 151
discourse, 33
discourse analysis, 33, 168, 195
dislocation, 212
dissertation française, 198
Dominica, 93
dominance, 9, 30-3, 41, 109
DOM-TOM, 84, 93
Dutch, *see* Flemish
dyadic interaction, 201-7

education, 14, 45, 47, 55, 63, 71, 90, 94, 117, 135, 151, 168, 176, 183ff, 198, 220, 243ff
elaborated code, 140
élite, 68, 108, 135
emigration, 84
English, 14, 180-2, 185, 231, 243
ethnography of communication, 5, 196
expansion, 84
expectancy pairs, 207
exposé, 198

Félibrige, 39-41
féminisation des titres, 120
feminism, 124
field, 213
Flemish, 9, 25, 29, 79-81, 87; regional French 25
formality, 175, 200, 208-210
francien, 12, 18, 22
francophonie, 5, 10, 82-112, 181, 223, 232, 245
Franco-Provençal, 11, 18
French language: developments in, 236; intrinsic qualities of, 106; Middle French, 12; Old French, 12; quality of, 116, 237; regional, 19, 22-26, 46; standard, 9, 18, 33, 88, 94, 139, 178
functional linguistics, 165

Gallo-Roman, 11
gender, 46, 118-25
generation gap, 45, 57, 113-18, 132, 157
German, 19, 25, 29, 50-9, 88
gestures, 202
Giordan report, 34, 144

Gothic, 11
Grandes Ecoles, 130, 135, 176, 184-6
grapheme, 211
Grégoire report, 15, 38, 220
Grenada, 93
group
    ethnic, 6, 158; interaction, 191, 198; primary, 2, 135, 163; reference, 130; secondary, 2, 163; task, 163
groupes d'expression directe, 168
Guadeloupe, 83, 93, 109
gypsies, 148-52

habitus, 141
Haiti, 93
Hebrew, 146

identity, 30, 32, 196, 236, 238
idiolect, 2
immigrants, 154-9
Indochina, 95
information, 197
Institut d'Etudes Occitanes, 40, 44, 48
intellectual, 139, 200, 227ff
interlanguage, 115
isogloss, 27, 28
Italian, 13, 77, 87

javanais, 161
Jews, 144-8
Judaeo-Spanish, 148

language, 26; attitudes, 2, 6, 13-16, 30ff, 84, 88, 90, 104ff, 123, 140, 222ff, 239; community, 5ff; contact, 7; continuum, 4, 26; insecurity, 22, 87, 238; legitimate, 141, 207; levels, 4, 215ff; loss, 8; maintenance, 7, 63, 75; mixing, 7; official, 84; planning, 9, 15, 30, 100ff, 120, 218-48; repertoire, 4, 6; shift, 8, 87; specialised (for specific purposes), 166; switching, 8, 56; vehicular/vernacular, 84, 91
langue, 1; *d'oc,* 12; *d'oïl,* 12, 19, 29; *minorisée,* 9, 33, 110, 151, 153, 157ff
Laos, 96
largonji, 161
Larzac, 38
Latin, 13, 27
Lebanon, 88

legal language, 168-75
liaison, 3, 208
linguistic
   capital, 141; distinctiveness, 141;
   market-place, 48, 141; variables,
   3, 122, 136-40
Lorrain, 20
loucherbem, 161
Louisiana, 96
Luxembourg, 86

Madagascar, 94
Maghreb, 83, 89-91, 152, 158, 208
Malherbe, 15, 219
Martinique, 93
Mauritius, 94
Mayotte, 94
message, 166
Mistral, 39
Mitterrand, 34, 62, 67, 152
mode, 213
monolingualism, 9
monologue, 198ff
Morocco, 89, 91, 109

nation, 6
negotiation, 201
neologisms, 161
network, social, 194
New Caledonia, 94, 95
norm, 107, 142, 238-40
Normandy, 21, 24

Occitan, 18ff, 25, 29, 37-49; regional
   French, 25

parole, 1
particularisme alsacien, 51
patois, 26
performance, 1, 216
phoneme, 3
phonetics, 3
Picard, 18, 21
pidgin, 83
Poles, 154
Polynesia, 94, 95
power roles, 31, 95, 124, 127, 191, 209
professional culture, 164
provençal, 12, 27, 39, 44

Quebec, 97, 99-104, 106

receiver, 166
redoubling, 161
regionalism, 30-5
registers, 213ff
restricted code, 140
Réunion, 94
Revolution, 13ff, 30, 50, 65, 76, 82, 145,
   218, 220, 241
ritualised exchange, 207
Rivarol, 15

Saint-Vincent, 93
Santa Lucia, 93
Saussure, 1
Scandinavian languages, 11
science and technology, 175-82
secret language, 160
sender, 166
Senegal, 91
sexism, 118, 119, 123-5
Seychelles, 94
slang, 117, 160
social
   attitudes (Life Styles), 123, 127, 134,
   238; categories, 4, 128ff; class
   practices, 134; class language usage,
   135ff; equilibrium, 127; mobility, 72,
   131-3; networks, 4, 194; outcasts,
   159ff; processes, 3, 126; roles 208;
   strata, 126; systems, 126; variables, 2
sociolect, 2
speech community, 5ff
State, 6, 30
symbol, 6, 30, 164
Syria, 88
Switzerland, 86

telegram, 187
telephone interaction, 205
telex, 188
tenor, 213
terminology, 168, 176, 182, 242
text, 1; types, 170-1, 179ff, 189
Tobago, 93
Trinity, 93
Tunisia, 89-91
turn-taking, 206

USA, 96
utterance, 1

Vanuatu, 94
variables, 3, 122; *see* language
   and social
variant, 3
Vaugelas, 15, 219
verlan, 117, 161
Vietnam, 96
Villars-Cotterets, 9, 13, 14, 38,
   218, 241

Walloon, 20, 24
written-spoken differences, 210ff

Yiddish, 148
youth culture, 117, 158

Bibliography

Aebischer, V. 1985. *Les Femmes et le langage*. Paris: Presses Universitaires de France
Ager, D. E. 1972. *Teaching Linguistic Register in French*. Unpublished PhD thesis. Salford: University of Salford
Ager, D. E. 1987a. *French Written Language 2, Course Manual* (unpublished). Birmingham: Aston University
Ager, D. E. 1987b. La Politique Linguistique de la France Contemporaine. *ACTIF, 1987*: 31- 40
Ager, D. E. 1989. La Francophonie. *ACTIF, 1989*: 19-33
Ager, D. E. 1990. La Francophonie: quels progrès? *ACTIF, 1990*: 64-72
Ager, D. E., and French, R. (eds). 1986. *La Francophonie*. Portsmouth: Association for French Language Studies
Allison, R., and Bradshaw, M. 1989. *The Concept of French Canada in a Geographical Context*. Plymouth: College of St. Mark and St. John
André-Larochebouvy, D. 1984. *La Conversation quotidienne*. Paris: Didier
Ardagh, J. 1982. *France in the 1980s*. London: Penguin
Argyle, M. 1972. *The Psychology of Interpersonal Behaviour*. London: Penguin (2nd edn)
Association pour Débattre Autrement (ADA), 1986. *Bilan de la France 1986*. Paris: La Table Ronde
Baetens Beardsmore, H. 1971. *Le Français régional de Bruxelles*. Brussels: Presses Universitaires de Bruxelles
Baetens Beardsmore, H. 1980. Bilingualism in Belgium. *Journal of Multilingual and Multicultural Development*, 1: 145-54
Bakhtine, M. 1977. *Le Marxisme et la philosophie du language*. Paris: Minuit
Balibar, R., and Laporte, D. 1974. *Le Français national*. Paris: Hachette
Ball, R. 1988. Language insecurity and state language policy: the case of France. *Quinquereme*, 11, 1: 95-105
Bastadas-Boada, A. 1985. La crise de la langue standard dans la zone catalane. In J Maurais (ed), *La Crise des langues*. Paris: Le Robert. 365-70
Bauche, H. 1920. *Le Français populaire*. Paris: Payot
Beauvais, R. 1970. *L'Hexagonal tel qu'on le parle*. Paris: Hachette
Bebel-Gisler, C. 1981. *La Langue créole, force jugulée*. Paris: Nouvelle Optique-L'Harmattan
Bec, P. 1967. *La Langue occitane*. Paris: Presses Universitaires de France
Bédard, E., and Maurais, J. 1983. *La Norme linguistique*. Paris/Québec: Le Robert
Beedham, C. 1981. *The Language of Management Case-Sudies*. Unpublished. Language Studies Unit. Birmingham: Aston University
Bentahila, A. 1983. *Language Attitudes among Arabic-French Bilinguals in Morocco*. Clevedon: Multilingual Matters
Bernstein, B. 1971. *Class Codes and Control*. London: Routledge and Kegan Paul
Betbeder, M.-C. 1985. Jeunes portugais: les vertus d'une double culture. *Le Monde de l'Education*, janvier 1985: 10-13

Biétry, M. 1985. Corse: le ciment de l'insularité. *Le Figaro*, 24.8.1985: 8

Blakemore, D. 1988. The organization of discourse. In F. Newmeyer (ed), *Linguistics: The Cambridge Survey*. Vol 4. Cambridge: Cambridge University Press. 229-50

Blanche-Benveniste, C. 1987. *Le Français parlé: transcription et édition*. Paris: Didier

Bloch-Lainé, F. 1982. *Bilan de la France 1981*. Paris: La Documentation Française

Bourcier, D. 1979. Le discours juridique: analyses et méthodes. *Langages*, 53, mars 1979: 5-32

Bourdieu, P. 1982. *Ce que parler veut dire*. Paris: Fayard

Bourhis, Y. 1982. Language policies and language attitudes: le monde de la francophonie. In E. B. Ryan and H. Giles (eds), *Attitudes towards Linguistic Variation*. London: Edward Arnold 34-62

Bourhis, Y. 1984. *Language Conflict and Language Planning in Quebec*. Clevedon: Multilingual Matters

Boursin, J.-L. (ed). 1981. *Le Livre scientifique et technique de langue française*. Paris: Imprimerie Nationale

Bouthillier, G., and Meynaud, J. 1972. *Le Choc des langues au Québec*. Quebec: Presses de l'Université de Québec

Broglie, G. de. 1986. *Le Français, pour qu'il vive*. Paris: Gallimard

Brown, R., and Gilman, A. 1960. The pronouns of power and solidarity. In T. Sebeok (ed), *Style in Language*. Cambridge, Massachusetts. MIT Press. 253-76

Brun, A. 1923. *Essai historique sur l'introduction du français dans les provinces du midi de la France*. Paris: Champion and Geneva: Slatkine reprints (1973)

Brunet, M. 1979. *Canadians et Canadiens*. Montreal: Fides

Brunot, F. 1966-72. *Histoire de la langue française des origines à 1900*. Paris: Armand Colin. 13 vols (original editions 1905-53)

Calvet, L.-J. 1974. *Linguistique et colonialisme*. Paris: Payot

Calvet, L.-J. 1987. La Guerre des langues et les politiques linguistiques. Paris: Payot

Carton, F., Rossi, M., Autesserre, D., and Léon, P. 1983. *Les Accents des Français*. Paris: Hachette

Cellard, J. 1984. Comment ils parlent. *Le Monde*, 17.8.84

Certeau, M. de, Julia, D., and Revel, J., 1975. *Une Politique de la langue: la Révolution Française et les patois*. Paris: Albin Michel

Chambers, J. K., and Trudgill, P. 1980. *Dialectology*. Cambridge: Cambridge University Press

Chambrun, N. de, and Reinhardt, A. S.-M. 1981. *Le Français chassé des sciences*. Paris: Centre d'Information et de Recherche pour l'Enseignement et l'Emploi des Langues.

Chapoulie, S., and Bosc, S. 1981. *Approches sociologiques des classes sociales*. Profil Dossier 536. Paris: Hatier

Charlot, M., Dias, M., Dupont, R., Metro, R., and Perotti, R. 1982. Vers une société interculturelle? *Pour*, 86

Chaudenson, R. 1979. *Les Créoles français*. Paris: Nathan

Chaudenson, R., and Robillard, R. de (eds). 1989. *Langues et développement*. Aix-en-Provence: Didier. (2 vols)

Chaurand, J. 1972. *Introduction à la dialectologie française*. Paris: Bordas

Chervel, A., and Manesse, D. 1989. *La Dictée*. Paris: Calmann-Lévy/Institut National de la Recherche Pédagogique

Chikoff, I. de. 1985. Alsace: écoutez la différence. *Le Figaro*, 23.8.85

Collins, R. 1986. *The Basques*. London: Collins

Comrie, B. (ed) 1987. *The World's Major Languages*. London: Croom Helm

Corbeil, J-C. 1968. *Les Structures syntaxiques en français moderne: les éléments fonctionnels dans la Phrase*. Paris: Klincksieck

Cordeiro, A. 1982. Assimilation ou stabilisation des immigrés en tant qu'étrangers? *Pour*, 86: 35-9

Corraze, J. 1983. *Les Communications non-verbales*. Paris: Presses Universitaires de France.

Crystal, D. 1987. *The Cambridge Encyclopedia of Language*. Cambridge: Cambridge University Press.

Dabène, L., Flasaquier, A., and Lyons, J. 1983. *Status of Migrants Mother Tongues*. Strasbourg: European Science Foundation

Damourette, J., and Pichon, E. 1911-33. *Des Mots à la pensée*. Paris: D'Artrey

Dedeyan, G. (ed) 1982. *Histoire des Arméniens*. Toulouse: Privat

Delsol, C. 1985. *Les Bretons bretonnants: des pauvres et des militants*. Le Figaro, 22.8.85

Deniau, X. 1983. *La Francophonie*. Paris: Gallimard

Desalmond, P., and Tort, P. 1977. *Du Plan à la dissertation*. Paris: Hatier

Desautels, C. 1983. Comportement verbal des hommes et des femmes en situation de conversation mixte et non-mixte; la courbe intonative et la phrase interrompue. *Revue de l'Association Québecoise de Linguistique*, 3, 2: 33-8

Descamps-Hocquet, M. 1988. Communication en milieu plurilingue. *Cahiers de l'Institut de Linguistique de Louvain*, 14, 2: 211-15

Deyhime, G. 1967. Enquête sur la phonologie du français contemporain. *La Linguistique*, 1: 97-108 and 2: 57-84

Dorais, L.-J. 1980. Diglossie, bilinguisme et classes sociales en Louisiane. *Pluriel Débats*, 22: 57-91

Downes, W. 1984. *Language and Society*. London: Fontana

Dumas, G., Bourassa, L., Taillefer, B., and Vaillancourt, P. (eds) 1986. *Promotion et intégration des langues nationales dans les systèmes éducatifs*. Paris: H. Champion

Duneton, C. 1978. *A Hurler le soir au fond des collèges*. Paris: Seuil

Dupeux, G. 1972. *La Société française 1789-1970*. Paris: Armand Colin

Durand, M. 1936. *Le Genre grammatical en français parlé à Paris et dans la région parisienne*. Paris: Bibliothèque du Français Moderne

Duranti, A. 1988. Ethnography of speaking: towards a linguistics of the praxis. In F. Newmeyer (ed), *Linguistics: The Cambridge Survey*, Vol. 4: *Language: the Socio-Cultural Context*. Cambridge: Cambridge University Press

Dutourd, J. 1986. SOS langue française ! *Le Figaro Magazine*, 11.1.1986: 11-17

Edwards, J. 1985. *Language, Society and Identity*. Oxford: Blackwell

Elegoët, F. 1973. Bilinguisme et domination linguistique. *Les Temps Modernes*, août 1973: 213-22

Encrevé, P. 1983. La liaison sans enchaînement. *Actes de la Recherche en Sciences Sociales*, 46, mars 1983: 39-66

Enis, B. M., and Cox, K. K. 1985. *Marketing Classics*. New York: Allyn and Bacon

Espérandieu, V., Lion, A., and Benichou, J.-P. 1984. *Des illettrés en France: rapport au Premier Ministre*. Paris: La Documentation Française

Espéret, E. 1979. *Langage et origine sociale des élèves*. Geneva: Lang

Evans, H. 1985. A feminine issue in contemporary French usage. *Modern Languages*, 66, 4: 231-6

Evans, H. 1987. The government and linguistic change in France: the case of feminisation. *ASMCF Review*, 31: 20-6

Fantapié, A. 1982. Historique d'une loi. *Médias et Langage*, 16: 14-17

Farandjis, S. 1986a, *Compte-rendus du Haut Conseil de la Francophonie; séances du 6/7 mars et 9/10 déc 1985*. Paris: Haut Conseil de la Francophonie

Farandjis, S. 1986b. *Compte-rendu de la session des 28,29,30 mai 1986 du Haut Conseil de la Francophonie*. Paris: Haut Conseil de la Francophonie

Farandjis, S. 1986c. *Etat de la francophonie dans le monde: Rapport 1985*. Paris: La Documentation Française

Farandjis, S. 1987. *Etat de la francophonie dans le monde: Rapport 1986-87*. Paris: La Documentation Française

Farandjis, S. 1989. *Etat de la francophonie dans le monde: Rapport 1988-89*. Paris: La Documentation Française

Fasold, R. W. 1984. *The Sociolinguistics of Society*. Oxford: Blackwell

Field, T. 1981. Language survival in a European context: the future of occitan. *Language Problems and Language Planning*, 5: 251-63

Fillmore, C. 1979. On fluency. In Fillmore, C., Kempler, C., and Wang, W. S.-Y. (eds), *Individual Differences in Language Ability and Language Behaviour*. London: Academic Press 85-102

Fishman, J. 1985. *The Rise and Fall of the Ethnic Revival: Perspectives on Language and Ethnicity*. The Hague: Mouton

Fishman, J., et al. 1966. *Language Loyalty in the United States*. The Hague: Mouton

Flower, J. (ed) 1983. *France Today - Introductory Studies*. London: Methuen

Fosty, A. 1985, *La Langue française dans les institutions communautaires de l'Europe*. Quebec: Documentation du Conseil de la Langue Française

Fouere, Y. 1977. *Histoire résumée du mouvement breton*. Quimper: Nature et Bretagne

François, F. 1983. *J'cause français, non?* Paris: La Découverte/Maspéro

François, F., et al. 1977. *La Syntaxe de l'enfant de 5 ans*. Paris: Larousse

François, F., et al. 1978a. *Syntaxe et mise en mots de l'enfant de 5 ans*. Paris: Editions du Conseil National de la Recherche Scientifique.

François, F., et al. 1978b. *Eléments de linguistique appliqués à l'étude du langage de l'enfant*. Paris: Larousse

François, F., et al. 1984. *Conduites linguistiques chez le jeune enfant*. Paris: Presses Universitaires de France

François, P. 1985. Francophonie d'hier et d'aujourd'hui. *Regards sur l'Actualité*, 108: 27-42

Gallouédec-Genuys, F. 1981. *Le Dialogue écrit administration-administrés* Paris: La Documentation Française

Gardes-Madray, F., and Gardin, B. (eds) 1989. Parole(s) ouvrière(s). *Langages*, 93

Gardin, B., Marcellesi, J-B., and GRECO Rouen 1980. *Sociolinguistique: approches, théories, pratiques*. Paris: Presses Universitaires de France

Gardner, R. C., and Lambert, E. W. 1959. Motivational variables in second-language acquisition. *Canadian Journal of Psychology*, 13, 266-72

Gardner-Chloros, P. 1985. *Choix et alternance des langues à Strasbourg*. Unpublished doctoral thesis. Strasbourg: Université Louis-Pasteur

Gardy, P. 1981. La Diglossie comme conflit: l'exemple occitan. *Langages*, 61: 75-91

Garmadi, J. 1981. *La Sociolinguistique*. Paris: Presses Universitaires de France.

Gauthier, G. 1982. La Corse. In R. Lafont (ed), *Langue dominante, langues dominées*. Paris: Edilig 109-21

Genouvrier, E. 1986. *Naître en français*. Paris: Larousse

Gilliéron, J. 1902-10. Atlas linguistique de la France. Paris: Honoré Champion

Giordan, H. 1982. *Démocratie culturelle et droit à la différence*. Paris: La Documentation Française

Girard, P. 1983. *Les Juifs de France*. Paris: Bruno Huisman

Goffman, E. 1981. *Forms of Talk*. Oxford: Basil Blackwell

Gordon, D. C. 1978. *The French Language and National Identity*. The Hague: Mouton

Grau, R. 1985. *Les Langues et les cultures en France: une approche juridique contemporaine*. Montreal: Editeur Officiel du Québec

Grillo, R. D. 1989. *Dominant Languages: Language and Hierarchy in Britain and France.* Cambridge: Cambridge University Press
Guespin, L. (ed). 1984. Dialogue et interaction verbale. *Langages*, 74, juin 1984.
Gueunier, N. 1985. La Crise du français en France. In J. Maurais (ed), *La Crise des langues*. Paris: Le Robert . 5-38
Guigo, D. 1989. L'adresse au bureau. *Travail et Pratiques Langagières - Communications*. Paris: Ministère de la Recherche. 185-201
Guillou, M., and Littardi, A. 1988. *La Francophonie s'éveille*. Paris: Berger-Levrault
Guiraud, P. 1978a. *Le Français populaire*. Que sais-je 1172. Paris: Presses Universitaires de France
Guiraud, P. 1978b. *Patois et dialectes français*. Paris: Presses Universitaires de France
Guiraud, P. 1980. *L'Argot*. Paris: Presses Universitaires de France
Guittet, A. 1983. *L'Entretien*. Paris: Armand Colin
Gumperz, J. 1982. *Discourse Strategies*. Cambridge: Cambridge University Press.
Gumperz, J., and Hymes, D. (eds). 1972. *Directions in Sociolinguistics: the Ethnography of Communication*. New York: Holt Rhinehart, Winston
Gwegen, J. 1975. *La Langue bretonne face à ses oppresseurs*. Quimper: Nature et Bretagne
Hagège, C. 1987. *Le Français et les siècles*. Paris: Editions Odile Jacob
Halliday, M.A.K. 1978. *Language as Social Semiotic*. London: Edward Arnold
Hamers, J. F., and Blanc, M. 1989, *Bilinguality and Bilingualism*. Cambridge: Cambridge University Press.
Hantrais, L. 1982. *Contemporary French Society*. London: Methuen
Harris, M. 1978. *The Evolution of French Syntax: A Comparative Approach*. London: Longman
Harris, M. 1987. French. In B. Comrie (ed). *The World's Major Languages*. London: Croom Helm. 210-35
Hartley, A. 1981. French, Québec, Francophonie. *Bradford Occasional Papers*, 2: 60-86.
Henry, J. 1984. La Louisiane francophone - une renaissance culturelle. *Universités*, septembre 1984: 2-6
Hérédia, C. de. 1983. Les parlers français des migrants. In F. François (ed), *J'cause Français, non ?* Paris: La Découverte/Maspéro. 95-126
Holveck, A., Mull, C., Neusch, A., and Reinbold, P. 1985. *Connaissance de l'entreprise: documents commerciaux*. Paris: Delagrave
Hudson, R. A. 1980. *Sociolinguistics*. Cambridge: Cambridge University Press
Hymes, D. 1972. Models for the interaction of language and social life. In J. Gumperz and D. Hymes (eds), *Directions in Sociolinguistics: The Ethnography of Communication*. New York: Holt Rhinehart, Winston
Irigaray, L. (ed). 1987. Le Sexe Linguistique. *Langages*, 85
Joos, M. 1962. The five clocks. *International Journal of American Linguistics*, 28, 5
Joscelyne, A. 1986. French language planning 1966-1986. *Language Monthly*, September 1986: 28-30
Kajman, M. 1985. L'identité française est à rechercher en dehors de toute position partisane: un entretien avec Fernand Braudel. *Le Monde* 24.3.1985: 1-8
Keating, M. 1986. 'Revendication et Lamentation': the failure of regional nationalism in Languedoc. *Journal of Area Studies*, 14: 27-32
Klein, P. 1984. Le particularisme alsacien. In M. Tozzi (ed), *Apprendre et vivre sa langue*, Paris: Syros. 37-42
Klein, P., Philipp, M., Bothorel-Witz, A., Finck, A., Klein, G., Foerflinger, M., and Nonn, H. 1982. *Alsace*. Strasbourg: Christine Bonneton
Kleinschmager, R. 1986. *Géopolitique de l'Alsace*. Fayard

Kocourek, R. 1982. *La Langue française de la technique et de la science*. Paris: La Documentation Française

Kramerae, C., Schulz, M., and O'Barr, W. M. (eds). 1984. *Language and Power*. New York: Sage

Lafont, R. 1974. *La Revendication occitane*. Paris: Flammarion

Lafont, R. 1977. *Clefs pour l'Occitanie*. Paris: Seghers

Lafont, R. (ed). 1982. *Langue dominante, langues dominées*. Paris: Edilig

Laks, B. 1983. Langages et pratiques sociales. *Actes de la Recherche en Sciences Sociales*, 46: 73-97

Laks, B. 1984. Le champ de la sociolinguistique française de 1963 à 1983, production et fonctionnement. *Langue Française*, 63: 103-28

Lamothe, J. 1983. Comportement verbal des hommes et des femmes en situation de conversation mixte. *Revue de l'Association Québecoise de Linguistique*, 3, 2: 23-32

Laver, J., and Hutchinson, S. 1972. *Communication in Face-to-Face Interaction*. London: Penguin

Lebon, A. 1984. La population étrangère au recensement de 1982. *Problèmes Economiques*, 1886: 3-9

Lefèvre, J., and Tournier, M. (eds). 1987. Le discours syndical ouvrier. *Mots*, 14, mars 1987

Lennig, M. 1979. Une étude quantitative du changement linguistique dans le système vocalique parisien. In P. Thibault (ed), *Le Français parlé - études sociolinguistiques*. Edmonton: Linguistic Research Inc. 29-39

Léon, P. 1971. Aspects phonostylistiques des niveaux de langue. In P. Rigault (ed), *La Grammaire du français parlé*. Paris: Hachette. 150-9

LeRoy, M. 1983. La Langue bretonne: aperçu historique. *Les Langues Modernes*, 4: 381-8

Lévy-Leblond, J.-M. 1990. Une recherche qui se fait comme elle se parle. *Le Monde Diplomatique*, janvier 1990 (Supplément langue et science): 25-26

Liégeois, J.-P. 1980. Le discours de l'ordre: pouvoirs publics et minorités culturelles, *Esprit*, 41: 17-50

Liégeois, J.-P. 1982. Bohémien ou personne d'origine nomade, où est le Tzigane? Pour, 86: 41-45

Lienhard, M. 1981. *Foi et vie des protestants de l'Alsace*. Strasbourg: Oberlin

Locquin, M. V. 1982. *Enquête sur la situation du français par rapport à l'anglais, l'allemand et le russe dans l'ensemble des sciences*. Paris: Centre d'Information et de Recherche pour l'Enseignement et l'Emploi des Langues.

Lucci, D. 1983. *Etude phonétique du français contemporain à travers la variation situationnelle*. Grenoble: Université de Grenoble

Maingueneau, D. 1987. *Nouvelles Tendances en analyse du discours*. Paris: Hachette

Maldidier, D. (ed). 1986. Analyse de discours nouveaux parcours. *Langages*, 81, mars 1986

Manessy, G., and Wald, P. *Le Français en Afrique Noire*. Paris: L'Harmattan-IDERIC

Marcellesi, J-B. (ed). 1986. Glottopolitique. *Langages*, 83, septembre 1986

Maresse-Polaert, J. 1969. *Etude sur le langage des enfants de six ans*. Paris: Delachaux and Niestlé

Martinet, P. 1945. *La Prononciation du français contemporain*. Geneva: Droz

Maugey, A. 1987. *La Francophonie en direct*. Quebec: Documentation du Conseil de la Langue Française, 2 vols

Maurais, J. (ed). 1983. *La Norme linguistique*. Paris/Quebec: Le Robert

Maurais, J. (ed). 1985. *La Crise des langues*. Paris/Quebec: Le Robert

Maurand, G. 1981. Situation linguistique d'une famille en domaine occitan. *International Journal of the Sociology of Language*, 29: 99-119

Méla, V. 1988. Parler verlan: règles et usages. *Langage et Société*, 45: 47-72

Mermet, G. 1985. *Francoscopie*. Paris: Larousse

Mermet, G. 1987. *Francoscopie 1987*. Paris: Larousse

Mermet, G. 1989. *Francoscopie 1989*. Paris: Larousse

Mettas, O. 1973. Les réalisations vocaliques d'un sociolecte parisien. *Travaux de l'Institut Phonétique de Strasbourg*, 5: 1-11

Milroy, L. 1980. *Language and Social Networks*. Oxford: Blackwell

Mimin, P. 1970. *Le Style des jugements*. Paris: Librairies techniques

Moatti, G. (ed). 1989. La France dans le monde. *L'Expansion* 6-19.7.89

Mongin, O. 1980. Vers un droit des minorités: L'exemple tsigane. *Esprit*, 41: 3-16

Morris, D., Collet,P., Marsh, P., and O'Shaughnessy, M. 1981. *Gestures*. London: Triad

Morsy, M. 1984. *Les Nord-Africains en France*. Paris: CHEAM/La Documentation Française

Muller, B. 1985. *Le Français d'aujourd'hui*. Paris: Klincksieck

Naaman, A. 1979. *Le Français au Liban - essai sociolinguistique*. Paris/Beyrouth: Editions Naaman

Naaman, A. 1984. Le français, langue d'élite. *Le Monde*, 29.11.1984

Newmeyer, F. (ed). 1988. *Linguistics: The Cambridge Survey*, Vol 4: *Language: The Sociocultural Context*. Cambridge: Cambridge University Press

Nichols, P. 1984. Networks and hierarchies: language and social stratification. In C Kramerae et al (eds), *Language and Power*. New York: Sage. 23-42

Nicolas, M. 1986. *Le Séparatisme en Bretagne*. Quimper: Beltan

Nouvel, A. 1978. *Le Français parlé en Occitanie*. Montpellier: Terra d'Oc

Pécheur, J. 1988a. Comment les français voient leur langue. *Le Français dans le Monde*, 218: 28-9

Pécheur, J. 1988b. La Francophonie, j'y crois: entretien avec Alain Decaux. *Diagonales*, 8, octobre 1988: 3-5

Perdue, C. (ed). 1986. L'acquisition du français par des adultes immigrés. *Langages*, 84

Peretz, C. 1977. *Les Voyelles orales à Paris dans la dynamique des âges et de la société*. Unpublished Thesis. Université René Descartes

Phal, A. 1971. *Vocabulaire général d'orientation scientifique*. Paris: Centre de Recherche et d'Etude pour la Diffusion du Français

Philipps, E. 1975. *Les Luttes linguistiques en Alsace jusqu'en 1945*. Strasbourg: Culture Alsacienne

Philipps, E. 1978. *La Crise d'identité: l'Alsace face à son destin*. Colmar: Société d'Edition de la Basse-Alsace

Pivot, B. 1989. *Le Livre de l'orthographe*. Paris: Hatier

Platiel, S. 1989. Les langues d'Afrique Noire en France: des langues de culture face à une langue de communication. *Migrants-Formation*, 76: 31-45

Ponthier, F. 1987. *Le Grand Livre de la correspondance commerciale et d'affaires*. Grenoble: Editions de Vecchi

Poole, A. 1985. The Fourons: a microcosm of Belgium's linguistic problems. *Journal of Area Studies*, 11: 22-5

Price, G. 1971. *The French Language: Present and Past*. London: Edward Arnole

Prost, A. 1983. *Les Lycéens et leurs études au seuil du XXIe siècle*. Paris: Ministère de l'Education Nationale

Reggi, M. de. 1984. Les sciences à l'heure de l'anglais. *Le Monde*, 30.12.1984: VII

Reynaud, J. D., and Grafmeyer, Y. (eds). 1981. *Français, qui êtes-vous?* Paris: La Documentation Française

Rickard, P. 1989. *A History of the French Language*. London: Unwin Hyman

Romaine, S. 1984. *The Language of Children and Adolescents.* Oxford: Blackwell

Roncière, M. C. de la. (ed). 1987. Jeunes d'aujourd'hui - Regards sur les 13-25 ans en France. *Notes et Etudes Documentaires.* Paris: La Documentation Française

Roulet, E. 1981. Echanges, interventions et actes de langage dans la structure de la conversation. *Etudes de Linguistique Appliquée,* 44

Rudder, O. de. 1986. *Le Français qui se cause.* Paris: Balland

Ruhlen, M. 1987. *A Guide to the World's Languages.* Stanford, California: Stanford University Press

Ryan, E. B., and Giles, H. 1982. *Attitudes towards Language Variation.* London: Edward Arnold

Sabourin, P. 1981. *Place et avenir de la langue française dans les sciences juridique, politique et économique.* Paris: Imprimerie Nationale

St-Robert, P. de. 1986. *Lettre ouverte à ceux qui en perdent leur français.* Paris: Albin Michel

Sandry, G., and Carrère, M. 1953. *Dictionnaire de l'argot moderne.* Paris: Dauphin

Sauvageot, A. 1978. *Français d'hier ou français de demain?* Paris: Nathan

Savile-Troike, M. 1982. *The Ethnography of Communication.* Oxford: Blackwell

Schiffrin, D. 1988. Conversation analysis. In F. Newmeyer (ed), *Linguistics: the Cambridge Survey,* Vol 4: *Language: The Sociocultural Context.* Cambridge: Cambridge University Press. 251-276

Schläpfer, R. (ed). 1985. *La Suisse aux quatre langues.* Berne: Zoë

Sebeok, T. (ed). 1960. *Style in Language.* Cambridge, Massachusetts: MIT Press

Sichler, L. 1979. Dites-moi tu. *L'Express,* 30.10.1979

Simoni-Aurembou, M.-R. 1973. Le Français régional en Ile-de-France et dans l'Orléanais. *Langue Française,* 18: 126-36

Sprott, W. J. H. 1958. *Human Groups.* London: Pelican

Stourdze, C., and Collet-Hassan, M. 1969. Les niveaux de langue. *Le Français dans le Monde,* 65: 18-21

Stubbs, M. 1983. *Discourse Analysis.* Oxford: Blackwell

Swales, J. (ed). 1980. *Episodes in ESP.* Oxford: Pergamon

Swing, E. S. 1980. *Bilingualism and Linguistic Segregation in the Schools of Brussels.* Quebec: International Center for Research on Bilingualism

Tabi-Manga, J. 1982. La dynamique de la langue française au Cameroun. In *La Prospective de la Langue Française,* Paris: Conseil International de la Langue Française. 91-101

Tabouret-Keller, A. (ed). 1981. Regional languages in France. *International Journal of the Sociology of Language,* 29

Termote, M., and Gauvreau, D. 1988. *La Situation démolinguistique du Québec.* Quebec: Dossiers du Conseil de la Langue Française

Tétu, M. 1987. *La Francophonie.* Paris: Guérin

Thélot, C. 1982. *Tel père, tel fils?* Paris: Dunod

Thorne, B., Kramerae, C., and Henley, F. (eds). 1983. *Language Gender and Society.* New York: Newbury House

Tozzi, M. (ed) 1984. *Apprendre et vivre sa langue.* Paris: Syros

Trotignon, Y. 1984. *La France au XXe siècle.* Paris: Dunod (2 vols)

Valdman, A. (ed). 1979. *Le Français hors de France.* Paris: Champion

Vandenthorpe, C. (ed). 1984. *Découvrir le Québec.* Quebec: Québec Français

Vandeputte, O. 1981. *Dutch.* Rekkem: Stichting Ons Erfdeel

Varty, K., and Davies, P. V. (eds). 1987. *Regional Varieties of French: Problems and Solutions in Teaching.* Glasgow: Glasgow University Language Centre

Veltman, C. 1987. *L'Avenir du français aux Etats-Unis.* Quebec: Documentation du

Conseil de la Langue Française
Verbunt, G. (ed). 1985. *Par les langues de France, Tome 2*. Paris: CCI/Centre Pompidou
Verdelhan-Bourgade, M. (ed). 1986. Communication et enseignement. *Langue Française 70*
Verdié, M. (ed). 1989. *L'Etat de la France*. Paris: La Découverte
Vermes, G. (ed) 1988 *Vingt-cinq communautés linguistiques de la France*. Paris: L'Harmattan (2 vols)
Vermes, G., and Boutet, J. (eds). 1987. *France, pays multilingue*. Paris: L'Harmattan (2 vols)
Viatte, A. 1969. *La Francophonie*. Paris: Larousse
Von Wartburg, W. 1971. *Evolution et structure de la langue française*. Bern: Francke
Walter, H. 1982. *Enquête phonologique et variétés régionales du français*. Paris: Presses Universitaires de France
Walter, H. 1988. *Le Français dans tous les sens*. Paris: Robert Laffont
Wardhaugh, R. 1983. *Language and Nationhood*. Toronto: New Star Books
Wardhaugh, R. 1986. *An Introduction to Sociolinguistics*. Oxford: Blackwell
Wardhaugh, R. 1987. *Languages in Competition*. Oxford: Blackwell
Weil, P. 1964. *Le Droit administratif*. Paris: Presses Universitaires de France
Whitcombe, E. V. 1980. *Cohesion in Radio French*. Unpublished MA thesis, Council for National Academic Awards
Winkin, Y. 1987. *Les Moments et leurs hommes: textes d'Erving Goffman*. Paris: Seuil
Wolf, L. 1983a. La normalisation du langage en France. In J Maurais (ed), *La Norme linguistique*. Paris: Le Robert . 105-37
Wolf, L. 1983b. *Le Français régional d'Alsace*. Paris: Klincksieck
Wright, G. 1987. *France in Modern Times*. Oxford: Norton (4th edn)
Wright, V. 1983. *The Government and Politics of France*. London: Hutchinson (2nd edn)
Yaguello, M. 1978. *Les Mots et les femmes*. Paris: Payot
Yaguello, M. 1989. *Le Sexe des mots*. Paris: Belfond
Zeldin, T. 1983. *The French*. London: Collins

1950 onwards. *Atlas linguistiques et ethnographiques de la France par régions*, Paris: Editions du Conseil National de la Recherche Scientifique
1981. *Pour l'occitan et pour l'Occitanie*. Toulouse: Institut d'Estudis Occitans
1982. *La Prospective de la langue française*. Paris: Conseil International de la Langue Française.
1982. *Rencontre internationale sur l'application des législations linguistiques dans les pays francophones*. Paris: Haut Comité de la Langue Française
1983. *Le Projet culturel extérieur de la France*. Paris: La Documentation Française
1983. Historique d'une Loi. *Médias et Langage*, 18: 14-17
1983. Dossier: les langues de France. *Médias et Langage*, 18
1983. La Bretagne. *France Informations*, 120
1983. Personal communication, ref SIGES 7/MG 313. Paris: Ministère de l'Education Nationale
1984. La Bretagne. *Le Monde Dossiers et Documents*, 107
1984. *Par les langues de France*. Paris: CCI/Centre Pompidou (2 vols)
1985. La population française de A à Z. *Cahiers Français*, 219
1985. Langue française: enrichissement du vocabulaire: textes législatifs et règlementaires. *Journal Officiel de la République Française*, Brochure 1468.
1985. *L'Avenir de la langue française - 2e rencontre internationale sur l'application des législations linguistiques dans les pays francophones*. Paris: La Documentation Française

1986. *Conférence des chefs d'Etat et de gouvernement des pays ayant en commun l'usage du français*. Paris: La Documentation Française

1986. *Les Minorités linguistiques dans les pays de la communauté européenne*. Brussels: European Community

1988. Le Pays basque. *Le Monde Dossiers et Documents*, 154

1989. *Travail et pratiques langagières - communications*. Paris: Ministère de la Recherche

1989. *Quid 1990*. Paris: Robert Laffont